FIRST PERSON FEMALE

—————— A MEMOIR ——————

MARIA FLOOK

FIRST PERSON FEMALE

A MEMOIR

THE PERMANENT PRESS
Sag Harbor, NY 11963

A note to readers: This is a true story. Some of the names have been changed. Eros is unrobed under bright lights, and at way-points of my life, in a narrative that is not always linear. It goes back and forth, or "in and out," so to speak.

For information, address:
    The Permanent Press
    4170 Noyac Road
    Sag Harbor, NY 11963
    www.thepermanentpress.com

Library of Congress Cataloging-in-Publication Data

Flook, Maria, author.
    First person female; a memoir / Maria Flook.
    Sag Harbor, NY: The Permanent Press, 2018.
    ISBN: 978-1-57962-515-3
        1. Flook, Maria. 2. Women authors, American—
    Biography. 3. Flook, Maria—Family. 4. Flook, Maria—
    Relations with men.

PS3556.L583 Z46 2018
813'.54 [B]—dc23   2017043373

Printed in the Unites States of America

"If a person's capacity for shame could be exhausted,
I would have exhausted mine."

—MARGUERITE DURAS

"The antidote to shame is not honor, but honesty."

—MAGGIE NELSON

PREFACE

I have never started a book with more misgivings. Writing about life in the first person is a repulsive thrill; a desire to expose one's own secrets becomes a kind of autonecrophilia. Arthur Koestler once told Robert Lifton, "With every book I write, I shed my skin, like a snake." But writing a memoir, with its writhing pages and carnivorous circling, is like a snake biting its own tail.

The day of our mother's death, my sister and I went to see our mother, Veronica, at a retirement community outside Wilmington, Delaware. My older sister had been estranged from her for some time and only recently had started to chisel through the ice shelf that separated them. Often she would throw up her hands and say it was impossible. But Veronica was failing fast, and at the last minute, Karen agreed to visit. I had always been the go-between, and this final reunion would be an important bridge for all of us. "It's easier to burn them than to build them," my sister said. I told her that maybe it wasn't too late to make peace.

7

I met Karen at the entrance of Stonegates luxury condominiums, a lavish bunker for the aging well-to-do. I noticed my sister's beat-up car. The security officer at the front kiosk looked her over for longer than he'd interrogated me when I had arrived in a late-model airport rental. Her clunker was an eyesore in their parking lot. The ceiling fabric had come loose to reveal the yellow foam insulation underneath. It was another reminder of how Karen's life was a little more shabby than most people's. Because our mother had favored one of us over the other, I sometimes thought I was responsible for each cash deficit that befell Karen.

When Karen got out of her car, her streaky blonde hair made her look sort of like an aging Indie movie type, a Vincent Gallo heroine or a victim in a docu-drama. Her face was more haggard than ever. She told me she'd been having some thyroid trouble, but I wondered if it could be something more serious. We embraced and I said, "How can you see out your rear-view mirror with that fabric hanging down?"

She said, "I never look at what's behind me."

Her words had buried meaning. But she knew I understood.

"I taped the fabric, but it keeps coming loose," Karen said.

"We should just tear it off completely, don't you think?"

So our first item of business that day was to strip the interior ceiling from her old Mercury Marquis. We yanked and tugged the synthetic bolt until it peeled away. I remembered when we had shared a room and Karen had taught me how to make my bed, careful to fold the top sheet down so its hem was even. My sister had few safe havens in life, and her car was where she would escape after our ordeal with our mother was over. Now, without the ceiling fabric, the naked roof seemed like a metaphor for secrets that finally should be addressed by us.

I waited while she stamped out her cigarette, in no hurry to go inside the building. We were nervous at this milestone—the impending death of our matriarch, the femme fatale and dangerous axis of our lives. So much harm can happen in a lifetime, how would we ameliorate all our wrongdoing in a mere teatime? After decades of our mother's indifference toward her, it was amazing that Karen had even showed up.

When she was just fourteen, my sister vanished.

Our mother had been moved from her pocket-of-posh apartment to the "Life Care" unit. We found Veronica propped up in a hospital bed. I thought, this is the sterile gateway most people are forced to depart from, and I'd rather die on a busy street corner. I was surprised to see that her lovely shoulder-length hair had been clipped by nurses, who thought a military hairstyle more appropriate for someone waiting on the tarmac of The Beyond. Seeing her with shorn hair instead of her Lauren Bacall coiffure, I remembered the first time she was hospitalized for heart surgery. She insisted that I go home to get a negligee from her armoire. She hated to wear a hospital johnnie. She had always been a coquette, even in the OR. I recalled watching her dress for cocktail parties. She wore black lace garter belts and seamed stockings, and I had liked to hear the little snapping sound when she pinched her garter tabs shut on their little tongues.

Veronica was happy to see me, but when Karen entered she blinked as if a pepper-ball deterrent had exploded in her face. Recovering her composure, she said, "Oh. It's you. What a nice surprise."

Karen said, "I'm missing work to be here."

"I didn't expect the casino would let you off," Veronica said.

"They'll dock my paycheck, but I guess I'm here now."

I saw that they would have a jousting match until they found their footing. But it wasn't a real battle cry, not yet anyway. Karen and I flanked either side of the hospital bed. I took one of my mother's hands and Karen took the other. I noticed how we were suddenly connected like a strip of paper dolls, the three of us holding hands again. We used to cross the city streets like this, our tripled shadow spilling across the concrete in a whimsical zigzag.

Karen felt the connection too. She's trying, I thought. This will work out. But Karen's childhood is like one of those meteor craters that formed at the bottom of the ocean. Scientists like to calculate how the world was different before and after the impact. My sister's disappearance was the linchpin event of her childhood, and it also had changed mine.

In my family, girls disappeared before their coming of age. As in the story of Snow White, our mother banished us as soon as we reached our sexual maturity. Our new, womanly bodies upset the apple cart. Having been abandoned by her first husband, the handsome Arrow Collar Man, Veronica felt threatened by other women, even her own offspring. When Karen left home, I knew that I, too, would be shoved out of the nest. It was just a matter of time.

Once I took a part-time job grading tests for a firm called National Educational Testing. The famous Iowa Tests were distributed to grammar-school kids nationwide, and the scoring was done by graduate students in Iowa City who assembled in three shifts at an old, abandoned A&P where they had set up Formica tables, Xerox machines, and coffee urns. We were grading a fifth-grade essay exam which asked students to describe what was happening in a line drawing. The picture showed a hot-air balloon floating beside a two-story bungalow. The balloon had a basket for passengers, but the basket was empty as it tipped against the eaves of the house.

Some children wrote that the balloon had arrived to take the family to a picnic; some wrote that it had just delivered a new baby, or a puppy. But others wrote that the balloon had crashed into the house and the mother had been killed, or the baby kidnapped, or that police were inside the balloon and had come to capture the father who owed money. Some even said that the balloon was really a bomb dropping onto the building. I might have answered, "The balloon took my sister away." Karen might have written, "The balloon came to rescue me from a wicked witch."

After Karen ran away, I maintained my neutrality in my mother's kingdom by acting like a tomboy or a stable urchin. As a saddle bum at a nearby riding academy, doing chores and whitewashing fences, repainting the sign that said RIDE AT YOUR OWN RISK, I masked my gender so as not to be identified as a threat to my mother.

When Karen became an overnight bombshell, Veronica sent her to the doctor to get diet pills to reduce her bustline. She bought her unfashionable jumpers that hid her figure. She sorted our Halloween candy and gave me all of Karen's booty. At twelve, I was the "cute one," still flat chested. Two years later, by the time Veronica started seeing me as a threat, Karen had become an FBI cold case. She had walked off without a word; we later learned that she'd met a man at the Bowl-o-Rama. He took her across state lines, where she worked at a porn theater and brothel in Virginia Beach. Once she had been raffled off as grand prize at Shriner Nite. My parents left it up to the authorities to try to find her, and I watched my mother to see if she seemed guilty. She'd sip her scotch and turn the pages of a new mystery novel. Veronica was hiding behind her normal routines, maybe for my sake.

I NOTICED our mother's eyes looked strange. She had once had gorgeous glass-green irises, rimmed in topaz with gold flecks. Our father called her "Green Eyes." But in her last hours, her eyes were flat slate buttons, leached of color. Karen recognized the change too. Whatever physiological aspect of the death process it was that had stolen her vivid eye color, the vixen at the center of our lives was, at last, neutralized.

A nurse brought a dinner tray. Tepid chicken goo, and a bowl of fruit salad. The peeled grapes reminded me of a childhood game where Karen blindfolded me and told me to hold "eyeballs" in the palm of my hand.

"You can't eat that," I told Veronica. "We'll sneak you back to your apartment. I'll make a real dinner for you."

She said, "A person's last words should be on an empty stomach." Veronica tried to rise to the occasion. Talking to her daughters "woman to woman" was not easy for her, but she said, "I'll tell you one thing about men. I once took a car trip with your father. Back roads all the way from Detroit to Chicago. It was a blizzard. The snow was coming down like chicken feathers and we got stuck. It was the middle of nowhere. I thought we would freeze to death that night. But you know what he did? He unbuttoned his coat and I got inside with him. We were together in one coat. They said if we hadn't worn the one coat, we might have died. That's my advice, find someone like that."

Our father had rescued Veronica after the Arrow Collar Man abandoned her with small kids. So I guess you could say he had saved her life. Karen stared at her in amazement. Veronica had said little about our father, who had succumbed to cancer eight years before. He'd chained-smoked Chesterfields and had been exposed to asbestos in the steel industry. But I wanted to think that her metaphor could go a different way. In one coat you could put man and wife, or mother and child, or even two sisters, right?

Veronica looked directly at Karen and said, "You know, I loved you." The past tense was confusing, but Karen nodded.

"Me, too," Karen said. That was going to be the sum total. Maybe it was good enough.

Before Karen went back to Atlantic City, she volunteered to go shopping to get something I could prepare for dinner, although she wasn't going to stay for it. It was my chore to kidnap Veronica from the Life Care unit. When the staff was busy, I found a wheelchair nearby and I whisked her off. I steered her through hallways and reached her apartment. Her last meal should be in her own surroundings, with her Limoges and high-end bric-a-brac. I moved her onto the living room sofa and arranged the pillows. I poured two fingers of scotch in her favorite tumbler and handed it to her. Karen had found lamb chops, and I broiled a chop and carved it into pink snips so she could chew it. I steamed asparagus, only the tips. A stray cat waited at the patio door. I let him inside and he weaved in and out of our legs. His fur was matted with impenetrable clumps that were too tender to touch and he hissed at us each time we tried to pet him. My mother said, "Some tangles are too painful to inspect." She was speaking in metaphors, warning me not to broach any last-minute topics. So I found a can of tuna and we watched the Tom devour it. When he wanted nothing more to do with us, we let him outdoors again.

I was there because a friend had told me to do the "Zen thing" at my mother's deathbed. I should praise my failing parent for all the gifts she had given me when I was a girl. It wasn't AA's "ninth step," which asks us to make direct amends to people we have harmed. The Zen instruction didn't ask me to apologize, but to offer thanks.

I tried to think of a few specifics. I told her, "Thanks for that great peach pie you used to make, the one with the slivers of melted cheddar that adds the right saltiness to all that sugar. And thanks for those bell-bottom jeans."

At the dawn of that fashion, when I couldn't find low-riding bell-bottoms in local stores, Veronica sewed the jeans for me, making the flared cuffs to my exact specifications. She bought denim, measured my hips, and drew her own pattern with a stick of chalk. She worked through the evening at her Singer sewing machine, until the pant legs ballooned according to my expectations.

I told her, "I know that you thought they looked ridiculous. But I was the first girl in Wilmington to wear bell-bottoms, and it was a political statement, you know?"

"Blue jeans?"

"If you wore bell-bottoms, you're antiwar. Sewing those jeans for me made me famous. I was an instant protester. Très chic."

"Oh, please," she said. She had had the same reaction when I was once detained with a group of demonstrators. We had stuffed ragweed and daisies into the fins of an antiaircraft guided missile that was left on display in a parking lot at the Merchandise Mart. When a picture appeared in the newspaper, I was wearing the bell-bottoms she had sewn for me.

"And thanks for teaching me how to wear French perfume," I told her.

A lifelong femme fatale, and French, my mother was expert in her preparations for men. She had had a complicated regimen with her toilette. She had always criticized me for my sloppy habits when I got dressed. I never could find a comb, and I often parted my hair with a pencil point or the tip of a ballpoint pen. This is something I still do. In my vanity drawer there's always a pencil or a pen for parting my hair. I sometimes don't notice that I've drawn a blue line an inch down my forehead until I go into work and I am asked, "What's with that ink on your face?"

My mother had instructed me about using perfume. She said to spray scent in *the air* and walk through the cloud. Don't overdo it. Spray just the hem of your dress.

Just the hem? I had asked her.

That's his way in, isn't it? And spritz perfume on the suitcase lining. Let clothes absorb it. Men don't want to lick it off your skin.

"Thanks for all of your pointers about men," I said, but I recognized it was a tragic thing to say when she had no current prospects, no suitor waiting in the wings.

She said, "If you feel so thankful to me, why did you write *that* book?"

In 1998, a few months before her death, I had published a memoir about my sister who had disappeared, and in that story Veronica didn't look very good. Her "narcissistic personality disorder" was a major thread in the narrative. The heading in the *New York Times* review said, "Waking from the Nightmare of Life with Mother."

I stared at my mother propped on three oversized pillows. Even hours before death, she was beautiful. The skin on her high cheekbones was smooth and tight. But I told her, "I had to write that book. It's for my sister, who can't speak for herself."

She said, "Do you really know who I am?"

"Sure," I said. "Of course I know who you are—" But her question made me think of Sybille Bedford's directive in her novel *Jigsaw*: an author must try to elucidate "Who is Who. Who is Half-Who. And Who is Not."

My mother smiled at me. She said, "You think you know all about me?"

"Yes."

"I am mother. I am daughter. I am bride. I am divorcée."

I was surprised to hear her say "divorcée" because, of course, after her first husband ditched her she had remarried, and with my father's death she also could have said, "I am widow." Her dramatic split with the Arrow Collar model was her lifelong talismanic explanation for everything. Against this irrefutable truth, she seemed to suggest that her marriage to my father might just be hearsay.

Veronica went on, "You are all the above, same as me, but to that list you can add 'liar.'"

A gardener outside the open slider must have overheard her, and dropped his snippers.

"I'm all the above? That's the index? Well, okay, but for me you have to say I am *writer.*"

"Writer equals liar."

I told her, "Dostoyevsky said, 'Lying is man's only privilege over all other organisms. If you lie—you get to the truth! . . . Not one truth has ever been reached without first lying fourteen times or so, maybe a hundred and fourteen . . .'"

"You both tell cheap stories," she said. She enjoyed lumping me in with the unfathomable Russian.

I said, "Memoir isn't just a story, it's a *known event.* I dramatize scenes to make the narrative coherent."

Veronica said, "Literature has many famous vixens and sluts. You think you rank with them? You're an everyday whore, same as me."

She knew me well. I recently had told her I was sleeping with my editor. All my literary affiliations are sexual liaisons, from my first "female poems" to my final draft of whatever we have here: a memoir, a Reid Technique confession, a "preponderance of evidence," and that requires that a defendant's story must be more likely than not—above 50.01 percent.

She didn't care about Dostoyevsky's instructions, but she often liked to paraphrase Somerset Maugham: *You think Passion doesn't count the cost? Honor is well-sacrificed and shame is a cheap price to pay?*

I loved her best when she turned to books.

But when she heard about my affair with my editor she said that she thought I was crazy. "You have a perfectly good husband," she said.

The adjective "perfectly" is a suspect qualifier. It means not quite unflawed but with *acceptable* imperfections.

She said, "I'll tell you one thing about men. I once took a car trip with your father. Back roads all the way from Detroit to Chicago. It was a blizzard."

"You already told us that story."

"It's a good one. They said if we hadn't worn *one* coat, we might have died."

Again, she was talking in metaphors. Marriage means *one* coat.

I was surprised to hear her say, "You know what I need?"

"What can I get for you?"

"I need a new Maidenform or Vassarette."

"You want a new bra?"

"Mine are all ratty. Do you think you can go to Wanamaker's and get me something nice?"

I understood that my mother wouldn't need any new lingerie for what lay ahead of her. At the funeral home, I don't think they bother with underwear when dressing the deceased. I guess they do what the family tells them to do. It all goes into the urn. But I thought I'd go shopping that afternoon to see what I could find. "I think I know your size, don't I?" I asked in a tiny voice.

"I'm not what I used to be."

"They have pretty things in all sizes. Underwire, front-snap, Cuddleskin? What do you feel like?"

"I saw an ad. Victoria's Secret, or what's-it-called, a Wonderbra? That showy push-up that's all the rage. Get me that."

I went to the mall.

At the lingerie department at Wanamaker's, I flipped through the light-as-bird-bone plastic hangers holding hundreds of diaphanous bras and panties. I sorted through silky items, holding them up against my own body, trying to choose one. "This is too pink. She's not into pink," I told the clerk. Despite all the reasons I shouldn't miss her, I knew her tastes. I bought a *black* bra. I left the store with a tiny paper sack, as light as a dandelion puff.

IN THE Life Care unit, she was losing her war with Hepatitis C and liver disease, and I found her drifting in and out of "sleep."

When I roused her, she said, "I've been practicing."

"Practicing for what?"

"Well, you know—"

I told her, "I found just the right bra for you. Not too much, but with support. Perfect for anywhere or anything. It's all you're going to need."

"That's very prescient," she said. "But I shouldn't have sent you out shopping. On a goose chase—besides, who's going to see it but us?" She always felt despair having no current man in her life. And being excommunicated since her divorce from her first husband, the Arrow Collar model, she didn't expect to get to Heaven where she might show off her togs to JC. She plucked sheets of white tissue from the little scrap of satin. "It's perfect," she said. "It's what I would have chosen myself. But this would look good on you. Maybe you should keep it."

"I bought it for you," I said.

"Oh, you're in the same shoes as me. It's just a matter of time."

"I'm writing another memoir," I said.

"Good grief. What's this one about?"

"About my writing life, my sex life—they're entwined, you know."

"A book about your dirty laundry? I don't think I'll hang around for that one."

"Maybe you can."

"Is it your story, or mine?"

GIOVANNI

The number one man in my life is flat on his back. I sit at my son's bedside in my sterile costume: rubber smock, rubber gloves, slipper-socks, and a pleated transplant survivor mask. I have to wear the space suit to sit beside him as he gets his third bag of high-dose chemo through an IV port. The port is a round metal disc implanted under his skin through a two-inch-long incision in his upper chest, right through his ink-black skull tattoo. The port is attached to a catheter tube that is threaded into the subclavian vein at the top of his heart. He has worn this port for more than a year of treatment. A tube invading his skull tattoo, the beloved totem of his favorite punk band, The Misfits, is an insult to his person.

By his third week in the Bone Marrow Transplant Unit of a Boston hospital he is pissing blood. His daily infusions are poison. Busulfan irritates the bladder, and Cisplatin causes nephrotoxicity (toxicity to the kidneys) and his organs are damaged. He gets up to use the plastic quart bottle each time he needs to pee, so they can measure *what is going in* and *what is coming out*. He has to maneuver his IV pole on casters, and take it with him into the tight bathroom. I wait by his empty bed. He returns from the toilet with a ruby-red carafe.

Facing my son's possible death, I have to reorder my life. I have to take stock. What was I thinking? Who did I think I was? I'm not looking for excuses. According to my own mother, I've been a liar all these years. If I write this down, I don't know if it will save him.

River-rat

M y editor meets me at my hotel. It's sometimes the Warwick Hotel, or the Fitzpatrick. The first time he showed up at my hotel room door unannounced, Random House had reserved a room for me at the InterContinental on Forty-Eighth and Lex. At the center of the hotel's grand lobby they had just erected a floral arrangement almost a full story high, as if for a Lady Di wedding or an unnamed ascension. As I checked in, they were adjusting a fiberglass ladder beside the pyramid of blooms, unfolding the ladder's big yellow frame in manageable sections. As the workers tucked the risers into submission, I felt my knees tremble. It's a delicious weakness that I welcome each time a man nudges my legs open. The clerk said that the flower arrangement is examined closely several times each day. Sagging petals are snipped with surgical precision, but before the display shows the slightest defeat, before the mountain of blossoms slumps, before my spaghetti string camisole slips off my shoulders, a brand new bouquet is brought in.

My trysts with my editor begin with dresses I wear just for him. A blue silk dress with a fitted waist and tucked front panels that cascade in vertical symmetry to the knee—I have dived into Lake Como and climbed out sheeted in its *chiaro azzurro* water. Or maybe I'll wear a sleeveless mini shift, a pink sarong, glove-tight. It follows from invisibly stitched darts at the breast, to the curve of my hips, and halts above midthigh. Its hem is a sharp crease that says, "Yes. You may cross this line." My glen plaid business suit was a lucky find at a designer outlet store. Its "seasonless" wool is feather-light, as if woven from our aroused breaths. He says, "Keep that skirt on." He gathers the hem into submissive folds and pushes the crumpled fabric over my buttocks until it's a tight belt above my waist, harness reins that he holds on to, double-fisted.

At the hotel, I unpack my dresses from my carry-on that's been spritzed with Guerlain's Samsara, so the dresses are suggestively imbued with it. I lay them on the bed to examine my choices. I can quickly steam a dress on the curtain pole just by turning on a hot-hot shower or I can press it with the hotel iron. The one I decide to wear rests on a wooden hanger until I slip it on, right before he arrives. Waiting for him, I sit on the edge of the bed with a straight-backed frozen posture in just my bra and panties.

Afterward the battered pink shift is jammed by its armhole on a bathroom hook. Or it's the Lake Como dress left in a careless puddle on the hotel room floor. He is called "charming," but she's "too flirtatious," a cock-tease, unladylike, louche. Although it's called *diction*, there is no male equivalent of the pejorative feminine noun "slut." She's christened by all antiquity: fallen woman, slattern, femme fatale, man eater, coquette, trollop, and strumpet. For him, we are more

affectionate. We call him a rake, a Don Juan, or a
Lover Boy. But she gets the direct barrage of one-
syllable baptisms in a *rat-a-tat-tat*: skirt, tart, piece,
ho, bitch, slit, gash. It takes two for a baptism. The
preacher dunks the new believer beneath him. He tugs
her hank of hair and pushes her under, the same gesture he makes with his belt open back in the hotel
room. He leaves her there, still naked, still wet; her
Lake Como gown evaporates into the air.

Have Gun, Will Travel

He meets me for a drink if I'm in the city for a book event, when launching my first novel, *The Arrow Collar Man*, and then the next one, *Open Water,* its title coming from sailors' slang that means you're so far out at sea, there's no land in sight, and the *next* white elephant, and so on. This time it's the nonfiction book, *My Sister Life, The Story of my Sister's Disappearance*. The book begins, "My sister disappeared when she was fourteen years old." She left home to become a child prostitute in Virginia Beach, completely dependent on her pimp as a surrogate parent.

The memoir is getting some attention and my editor and I will celebrate our initial success. When I enter the hotel room at the InterContinental, I find a tureen of flowers, fat blue hyacinths standing erect like phalluses, with a teensy white card attached. Delivered to the wrong room, I think. Or perhaps my husband is repentant after being in a grouchy mood at my departure. We have a fire that will never go out. But he isn't the type to think of flowers as a bridge between two burning shores. I don't think it is him.

It's River-rat who sent the vase of flowers to the room ahead of my arrival so I would find them waiting for me. I have not yet put down my bag when I rip open the little white card. The note says, "From your flea-bitten editor."

River-rat had penned the coy signature because I often ended my notes to him by signing, "Your Flea." The nickname comes from my being a pest, asking him questions about his blue pencil marks on my manuscripts, biting his ankles about changes he wants, but my complaints are never too serious. I like his blue pencil marks. I told him about the movie, *Closely Watched Trains*. In my favorite scene, the stationmaster takes a vintage rubber stamp with a wooden handle from an office drawer. He inks the antique contraption on an ink pad and he gently stamps his beautiful young assistant across her thighs and buttocks. In the same way, I can feel every mark River-rat makes on my pages—the brackets, squiggly delete marks, indents, little slashes and long-tailed arrows, the double-sphered hard periods, the crossed-out sections and insertions—as if he had written everything on my skin. His editorial markups are almost erotic. I want him to make little notes on *me* with his blue pencil. Circle my nipples. Make dotted lines from my white throat to my triangle. I want to feel the thrilling decisiveness he uses when he scribbles on my text, but on every part of me. Like the scene in *Open Water* when Rennie lovingly circles Willis's flea bites with a ballpoint pen, in order to tabulate any new red spots he might get overnight, I wanted my editor to write on me.

OTHER WRITERS have difficulty accepting an editor's comments. One of his authors reacted strongly to a critique River-rat had sent her. She sent his letter back to him riddled with bullet holes. She had tacked the page of Random House stationery to a fence post and shot it up until it was Swiss cheese. I was impressed. I never get very angry about his editorial suggestions. He has some helpful perceptions, but if I don't agree, I ignore him. He had once telephoned me when I was in Vermont, teaching at the Bennington Writing Seminars. It was during a severe cold snap, and he reached me at the faculty house where I was staying. I had had the misfortune to be assigned a small apartment in an old farmhouse. In subzero temperatures, the field rats left the pastures and entered campus housing. I called it the "rat room" because at night, when I was in bed, the rats emerged and scrambled across the bedroom floor. When I turned on the light, they slipped behind the wainscoting. I kept the light on, but if I fell asleep, they returned. They found a package of saltines in my jacket pocket and had nibbled through the lining. They even chewed my bar of soap where I had left it in the soap dish. I was most upset when, in the classroom, I peeled the cellophane from a cough drop and discovered that the lozenge had been gnawed.

I was sitting at my desk in the "rat room" that morning, when River-rat called. He had just finished reading the final draft of my novel *Open Water*. He said he was having trouble with the protagonist, a handsome twenty-something short-con operator. He told me, "Willis is despicable!"

"He's despicable?" I said. These were not words of praise. Okay, the character had some social problems.

He was a petty thief, stealing expensive tools with his sidekick, Fritz, and he was hooked on morphine suppositories that he swiped from his grandmom, Rennie Hopkins; he had a broken arm, in a cast, that never healed because he kept smashing the cast in fits of anger, and he had a sexual obsession with his next-door neighbor, a divorcée named Holly. Holly says, *"Your editor's right about Willis. I thought he was despicable too. Worse than my last disaster. But then I got to know him. He's a sweetie, really."*

I'm shocked to hear one of my characters talking to me from out of the ether. Holly knows what she's talking about, after all, she had set fire to her husband's bed to prove a point. Holly is right. Willis is lovable. I write about the attractive nobodies of the social fringe. I follow Thomas Hardy's instructions: "The business of the writer is to show the sorriness underlying the grandest things, and the grandeur underlying the sorriest things." River-rat always had mixed feelings about my ne'er-do-well characters. His squeamishness about these hardscrabble toughs that I write about has something to do with his concern about sales. My work has no commercial appeal and each time he published my books, his back was against the wall. Last year the erotic romance title *Fifty Shades of Grey* made so much money for its publisher that the company awarded a $5,000 bonus to all of its employees. The bonus was not just for editors with their blue pencils, but for the company's warehouse workers who use box cutters, Windex, mops, and brooms. Except for my one *New York Times* Best Seller about a murdered fashion writer, the books that I write often don't show a penny.

My fans are few and far between. One reviewer in the *Chicago Tribune* said about my novels, that if my edgy characters approached her on the sidewalk, she would cross the street to avoid them. River-rat felt a similar aversion. But I never changed a word about Willis.

I never sent River-rat's letters back to him with bullet holes or with their edges burned. It was later, when we were lovers that I acted out like his other author. He once gave me a beautiful antique Hamilton wristwatch with a snakeskin band. The gorgeous watch had to be wound by hand, with a teensy knob. When winding it, I was careful to monitor the delicate but strident resistance of its little spring. With rising admiration for the mechanism, I turned the little knob using extra caution not to go too far. The operation of gently twisting it tighter and tighter was an increasingly erotic sensation. Yet I wanted to smash its crystal with a ball-peen hammer. The ticking watch just reminded me of the trap I was in. Its snakeskin band coiled around my wrist like a jungle vine. I should nip it in the bud! Instead I sent the watch back to him. I walked to the Random House mailroom in person to give the watch to the mail sorter. I instructed him to hand deliver it to his floor that very afternoon, the very same day River-rat had visited my hotel room.

I returned the watch to him, but the next week River-rat sent it back to me in a Jiffy Bag. I opened the padded envelope and immediately put the watch back on my left wrist. I pressed its tiny crystal to my ear to hear it tick. Its winding mechanism always needs adjusting, so to speak.

I BORROWED my nickname "Flea" from something I had learned from my husband. He explained that the word flea, in Italian, is a feminine noun pronounced *mosca*.

Mosca can mean "a little fly" or a "flea," but my husband said that "Mosca" was poet Eugenio Montale's pet name for his common-law wife. I liked the story, believing the pet name was romantic. In an e-mail, poet Jonathan Galassi told me not to be fooled. He said, "One of Montale's nicknames for his common-law wife (not to her face) was *'Hellish* Fly.'"

My husband never calls me "Flea" or "Mosca," but when standing to embrace me he always seems surprised by how I fit right under his chin. He says, "You are so tiny." At five foot seven, I wasn't that small, but he uses "tiny" as a superlative. And he gives me many nicknames of his own. He calls me "Marina Bay" after the name of a seaside dive where they offered Twin Lobster specials for $14.99. The waiter brought two lobsters for each of us, except that each lobster was a scrawny cull. The maimed one-armed lobsters soon became an emblem of our long-term partnership. After a friend once said that I have a slight resemblance to the actress Greta Garbo, my husband calls me "Greta Garbage." Or he teases me again, and calls me "Mal de mer." And then he uses Lorca to mock me in sex play, when he says, "Verde, Verde, come here." That's from Lorca's line, "Green, green, I want you green," in the English translation.

One day my husband will kill me. He attended an afternoon class at the police station, took the test, and received his gun license. His score was perfect. He is qualified to carry the most dangerous, automatic weapons on his person and was awarded a "*Class A:*

Large Capacity Concealed Permit." I don't recognize the photo ID on his laminated gun license. A Luciferian apparition emerges in a sheen of light as you flip the holographic card back and forth under the lamp. This was before he went to the Powder Horn to purchase his Taurus 850 CIA "Carry it Anywhere" five-round .38 Special for concealed carry.

RIVER-RAT HAD not yet called me "Flea," until he sent the vase of flowers.

I had named my editor "River-rat" after he gave me an important book, *The Bottom of the Harbor*, by Joseph Mitchell, a masterpiece about New York Harbor, the Hudson, and its mysterious tributaries. The book begins with a description of filth. Mitchell tells us that New York waters are poisoned by "silt, sewage, industrial wastes, and clotted oil." Where I live, the sea is Coke-bottle green, but Mitchell describes the Hudson's underwater "rot" that creates basketball-size "sludge bubbles." Sludge bubbles are both literal and metaphoric. They represent all the human hubbub and misery that surfaces along the shoreline, the unfortunates, the lost, everyone who is discarded, like trash that hugs the jetties and the pilings. This is what I love to explore, the unpleasant settings where our souls are born, just like Thomas Hardy showed me.

Mitchell also tells us that fish return each year despite the filth, so a story must have optimism, despite our cynical expectations. River-rat loves rivers more than the seven oceans. He told me that he didn't like the sulkiness of tides. He said that he could see the Hudson River from his house where he viewed the

night surge from that chalice, and, at morning, saw its
golden hydraulic light refill it. Watching the river is his
one sliver of daily introspection. "You are always writing about the sea," he teased me, but I sensed he had
a respect for my authentic feelings. Even the names
of my books reflected my obsession. *Open Water*. *Sea
Room*. And even my short story, "Riders to the Sea,"
was a title I borrowed from John Millington Synge's
play of the same name. River-rat's love of freshwater
lakes and rivers was also authentic and quite charming.
Joseph Mitchell was his hero, and almost like a father
figure to him, although Mitchell was recently accused
in a *New Yorker* article of having invented nonfiction
details in his famous book, *Joe Gould's Secret*.

In a memoir, there isn't the snow fence of fiction
but a storm of true details. But truth wants to be
manipulated and coerced; it invites the lyric interpre-
tation and dismisses the factual. Truth's membrane is
subdural and elastic. Matisse told his students, "*Exaggerate* in the direction of truth." Gauguin instructed,
"Because your canvas is smaller than nature, you have
to use a greener green. That is the falsehood of truth."
Picasso said, "We all know that art is not truth. Art is
the lie that makes us realize truth." He explains that the
subjects of paintings often disappear. Describing figures
in his paintings, he said, "The 'vision' of them gave
me a preliminary emotion; then little by little their
actual presences became blurred; they developed into
a fiction and then disappeared altogether, or rather
they were transformed into all kinds of problems.
They are no longer two people, you see, but forms and
colors: forms and colors that have taken on, mean-
while, the idea of two people and preserve the vibrations of their life."

When writing a memoir for my editor, a blizzard of erotica swirls over him. I have unbuttoned my blouse; my hair falls loose to my shoulders in dirty-blonde fronds, in the straight-haired shiksa disarray that he seems to adore. The elastic sliver of my French cut panties saws into my slit, for *him*.

As I am writing the sister memoir, from the get-go I sensed I was selling myself. My book/my body! I have to acknowledge that from the very beginning I might have encouraged him. During our introductory telephone conversation when discussing my very first novel, I had used a sexual idiom.

At that time, my agent at Janklow & Nesbit had submitted my manuscript, *The Arrow Collar Man,* to an editor at an imprint at Random House. The novel was about a brother and sister who, in adulthood, unite to search for an estranged patriarch, a handsome cad who had once been an Arrow Collar model. The father had been immortalized in the famous J. C. Leyendecker illustrations in *Collier's* and in the *Saturday Evening Post*. My agent called to tell me that an editor at Random House was quite interested in the novel. "He's not ready to get into bed with you yet," she said, "he's writing a memo."

"He's doing what?" I asked. I was unfamiliar with the specific meaning of the publishing jargon "memo" which I soon learned usually means a bitch or complaint about something. "Why is he writing a memo?" I asked.

She said, "He has some questions, I guess. Maybe you should just talk to him and head him off at the pass. What do you think?"

I didn't understand the vernacular, "memo," but I recognized the old Hollywood western lingo, "head him off at the pass," a phrase which conjured a posse seeking a fugitive. That very year, I had made a personal acquaintance with Richard Boone's widow, who lived in the same retirement community with my mother in Ponte Vedra, Florida. Richard Boone was Paladin, the beloved gun for hire in the TV western *Have Gun—Will Travel*, a gentlemanly but mercenary gunfighter, a polyglot, who always dressed in black. He looked more like an Eastern dandy than a cowpoke, and Paladin's widow gave me many signed photographs of the TV star. So I thought of Paladin when my agent told me to call the editor and to "head him off at the pass." I dialed the Random House switchboard and asked to speak to this guy writing a "memo" to me.

Some women swear it's a man's eyes. His clear and deeply seeking gaze, maybe just slightly hooded with a hint of bedroom intentions. Other girls say, it's his powerfully defined mouth, or his long-legged swagger on the sidewalk, when he shoves you to the inside stream of pedestrians, out of harm's way. He strides along the curb to fend off taxi doors swinging open. He alerts you to any open grates. His shoulders are level and squared, making an even V-shape of his upper torso, a full-grown man, without the lopsided slouch or sloped shoulders of a backpack-carrying twenty-something.

There are a lot of possible lures, but a man's *voice* is the bedrock of my attraction. The hetero grumble can be heard in everything attractive. The male voice evokes a cross-continental authority of selfhood, as in Pablo Neruda's poem, "We Are Many." I hear it in every engine turning over, in long-haul semis with double-clutching nine-speed transmissions, in silences like a river's swirl and in ocean suds, in the echo of empty silos dotted across transcontinental prairies, in clattering bamboo forests, in a wall of wind. I hear a constant hetero vibration in every setting, in every background, a throbbing roar like a beehive in an abandoned pipe organ.

River-rat's voice hits me below the waist, and I like to hear him clear his throat of all those honey-clogged notes, both before and after sex.

In our first conversation, twenty-five years ago, we spoke fledgling novelist to fledgling corporate pencil pusher. After starting out as a young editor at *Readers Digest*, he was soon becoming a notable Random House guru. I already had published a small edition of short stories, and two collections of poems.

But I was AWOL from poetry.

Talking to River-rat, his voiceprint was instantly seductive, its timbre rich and smoky with Karo vowels and closeted eroticism. He told me that he loved my novel *The Arrow Collar Man*. I was thrilled to hear this. Here was a man who was saying that he connected with my book, with my vision, with my *reason for living*.

Yet he said that before he could make an offer on my first novel he wanted me to make changes to the manuscript. He wanted me to shift a third-person narrative to the first person.

I wanted to please the new Paladin who had said he "loved" my novel, but I told him, "I don't think the novel would work in first person. Remember those explicit scenes between the couple? That sort of thing needs the third person don't you think?"

"Scenes between the couple?"

"You know? The *sex* scenes?"

"Well, maybe you can try to tone down all those third-person introspections. When you write, 'She *felt* this . . . She *felt* that.' And I think that the novel should start at the second chapter."

I said, "You want it to start at the second chapter?" That would dismiss the interior point of view of my female character which creates immediate sympathy for her.

"We don't need the first chapter," he said. "The second chapter gets right to it."

He was talking about the sex.

The second chapter begins, "In April, Tracy moved in with Margaret. It was the same week he joined Sex Anonymous." In the very first scene of the second chapter, the heroine's man-friend is fingering her nipples.

River-rat wanted me to make changes, but he had not yet made an offer on the novel. So I told him, "Do you want the book, or not? Because before I make any changes to the manuscript, let's pop the cherry on this first."

I used the sexual idiom, "pop the cherry," in my very first telephone conversation with him.

It came out of nowhere, seeded by our discussion. His voice had evoked my dirty mouth. From that moment on, my whole life at Random House would be fiercely sex-driven.

He might say I had started it all by using the sexual idiom. My words promised him something. But I think that *he* started the pattern, asking me to work for him for free, without payment or commitment. Either way, I didn't change my novel from the third person.

I am writing about him in the first person now. How do you like it, baby?

ICE

There is a distinction between my secret life and my real life. My secret life has no foundation, no bulkhead, no stone stairs, no crossbeams or attic framework to support its shivering temple. It is of the mind, or in the mind, what I have come to recognize is the "mind's mind." It takes bodily form only on the soiled synthetic hotel coverlet in every unsanctioned setting where we meet. Outside our trysts, it doesn't exist.

In 2011 my real house was destroyed in a manner I could not foresee.

My twenty-five-year-old son became very ill. It started with a lump on the side of his throat, the growth sluicing toward his shoulder. He had a doctor look at it, and they said it was nothing. It was a "lipoma," or fatty deposit, just below the skin. They did not order an ultrasound or other diagnostic tests. We had a friend, Hunter O'Hanian, the director of the Fine Arts Work Center in Provincetown, who also had a "fatty lump" on *his* shoulder. In summer, he sometimes wore sleeveless "wife-beater" T-shirts and people liked to tease him about his fatty lump. We poked it with a pointer finger. Because of Hunter's fatty lump we accepted Giovanni's diagnosis.

Months later, Giovanni was feverish and couldn't get out of bed. He was having night sweats. The lump on his neck was even larger. He went to Massachusetts General Hospital to get another opinion. After four days in the hospital, he was diagnosed with advanced stage lymphoma, what they called "fourth stage lymphoma, *bulky.*" That means that the tumors were large and had a foothold in his other organs. Tumors had invaded his rib cage. When they operated to extract the tumor from his throat to get a biopsy and to rake out as much infected tissue as possible, he awoke during surgery. They had not administered the correct anesthesia. He told them, "Hey, I can feel that!"

He would have to begin a first regimen of chemotherapy called ABVD, to be administered biweekly for six months in visits to the chemo factory on the eighth floor of Mass General's Yawkey building, named after Red Sox owners Tom and Jean Yawkey. Every hospital in Boston has its own Yawkey buildings, and patients who visit the city for treatment are faced with this confusion.

And then there's the bothersome acronym "ABVD," a word that's made up of the first initial of each deadly drug they would load on: Adriamycin, Bleomycin, Vinblastine, and Dacarbazine, and because he was fourth stage they added yet another drug called Avastin, so it was ABVD-A. The drugs were administered in succession by IV, one after another, requiring six hours in the hospital, every other week, from October to April. Treatment causes infertility, and before he could begin, he had to make an appointment at a sperm bank. In his poor condition he was expected to show up at an office at New England Cryogenic Center. They sent him into a cubicle where he was ordered to masturbate. In his condition, he wasn't in the mood. He was asked to make two appointments, so they could be sure to get a viable sample.

With ABVD therapy, the drugs cause side effects. He soon lost all his hair. He shaved his head, so he wouldn't have to watch clumps of hair falling out. His blood counts dropped and he risked serious infection, so he was told to stay locked up at home, out of public places. He couldn't take the subway or go inside busy buildings. He had to stay out of clubs. He dropped out of his band, Street Sweeper, which was doing regular shows in crowded underground settings: at Elks clubs, in basements, in backrooms of low-rent taverns across the state. Besides, with ABVD, neuropathy soon takes hold, and he lost sensation in his fingers. He could no longer play his guitar. He shoved his guitars under the bed. He couldn't stand having his equipment nearby, reminding him of his uselessness. He decided to lend his guitars to his replacement.

After six months, he was bald and weak. ABVD didn't work. He was not in remission.

Next he faced a more dangerous regimen, the one called "ICE," again named for the initials of the names of three new medications, a combination chemotherapy regimen used to treat progressive and poor-risk recurrent lymphomas. This protocol has a higher incidence of fatal consequence. Side effects can include leukemia, bloody urine, hallucinations, numbness, confusion, ringing in the ears, and tissue damage if the drug leaks from the IV onto bare skin!

Each day, when driving to Mass General Hospital to sit with Giovanni, I passed a roadside stand. A large white plank on a tripod displayed a sign with tall black lettering that said *ICE*. Fishermen could stop to buy bags of ice cubes for their coolers to take on day trips. Seeing the ICE sign each day always took my breath away. I wanted to steal the sign or perhaps even purchase it, so that I could throw it off the wharf and watch it sink or float away.

Leaving town to join my son at the hospital, I also have to pass another upsetting vision. The summer before, a teenage boy tried to cross Route 6 on his bicycle at a busy Wellfleet intersection on Cape Cod. The kid had worked at Hatches fish stand, and was beloved by both the locals and summer residents. He was fresh-faced and always friendly, even when penny-pinching oldsters asked him to cut off an extra tenth of a pound from a quarter-pound piece of cod. On his break, the kid biked to the convenience store to buy snacks or an iced coffee. One afternoon he was hit by a car and killed.

Friends erected a memorial to the fish boy. They placed a ten-speed bike just off the shoulder of the road where the boy had been struck. The bike was spray-painted ghostly white. It looked boldly skeletal in its white outlines. When I drive to the hospital, I pass the *ghost bike*. The ghost bike was not just an icon to the fish boy, but soon became a symbol of my son's fight not to die.

These ghost bikes are not uncommon, and we find them here or there across the nation's highways. If my son dies I might paint his very first electric guitar, the one on which he had learned to play the first covers of his favorite songs. I imagine the beat-up Telecaster sprayed clay white. If I died, they might set up my old typewriter, its keys smeared with chalk. Or even more appropriate, my kitchen broom. My string mop.

Before he was readmitted to the hospital for ICE, Giovanni and I had breakfast at a high-end hotel one door over from Mass General. The building was the infamous Charles Street Jail. Some of the original cast-iron grills and jailhouse accessories were part of its decor. And with sarcastic exuberance or with a hats off to Boston's law enforcement, developers had named the five-star palace The Liberty Hotel, and its posh restaurant was called "Clink," an insensitive joke about the jailhouse idiom that arose from the actual "sound" an inmate hears at lockdown.

When Giovanni and I were seated at Clink and after ordering our eggs, (we declined to sample their lobster omelet), we were surprised to see Larry David, sitting alone at the next table, buttering a muffin. The Hollywood celebrity was in Boston because his daughter had just enrolled at Emerson College. Sitting with my cancer-stricken son so close to the renowned comic, whose overt cynicism had been a welcomed palliative in years past, seemed to lend our situation an absurd twist. Giovanni had grown up soaked in the Chekhovian subplots of David's *Seinfeld* series, and he admired its mastermind. Giovanni was a big fan, but he didn't want to bother the TV icon. But on our way out of the restaurant Larry David called over to *us*. He had heard us discussing Emerson College, and his ears were pricked. He asked my son about the college. The actor examined the kid standing before him. Giovanni is tall and lanky, with gorgeous eyes and high cheek bones. But he was bald. Yet, with his deep voice and a killer smile, he was a young man who Larry David's daughter might like to meet. Perhaps because it was a current fashion trend for young men to be skinheads, Larry David didn't see a cancer patient. He didn't imagine the plastic vials and IV bags of poisonous ICE that were to be mixed and measured at that very moment, and set aside for my son.

We had enjoyed meeting Larry David at the next table, but the comic was forgotten when I sat beside Giovanni in the ICE unit, in a brand-new oncology wing at Mass General. The unit was for end-stagers and hopeless cases. We were funneled into the new wing, that, in fact, looked like an ice palace, an entirely glass enclave with modern decor quite like a Trump tower hotel. Floating chandeliers dangled in the circular six-story lobby like giant glass jellyfish. The walls of his room were nine-foot-tall, dust-free glass panels. The room was very cold and dimly lit with mood lighting like an Icelandic casbah.

"We have to stop meeting like this," I told him.

"Yeah, right."

I handed him another bottle of Aquafina. ICE patients are not permitted to drink ordinary bottled water; they have to drink *distilled* water. Whenever Giovanni comes home he cannot drink my well water. An underlying darkness envelops me when I recognize that my well water is somehow metaphoric for my maternal nurturing. It was off-limits to him. It could poison him. This well-water restriction seemed to represent my helplessness and the tragedy of everything unfolding.

THE GARDEN

After working with River-rat on four books together, a dramatic change occurred with the release of my memoir, *My Sister Life*. When writing a memoir, your editor gets involved, with the probity of a schoolmarm, or like a bossy uncle, or a lover—

Now he will learn about you, your debauchery, your low-life itinerary, the grim facts about your sister who was a child prostitute, a "baby pro." These things unnerve him, but he wants more; engaging in my memoir he'll live out his shadow side without consequences. Writing the memoir, you materialize before him—in the flesh. You have unbuttoned your blouse; your hair falls from its comb. You're the live article. And he, too, is real—unlacing his wingtips in the dark.

It's "Searing . . . Harrowing," says the *New York Times*. So what? My friend, the writer Judith Grossman, tells me that all of my books are about the disappeared. Lovers, fathers, and siblings go missing. She says my sister's mysterious departure was the linchpin event of my coming of age. Many years later, I am writing a sequel to that book about my missing sister. It's a *memoir of a memoir*. I owe it to that first book to write this one. It's going to be a love story, but not *that* kind of love story. Every book I write should bring me grace, but this one is going in the opposite direction. Yet with memory, if the glass is half full, the sediment in the bottom grows deeper, more savory. The elixir ferments, becomes golden and transparent. Despair just increases its potency.

My life as a writer spans almost a half century. Those years are entwined with sexual liaisons and broken bonds, book after book. This book will be just as "Gripping . . . Startling" (*Newsweek*) as the first one. My old friend, poet Stanley Kunitz, once said about my first book, *Reckless Wedding*, "This is her book of chances and dangers." The writing life is a dangerous occupation. Stéphane Mallarmé said writing "is the language of a state of crisis." But I asked Stanley, "What kind of dangers are you talking about?"

"Telling the truth is dangerous," he said. "Be careful. There are *ways* of telling the truth."

Other friends suggest that I should be writing a feel-good book about my English gardens. My gardens are in full maturation and have had several magazine stories published about them; foppish horticultural busybodies have toured my sunny garden tiers and shady theaters to write rave reviews, with full-color pictures. In the garden's green rooms, I am sage, straightforward, and without fault. As Edenic sylph or matron, I'm truly pure of heart. All right, I will include entries about my flower beds. But I'm going to write a *tell-all* gardening book.

Hibiscus Syriacus

O ne of the staples in my garden has a history that
dates back to biblical times. In Song of Solomon, the most erotic section of the Old Testament, the
little shrub Hibiscus Syriacus gets its common name.
The text says, "I am the rose of Sharon," and in direct
statements we hear mutual praise by the two lovers.
"Let him kiss me with the kisses of his mouth . . .
Thy lips are like a thread of scarlet." "Thy name is
an ointment poured forth; therefore, do the virgins
love thee."

The Rose of Sharon is a reluctant little vase-shaped
tree that doesn't leaf until late spring. It stands naked
for weeks like an unwilling ingenue after everything
else is in bud. The inexperienced gardener might think
the virginal item is not worth the wait, and dig it up.
In time, a latex frizz erupts like number-two pencil
erasers; tiny green nipple tips poke out on staggered
branches. With real June heat it thrives, leafing bright
green, but it waits until summer's end to please us.
Finally it decides to flower. Hundreds of flouncy handkerchiefs unfold; four points billow out, each gathered
by a single stitch at center. Erratic stars, Kleenex-white.

Like when a man shakes out his pocket square and offers it to me to line my panties after a secret tryst. In Song of Solomon *he* says to her, "The joints of thy thighs are like jewels."

My father once said that Rose of Sharon is a dirty tree. Hibiscus Syriacus flowers survive for only one day. By evening their petals close up and crumple into moist clumps and they fall, like wadded cum rags dropped behind in bed.

1960

My mother comes into the garden bare breasted, in just her silk panties. Holding the backs of her wrists against her nipples, she's gloriously in her sublime nothing. She wants my father to leave his lawn chores and come into the house to fuck her. Or she wears her tight green stretch pants. She snaps the waistband once or twice to remind my father what waits for him.

Sometimes she tends her kitchen garden, plucking hollyhock blossoms one by one, to float the fluffy bells in the wading pool. "There she is: the queen, and her entourage," she tells us, as we watch the inverted blossoms glide by like fine ladies dressed in formal gowns.

Our mother is the goddess of the garden, the sex goddess. My father mows our two acres more than once a week in summer. His mower doesn't have a bag to catch grass clippings and one of my chores is to follow my father as he mows the lawn in sections and to rake the newly cut grass into piles right behind him. My sister and I work together to create distinct, sizable mountains of grass, little hills that grow almost as tall as I am. After big heaps are formed, we sweep them into a large compost wagon, a big scoop of nylon mesh on an aluminum axle with two back wheels. Together we maneuver the awkward hamper to a secreted compost theater on the opposite side of a hill, out of sight. It's an afternoon's work for two little girls. Sometimes our mother steals our father away and tells us to keep raking grass until she is finished with him.

One summer I caught a virus. The doctor called it "Slap Cheek Syndrome" because I had raised red patches on my face, the size of the palm of a hand. It was a "parvovirus," and not as serious as rubella or scarlet fever. But my fever spiked to 103. I was sent to bed where I was entrapped in repetitive fever dreams: I stand on our back lawn. My father asks me to move a mountainous pile of grass from one side of the yard to the other side.

He says, "Take only one blade of grass at a time."

"One sliver of grass at a time?" The task seemed monumental.

"Choose the best one first," he said.

I examine the pile of grass to find the most perfect specimen. I pinch the tiny snip in my fingers and run across the lawn to the other side where I deposit it to create a new heap. I go back to the first pile to get another single blade of grass. I trust my father. I believe he must have some manly reason to transfer the mammoth grass pile from one side of the lawn to the other, one blade of grass at a time. Back and forth I go. Sometimes I drop the weightless flute of grass and search for it, but I have to go back to get a different little green fleck. I do this for hours.

My mother watches from the kitchen steps, her arms crossed beneath her prominent décolletage. Her bosom grows more substantial as my fever climbs higher. Dressed in her tight green stretch pants beside the tall hollyhocks, she is the main attraction. My mother is a French femme fatale. She is "drop dead" gorgeous, but she liked to say that all other women should "drop dead." I take after my mother. I have some of her beauty in most of the same ways, but it's not as flawless. My nose is not as straight as hers, and it's a little more than a "button" nose. But I utilize my good fortune of being born fully half French, and that has some wallop, believe me. The monotonous task of my fever dream when I suffered Slap Cheek Syndrome is a metaphoric instruction of an importance I will discover in years to come. For women, fevers erupt at every transformation. But there in the wading pool, rafts of inverted hollyhocks twirl like petulant girls in party dresses; in them, I see my mother's secret intentions.

ALL SPACE AROUND THE GIRL

In the lobby at the Warwick Hotel, sitting on a leather bench across from the reception desk, I felt self-conscious. I was a *woman waiting for someone.* I tried to be invisible, but I must have stood out. I wore a tight tailored suit, with a short skirt. I kept my legs crossed in a high swipe that showed my slender calf, a long and tapered invitation. Of course, I always wear silky hose in "nude," the most seductive flesh tone. A few years later, I sat with my legs crossed in the very same manner on the *Today Show*. My long leg on the TV monitor was an eye-stopper on national TV as Katie Couric questioned me about "premarital sex and single women" when discussing the murder victim in my book *Invisible Eden*. Couric was waxing with moralistic accusations about fashion writer Christa Worthington's reputation as an unwed mother and man killer. I said to Katie, "But you're single, aren't you? Don't *you* have a sex life?" There was a sudden explosion. Very loud. *Pop. Pop.* The morning talk show hostess was startled from her seat. Just months after 9/11, she believed that we were under attack. Two of the high intensity spots had shorted out. It seemed to be in direct response to my query, "Don't you have a sex life?"

Waiting for River-rat in the Warwick's lobby, I wanted to appear lovely, unforgettable, upon the very first instant his eyes found me. That moment was of great importance to me. I took to heart the painter Robert Henri's instructions about the importance of painting backgrounds in pictures. He says, "With the model before it, the background is transformed. All the beauty that can exist in the background rests in its relation to the figure." Waiting for my editor I was very conscious of the background setting I had placed myself in.

Expecting his arrival, I am the only female in the world. *The background is the sensation of all space around the girl.* He will enter the lobby from the Sixth Avenue door, walking through Randolph's. I really like that bar. But he's always in a rush and he usually takes me somewhere near Grand Central where, after his business with me, he hops on a train before his wife will notice that he gets home later than usual.

And Suddenly it's Evening

The first time River-rat arrived at my hotel room unannounced, I was surprised to hear a stifled knock on the insulated door. I saw his face through the peephole—troubled, handsome, as he searched the long hall, looking to the left and right, like a pup trying to avoid the dog officer's choke stick. He looked haunted, or maybe a little woozy, too, as if in my hotel door he saw his distorted reflection in a funhouse mirror. This was a man of such great importance to me, but he presented me with emptiness, an extensive abyss that would be my duty to fill. It would own me.

I grabbed my purse, pulling on my high heels since I hadn't finished dressing. I hadn't combed my hair. I forgot my coat. I tugged the heavy hotel room door open—stopping to release the phallic prong of its safety lock. But I didn't invite him in. I stepped into the hall, letting the door spank my bottom. Face to face, he looked even more haunted. People who try to bury their feelings instead seem to wear their feelings all over them. I felt the same way. We recognized one another. But I said, "What are you doing up here? You didn't ring me from downstairs?"

I had *wanted* him to arrive at my door, his eyes said.

After four books together, I still can't tell you the color of his eyes. They are pale blue, light brown, maybe metallic grey. A smelted, hot amalgam that burns into me. He once told me why he was attracted to me; he said, "I get so turned on because *you* are so hot for me!" It was his nature to blame others. But his arousal is spiked by a bashful vanity, that with me, he is willing to bask in. I too felt the pleasure of being wanted by him, to be, as Marguerite Duras once said, "the white-hot center of his world." Marguerite Duras wrote many instructions to me. Reading a line by Duras is a prescription for a high-dose potion or salve. I started to think of Duras as my secret primary care physician, my PCP; all my written-under-the table scripts came directly from my MD. Like Duras, I would write about *one* lover, again and again, in many different texts and in all my novels.

He would be the one.

Duras's books, *The Sea Wall, The Lover*, and *The North China Lover,* tell the same story about one exotic liaison, about its awkwardness, its passion. Its eternity is revealed in repetitions. The story of her "lover" begins with a true event in her youth. She said, "No other reason impels me to write of these memories, except that instinct to unearth. It's very simple. If I do not write these down, I will gradually forget them. That thought terrifies me."

Standing before River-rat in the dim hallway, I said, "Okay. Just kiss me. Get it over with."

"Not out here," he said. "Let's go into your room." He poked the weighty door with his fingertip. It easily

swept open and he gently sidestepped me into the room.
The heavy door plowed shut onto its tight threshold.

I saw my open suitcase on the floor with all its
jumbled contents. I didn't want him to see my tat-
tered half-slip that I sleep in, or my ratty hairbrush
that I forgot to use, or my copy of Flaubert's *Senti-
mental Education*. I didn't want to hear his opinion
about what I was reading. He wasn't interested in my
book, yet his eyes darted around the room. The sheets
weren't yet turned down so I yanked the spread open.
A tousled bed would seem less fearsome.

River-rat is very handsome; his refined features have
an imperious glow that reminded me of my mother's
rare Haviland French china that gleams in the corner
cupboard and *dares* you to eat off of it. As children we
were scolded if we lifted our plates before our noses
to lick the frosting off the Limoges. But despite his
nice features, this is a man with no outlines. Standing
before me is a black gulf I will never understand. He
presents a great library of absences and threatening
losses. They are suddenly in my hands.

Teen girls might say, "He's so cute!" It's the way
girls talk about unseasoned boys who show no signs of
wear and tear, no gravitas. My husband is Latin; he's
half English and half Italian. Even as a teenager, he
looked world-weary. Despite his English father, his Italian blood overpowers his roots to the United Kingdom.
He's inherited a burdensome oversexed machismo
from his maternal ancestors in Bedonia. His presence
exudes carnal energy wherever he stands; it percolates
at the podium, in the conference hall, when pitching a
ball, or tossing little babies into the air. There's a tingling hetero current in the air around him. I shouldn't

be thinking of him. But certain men set a standard that can't be met or overtaken.

Finally River-rat kissed me. He had never learned how to kiss a girl. In his forties, he was inexperienced. His kiss enveloped my mouth in an awkward bathroom plunger effect, instead of meeting my lips. I stopped him. I pulled his chin slowly to my face, encouraging him to find my lips with his lips.

River-rat has a beautiful mouth, with a classic vermillion border of the upper lip, or what they call "cupid's bow," but his lower lip has a minor anomaly. On the left side, there's a small lump—or in medical vernacular, it's known as a "Venous Lake." It's a small round bump, the size of an English pea, but it's very deep blue, like a sapphire shimmering through the epithelium. I once told him that he could get it removed with laser treatments at the dermatologist, but the idea of laser therapy made him queasy. I found the little sapphire mysterious and appealing. So I kissed him again, gently sucking his lower lip with drawn-out tenderness.

I often think of music lyrics to rationalize my actions and desires. Right then I thought of my son who had taught me the Misfits lyrics: Anything you want / anything the world has to offer / I can give you / if you just reach out to me / take my hand / everything a kiss cannot bring / I will give you / if you just say you will.

But River-rat interrupted my train of thought and said, "You must think that I'm so bourgeois."

I thought I knew the meaning of the word, although I often fudged the spelling. Calling our first kiss "bourgeois" showed self-knowledge, but it also knocked our first kiss down a few pegs, didn't it?

I wondered if he was serious about me. Then I thought *"serious"* is a prognostic label used in emergency room triage or in an ambulance ledger.

He said, "I have kids."

"At our age, who doesn't?" I said.

"The enlightened, I guess."

I didn't agree with him. Although my son had not yet become sick, my kids illuminated my understanding of my mortality. Without children I would never have understood a little poem by the Italian poet Salvatore Quasimodo: *Each of us alone on the breast of the earth / pierced by a ray of sun / And suddenly it's evening.*

River-rat had had three sprouts in just five years. His wife had had *save-the-date* cesarean births for all of them. She must have been out of service much of the time. His wife has a very unnerving name. He called her "Weensie." It was a playful nickname she'd been given as a child, a cutesy appellation born from her being the youngest one. There was a sexist ring or some kind of oppression behind the name. How could someone named Weensie have any say in household decisions? Her childlike name always made me feel uncomfortable, if not directly guilty. His wife had once been a painter but had later changed her career to become an ESL instructor. For Weensie to leave the art life behind to teach English as a second language was a sad story. But I understood that River-rat and I had a "second language" of our own.

If he felt he had to tell me about his wife and kids he was talking to himself, not to me.

He looked beleaguered by self-inflicted forces, as if a great prehistoric bird had alighted on him, its talons pinching his shoulders. I didn't think our kids had any place in the equation. He leaned back to look at me, with both curiosity and wariness, as if I were an invasive weed or wildflower, an all-too-natural detritus, like a sticky burr that might attach to the socks of his children. He didn't want my prickly sexual Velcro to adhere to his home life. I had to be kept separate. But for some reason he needed to describe his beautiful house in Hastings. He said, "It has two porches on opposite ends."

"Two porches," he said again, as if picturing his two porches and all the family gatherings that took place on summer evenings. These porches represented everything he might lose if he were found out. But I wanted to know, are the porches glassed-in or open? Did he mean terraces or screened breezeways? Are they like the sleeping porch of my childhood, where summer trumpet vines crisscrossed the screening? I saw lounge chairs. A Ping-Pong table for his kids. A gas grill with a quilted mitt dangling off a hook. The elegant wrought iron furniture that looks gorgeous after a snowfall. A few years later, when I wrote my novel *Lux*, for *him*, a minor character had the same obsession about his trophy house. I had nicknamed the character "Mr. Two Porches."

River-rat kissed me again.

He knew I would ignite in an instant. *I* was to blame for it, he believed. It was a case of "the firefighter as arsonist."

Blamers are tortured people. My heart went out to him.

Despite his excitement, he tries to remain cool, like a block of ice. Ice is a vulnerable medium. Ice sculptors attest to its responsiveness to human touch. It begins to liquefy with the artist's first intellectual spark or creative thought, a mere human instinct can dissolve the surface layer. That's what I'd been doing for years. My words are intimate taps and prods, chipping like burr bits, shaving with a V-shaped chisel; everything I said to him carved an illicit figure in the unforgiving block of ice. In our telephone conversations, a statue of Eros emerged with the heat of our entwining voices, word by word.

Just days before our first tryst, we had talked on the telephone about having recently seen the movie *L.A. Confidential*—with our own spouses. In the movie, a politician's sexual liaison with a boy cupcake ended in the murder of the young man. Detectives described how forensic examiners had found semen in the victim's gut.

I told River-rat in a whisper, "You know that scene in the movie where the kid is killed? You remember what the cops found in his stomach?"

River-rat said, "Yeah. I remember that scene."

"I want that in my stomach too. Can you help me with that?"

"We'll see what we can do," he said.

Our conversation wasn't very veiled.

He fell back on the bed, his head on the pillow, legs stretched out. He looked like a platter of gold. "This will change us," I said. But nothing was changed. I unbuckled his belt. The two side panels of his zipper uncurled like lotus petals in slow-motion time-lapse photography. The tip of his cock was already sweet, weeping a pearl as it brushed past my lips. My tongue fit the silky notch of his glans and followed its taut seam up to its brimming head and back down again. I let him glide it all the way back to the meaty snarl of tonsil and epiglottis—as deep as he wanted. A doctor had once told me, as he examined the back of my throat with a wooden tongue depressor, "Your gag reflex control is phenomenal!" The doctor imagined my carnal expertise as I endured his prods with a balsa stick. "Your throat looks good," he said.

Fellatio is a pleasing, mutual sensation that reverberates deeply through me; I can feel its power and girth deep in my breast, in my trunk, and into my perineum. My style isn't rushed or half-hearted, and never too studied.

He wrapped a hunk of my hair in his hand and tried to control the ending, prolonging the explosive moment, trying to keep it from concluding. The *more and more* brought us very close. Meeting flesh to flesh has a spirituality that is not often acknowledged, but is very prayerlike. I was too willing. I remembered Blake's instructions: "The cistern contains; the fountain overflows."

We had not removed our shoes and had not even undressed. If the shoes come off, it's *serious,* I guess.

He took me for drinks at the Bull and the Bear. At the little table, sitting across from me, his expression said, "This isn't going anywhere." At that instant I was lucid. I had science on my side. I was looking at an organism on a microscope slide.

The contagion exclaims, "I have infected you forever!"

I should have resisted him. I should have shut it down at each turn. I think of the little spring in the

Hamilton wristwatch. Wind it up just so far, and it ticks happily, with joy, for hours.

All of my writing belongs to him. Books I already had written, and books I have yet to write are for his eyes only.

I smiled.

EMTs call it "smiling death," when accident victims grin at first responders, giddy to be rescued, but secretly bleeding from fatal internal injuries. He had driven the first sword, a beautiful *espada de toros*, into my belly. The tip of its silver blade remains embedded in me. He meets me at hotels for fifteen years. Our children grow up and go to college. But the game is on. The starting flag unfurls at our eternal *course de nuit*.

BOY LEADING A HORSE

I have always understood that an art life is imbued with a sexual consciousness. At a very early age, I was seduced by both worlds. As a child I was involved in a ruckus at the Philadelphia Museum of Art that was written about in all of the Philadelphia papers. In February of 1958, when I was not yet six years old, my mother took me to a famous exhibition of Picasso's work at the museum. The show was called "Picasso at 75," a reference to the artist's age at the time.

The show was fully comprehensive, including a representative retrospective of the complete Picasso oeuvre, on canvas, in prints, ceramics, and illustrated books. I wandered through the galleries with my mother, but I became separated from her. All on my own, I came upon a narrow panel called *Boy Leading a Horse*, Picasso's famous 1906 portrait of a frontally nude young man walking beside a beautiful grey horse, its front leg lifted in an elegant prancing motion. I was horse crazy, like many little girls, but I was also curious about the naked boy. I walked up to the painting. The panel had been displayed in a gallery space by itself. I huddled near it, stepping up close to the horse's face. I traced its muzzle with my fingertips. With my pointer finger I inspected the boy's curious-looking scrotum. Without anyone to stop me I embraced the canvas. The painting was slightly wider than my open arms, but I gripped one side with my tiny fist, and flattened my cheek against the masterpiece in a melting adoration for the horse, ignoring the naked boy.

Security staff and docents surrounded me and pulled me away from the panel. I had done no real harm, although the curator ordered that the painting be gently wiped to remove any sticky residue left from my fingerprints. The very next day there were letters to the *Philadelphia Inquirer* complaining about my assault on Picasso's great painting. They said, "The museum board must establish new rules. Children should not be allowed to attend important exhibitions at the PMA." "Where was the little waif's nanny?" And, "Does this demon child have no one willing to step forward and take responsibility?" At cocktail hour, my parents read the newspaper's Letters to the Editor out loud, enjoying the absurdity of their sudden fame. One person had written to the paper praising my parents for bringing their children to see fine art, so they felt justified, and they didn't seem angry at me.

I HAVE always been a writer. My writing life started early. At eight years old, my second-grade teacher encouraged it. In fact, she was my *second* second-grade teacher, named Mrs. Tindle. My first second-grade teacher, "Miss Loveless," had kept me back. I had to repeat second grade because of my behavior problems. Mrs. Tindle entered the classroom prepared to deal with me. She came to work equipped with a strategy. She arrived each morning wearing several scarves looped around her neck. Every day she unwound her long chiffon veils and wrappers and used them to tie me to my chair, because I wandered from my seat. This was before children were diagnosed with Attention Deficit Hyperactivity Disorder, or ADHD, before prescriptions for Ritalin, and before educators believed it important to create an individual educational program for either gifted or hyperactive students, what they call an "IEP." My academic troubles in grade school, when my teacher tied me to my chair, might have arisen from my having been born a "premie." My mother was a heavy smoker, and I was less than three pounds at birth. In those days there were not any high-tech neo-natal units at hospitals. Instead I was placed in a glass incubator that had stiff rubber gloves attached to arm holes in the glass. Nurses were not allowed to touch me with bare hands, and they had to insert their arms through the glass and into the awkward gloves in order to change my diapers or to give me sustenance from a tiny glass bottle. I was not breastfed, cradled, or held in someone's arms for more than five weeks. I started my life as an untouchable. Sometimes my mother could stick her arms into the incubator's rubber gloves to rub my little shoulder blades, but soon she was discharged from the hospital and I was left to the staff. Experts believe that neglecting to cradle and embrace a newborn infant can have lifelong repercussions. The child might grow up "acting out" or the child might grow up to become a writer. A psychiatrist once told me that the psychic residue of being touched only by those rubber gloves would be hard to dispel.

When the second-grade teacher kept me bound by the waist to my seat, my chair was pushed into the back of the classroom, a secondary insult. But from my roped desk, I could reach the temperature dial on the tropical fish aquarium and I liked to fiddle with the tiny lever. I adjusted the heater higher and higher. Within just an hour an angel fish floated to the top of the aquarium. Then a neon tetra drifted sideways. A loach rolled over on its back. All the fish died.

When shackled to my chair, I amused myself by writing short stories. The teacher was impressed by my intensity. I scribbled several pages before lunch hour. So she sent me down the hall to read my fantasy tales to first graders. They were a captive audience, she said, and she was happy to get rid of me for a spell.

Twenty years later, in 1981, I published my first short story. It was a piece that the writer Ray Carver had helped me edit when he visited the Fine Arts Work Center in Provincetown. Ray had recently quit drinking. In his sobriety he had acquired a couple new addictions. He was smoking a lot of pot but even more concerning, he was eating three or four boxes of Fiddle Faddle each day, a store-bought confection of sticky-sweet caramel popcorn and peanuts. He sat beside me at my makeshift desk, an antique Singer sewing machine stand that with its lid shut could support my Smith Corona. The makeshift sewing machine-typewriter stand was a perfect sarcophagus for my enslaved domestic life with my first husband.

Ray crunched handfuls of peanuts and caramel corn as we looked at my story, line by line. He said he liked the story but he thought I should give it a different name. Its original title was too long-winded:

"The Effect of Live Radio on a Nude Girl While Bathing." In fact, I'd thought up the wordy title in imitation of Ray's often effective but very long titles like "So Much Water so Close to Home" and "What We Talk about When We Talk About Love." And Ray told me that he, too, had invented his wordy titles having been influenced by early James Purdy stories, like the one called "Why Can't They Tell You Why?"

"We are victims of influence," Ray said, shaking his head slowly, side to side. But Ray also had invented some very terse and succinct titles like his famous story "Fat," and a later one he had called "Cathedral." Ray decided to rename my story with a one-word title too. He called the story "Clean."

"'Clean'? That's a great title," I said.

"You like it?"

"I love it!"

"It's yours," he said.

"No kidding? Thanks a million."

After he left my place, I had to take out the broom and sweep the kitchen floor. He had spilled a lot of Fiddle Faddle, and it would attract mice I was certain.

When "Clean" was published in *Playgirl* later that year, I was paid $500. It was a huge chunk of change for me at a time when I was waitressing tables at a seaside café in Provincetown, banking my pay from tips in plastic bags of loose change secured with twist ties to the annoyance of the bank tellers.

The three-page centerfold in that issue of *Playgirl* was a photograph of men dressed in snappy airline uniforms, wearing their official blue sport jackets with snazzy epaulets, but without their pants. The story was called "Pilots in the Cockpit."

The fact that my first published story appeared in a magazine with naked airline pilots seemed comical then. But there always have been "pilots in the cockpit" at every turn in my writing life. Since the very beginning, with Picasso's naked boy leading a horse, in every literary arena I entered, my liaisons in the writing world often became sexual. It's not politically correct to admit it and it might seem antifeminist, but my allure was on every page I wrote. It was my first introduction, my sole identification, long before I walked into the college classroom, into any office setting, into local bars where writers and their patrons gathered, elbows up, and it preceded me into the towers of Random House. My editors, my teachers, my mentors were waiting for me, already fluffed and primed. It wasn't a calculated method of gaining entrance, but the sexual edge that young female writers display on their pages has to be factored in at every stage of the game. Marguerite Duras is famous for saying, "Very early in my life it was too late." She was born female and had had no say in it. Her fate was mapped. She would get what was coming to her.

There were always men waiting for us.

THE TIGHT WHITE COLLAR

I am interested in how I found my writing influences. We are "victims of influence," Ray Carver
had said. Carver was helpful to me, but I did not follow
his example or write what came to be known in the
eighties and nineties as "Ray Carver" stories. Carver's
stories are frank portraits, with direct dialogue and
action, very minimalist in their sparse inclusion of
background information or interior remarks. His minimalist observations became quite popular and they
have even developed contests where writers compete
for prizes for writing the most "Carver-esque" narratives. I'm more of a maximalist. The first writers who
influenced me are a diverse group but they didn't write
minimalist fiction. Thomas Hardy's *Jude the Obscure*,
Joyce Carol Oates's *Them*, Edna O'Brien's *Night*, Jean
Rhys's *Good Morning, Midnight*, Philip Roth's *Good-
bye, Columbus*, and Carson McCullers's *Reflections in
a Golden Eye* were very early examples to me.

My influences came from many places, not just
from literature. My vision isn't just book-learned but
comes from a "lived life." President Obama's choice
for a new Supreme Court justice, Sonia Sotomayor,

talked about the "richness of her experience." One definition of "experience" is "*contamination* of foreign influence."

And, in fact, the word "influenza" is from the Medieval Latin *influentia*—a belief that epidemics were due to the *influence of stars*. A writer's influences are like viruses that can contaminate and threaten unless put to work. Importantly these germs of influence "morph" into new organisms, into our individual voices, into our own idiosyncratic points of view.

As a young writer, I soon understood that observation is not a passive activity. Observation is an action full of intention. Recently I accidentally reversed a common idiom in conversation when I said, "I'll see it when I believe it" instead of the usual "I'll believe it when I see it." But this reversal makes sense to me. "Seeing" requires that we have innate belief. What a writer sees is sharpened, transformed, or even warped by her own anxieties and obsessions. My colleague at the Writing Seminars at Bennington College, the writer Amy Hempel, once said in the classroom, "A writer's voice is established by what he notices." The word notice means to "take note, write down." With experience we grind a lens, but our innate turmoil is what triggers our attention to detail; our preformed obsessions are what will magnify, clarify, and tint a writer's vision. The act of "noticing" requires we make choices about what to look for. Noticing has attitude.

Writing is like a hornet's nest. Craft is the structured hive itself, yet a writer's idiosyncratic bank of impulses is a swarm of dangerous stingers. Another colleague, Betsy Cox, is more generous and she makes writing seem more uplifting. She says we should imagine a little wren building a nest. "It uses the pounding of its own breast, its own heartbeats, to shape a tiny bowl in the grasses it has collected." Craft, itself, is a scheme or vessel that is built by the writer's interior desire.

Vincent van Gogh wrote, "Count the wren and the oriole among the artists," and he, in fact, kept a cupboard with more than thirty bird's nests in his studio.

At a young age, I learned that I could choose to be victimized by circumstances or I could horsewhip my circumstances and could dominate events by the mere act of writing annotations about what I experienced. The writer should never be above the fray, but find a proper place in it. With my sister's disappearance I was thrust into the role of witness. I traded up, and from "witness" I became "writer." Our tentative grip on our self-esteem made me write things down; it made my sister run.

There were two books I read as a young girl that were great examples to me. These titles introduced me to some basic elements of stone cold realism. I was attracted to realism. I never liked fantasy, and I didn't read classic books such as *Narnia*. The colorful unreality in its pages was rather boring, and I never read beyond the first few pages. Instead I found a book by Grace Metalious, the author of *Peyton Place*, on my parents' bookshelves. It was a novel called *The Tight White Collar*. Its title sent a shiver up my spine. But one scene in that book in particular had greatly impressed me. Metalious wrote:

"Sometimes Lisa could pretend that Chris was not touching her at all. She could think her own thoughts with most of her mind, leaving just enough of her brain free to moan at the proper time. But then she was back in bed with the broken spring in the mattress poking her back, and with Chris who hadn't taken a shower that day. He had arrived in bed with his itchy armpits."

Reading about the lover's "itchy armpits" and the "broken box spring" awakened me to an idea that fiction could evoke uncomfortable settings and situations. Fiction could be very similar to the unpleasant, sometimes exasperating real-life experiences I was enduring. I felt a great connection to literary realism. It seemed to give me a kind of validation for surviving unpleasant world experiences of my own. For years I carried around the idea of the character who had had "itchy armpits," and who had not showered before making love to his girl. I was certain that a situation like this was soon going to happen to me when a man would take me into his rumpled bed, and I both feared and desired that probability.

Spurs for Suzanna, by Betty Cavanna, sounds like a bondage and discipline title, but it's a book about horseback camp. For almost fifty years I've remembered the opening scenes in that Young Adult novel. The writer describes a girl coming home from school to "a dry, stale odor, the indescribable, unpleasant smell of a tenantless house. The chintzes on the couch and wing chair looked dingy, the drawn venetian blinds showed a thin film of dust . . ." I liked how the author described *dirt*. That was new to me. The next scene describes the same teenage girl sitting in a gloomy Philadelphia restaurant having a tense argument with her mother. They are eating Chicken Croquettes (what they now might call Chicken McNuggets). I learned how a writer can evoke a character's anxiety in a few lines of physical description. She described the girl like this: "She picked up a spoon and ran its rim along the tablecloth, leaving a thin indentation. A line as thin as the spoon's tracery appeared between her mother's eyes, but her smile remained even." This little description of mother-daughter tension was familiar to me.

At an early age, I was seduced by the aura or ethos, or let's even say the eros of books. The moment when as a child I first recognized I could read on my own, one sentence, and then the next sentence, letting the narrative pull me along, is an indelible recollection. One word led to another. Words no longer seemed disjointed or awkward standing on their own. I was suddenly bestowed by a supernatural power; I could connect the audile pleasure or sound of the words with the tactile, full-bodied sensuousness of images and details. Flannery O'Connor wrote, "Fiction operates through the senses. . . . Fiction deals with reality through what can be seen, heard, smelt, tasted, and touched." She also explains how a writer's "judgment begins in the details he sees and *how* he sees them."

It's funny that with my nickname "Flea," that the very first story that I had learned to read on my own as a child was *A Fly Went By*, a picture book by Mike McClintock. The book describes a frantic chase; one creature stalks its prey, only to be pursued by another predator, larger than he—a fly, a frog, a cat, a dog, etc. The rising tension was elementary, yet the narrative bubbled along using exact rhymes in a maddening singsong. "The fly ran away in fear of the frog who ran from the cat, who ran from the dog . . ." I distinctly remember the summer afternoon when I sat in my living room beside the big window screen that allowed the scent of the garden to sweep over me. As I was reading on my own for the very first time, my father and older brother were having a vicious argument. My brother had driven the family car, a new 1958 Chevy Biscayne, into a streambed behind the high school parking lot. The wheels got stuck in the mud when he had tried to back it out of the water, shifting it into "reverse" and then into "drive" several times, digging the wheels deeper into the slop and making matters worse. He left it there and walked home hoping to avoid interrogation before returning with friends who might help him push it out of the gully. He had had no idea that twice a day the city opened the storm drain valves from two "reclaimed water" sewers that emptied into a nearby spillway. When that happened, twice a day, the ten inches of water in the gully became a three-foot surge where the car had been abandoned. The water rose up to the door handles and drenched the engine block. The Chevy would never dry out without costly professional renovations, and the car might be totaled.

As I was turning the pages of my picture book, my father stalked my brother, room to room, kneeing my brother in the back of his knees, knocking him down, again and again. My brother stood up and my father pursued him throughout the house, charging through the dining room, into the kitchen, and again into the living room. Around and around the suburban race course they paced, both of them screaming epithets to one another. I kept my head down, reading the book, but once I looked up and asked my brother, "Hey, what's going on?" He was in such a state of helplessness and anger that he grabbed my hardbound copy of *A Fly Went By* and struck me over the head with it. It wasn't beyond me to see that my father and brother were illustrating the very premise of *A Fly Went By*: the larger beast attacks the smaller one, and the smaller one attacks the tiniest one. But even at a young age I recognized emerging family tensions and human contradictions that would be in familiar tandem for much of my life.

My brother's nose was bleeding. My father had clocked him to end the row before my mother returned home from her bridge club. It wasn't merely the submerged Chevy Biscayne that had caused my father's anger. My half-brother was not my father's son. He was the residue of my mother's first marriage, the forfeited progeny of the Arrow Collar Man, and he and my father had a lifelong hatred for one another. The eruptions between them became worse and worse, until my brother enlisted at sixteen, lying about his age. He was sent to Korea after the war was over but American troops had remained to uphold the armistice between South and North Korea. His main duty was to give blood. Like me, he had a rare Rh-negative blood type that was in demand, even though the fighting was over. Although there were nine years between us, my brother and I were very close, and I missed him. Of all the kids, he and I took after our mother. We *looked* like her and we had superiority in other aspects, in our independent ideals and caustic attitudes that were spawned from a heightened intelligence. We recognized this distinction, feeling its blessings and its secret dangers. From Korea, he sent me a black enameled jewelry box with exquisite Japanese gardens painted on the cover. I did not have any jewelry yet, but I kept my fragile china horses inside its velvet-lined box.

Seeing that I was an avid reader, my mother enrolled me in a book club which sent new books to me every month. These were hardcover volumes, with full-color glossy jackets and delightfully stiff pages of expensive furry paper, published by major publishers. One of my first pleasures with books was to hold them in my hands to measure what each one weighed. I liked a heavy book. Its weighty block promised so much. Years later I discovered that skinny poetry volumes, at only sixty pages, can pack a punch. I also liked to examine the spines of all the books. I found it interesting to see if a title and the author's name were written *vertically* in the tight space of the spine, one line above the next, or if the title had been given its freedom to travel *horizontally* down the length of the binding with all the elbow room it required, but of course that demanded that we tilt our heads when examining the bookshelf. I liked to find the hallmarks of the many different imprints. The borzoi sighthound on Knopf bindings. The jagged flames on Scribner's. F.S.G.'s three symmetrical fish. The shaggy sun with a crooked grin on Vintage. The penguin, the anchor, the Viking ship, and my favorite, the leaping dolphin, on Houghton Mifflin's jackets. Little did I know then that Houghton Mifflin would publish my first book. I found these emblems very exciting: a promise that the pages inside the book had earned a rubber stamp of approval from the powerful animal icons of each press.

In my early years, I think my storytelling impulse was also influenced by my father. He told me many stories about working in the steel industry, complex step-by-step narratives about open-hearth melting practices at Carnegie Mellon steelworks in Chicago, where he was a foreman. I was the only kid in grade school who understood that steel wasn't mined, it was man-made. I learned about the gothic thrill of metallurgy. My father told me about "semi-killed" steel and "dead-killed" steel. He discussed "slag viscosity" and the "Theory of Solidification." But he told me incredible, hair-raising stories about the dangers of the open-hearth factory where he was in charge of fifty men each shift. He had saved many workers who got into jams. He told me, "Trojanowski was snagged on a ladder just as a ladle was ready to pour."

"You mean a ladle of molten steel?"

"That's right. Now, I have to figure—I can get over to him by going up to the second tier and coming down the other side, but the shortest route to get to Trojanowski is to run beneath that ladle before it tips. The nozzle is full, but I'm thinking I can do it—"

My father's stories about steelworkers taught me to structure scenes and develop pacing, believe it or not. And from him, I learned a certain cynicism. He had lost his job in the steel industry when he was promoted to be a head cheese at US Steel, but in his second year there ran into trouble. Because of his high-end position, his signature was needed when his colleagues were making suspicious transactions. They had asked him to help "cook the books" and sign off on necessary documentation. He had just reentered the country after being in exile for five years. His first wife couldn't serve papers on him outside the United States and that's the reason why my sister and I were born across the border in Hamilton, Ontario. And that's why, in 1972, I had to apply for American citizenship and recite the oath in order to be able to vote for McGovern. But my father had been trying to make a new start with my mother, and had just tiptoed back onto solid ground in the US again, so he refused to sign the fudged US steel contracts. Instead he took a different job as a steel engineer at Fiat and we lived in Turin for the next few years. The Italian auto manufacturer prized my father's American know-how and they assigned to him two personal translators, one at either elbow. But he joked about the origin of the car company's name. He liked to say that FIAT meant "Failure in Automotive Technology."

Living in Torino, we rented a place owned by a "Contessa" and I have since learned that our house was just a few blocks from where Primo Levi had been living at the same time. I wonder if I had ever passed Primo Levi in the street when out walking with my nursemaid, Madelina. Perhaps he had stopped to speak to the little American girl to ask her why her legs were bloodied. I was often chased and pecked until bloody by a cock rooster. I was a threat to his hens whenever I entered the garden outside our apartment building. This went on for some time, until my mother opened the front door to find a roast chicken in a bed of polenta, with a handwritten apology stabbed on a toothpick, a gesture made by our contrite neighbor. But it was worrisome to my mother when we came back to the states and my father signed a loan in order to take over several chicken farms in southern Delaware, in rural Sussex County, the poultry capital of the US. The chicken complex was the same farm that later became the Frank Perdue empire. Perdue found success when he ingeniously decided to rename the product. Instead of calling his chickens laying hens he called them "broilers." But my mother refused to go to the rural fields of Delaware to be the wife of a chicken farmer. My father had to get out of the contract without "ruffling feathers" at the bank that had approved his loan, he liked to joke. My father had a lot of stories about the American experience, usually ending with how he had survived a lot of red tape and bureaucracy. But his business savvy had actually helped save our lives. Because of his position at Fiat, he was able to change our reservations on the Italian ocean liner that was bringing us home from Genoa in 1956. We had had reservations on the SS *Andrea Doria* for the date of her fatal voyage but he used his Fiat credentials to wedge us on an earlier crossing on the SS *Giulio Cesare*, another ship from the same line. My mother kept our original ticket vouchers for the *Doria,* the doomed ship, complete with the historic dates and cabin numbers. We had had the adjoining staterooms, 52 and 54, on the starboard side, right under the promenade deck. In fog, the liner SS *Stockholm* had steamed straight into the *Doria*, ramming these exact sleeping compartments. My mother said, "You girls would have died. We couldn't have saved you. We would have been dancing in the Belvedere Lounge. There's always a big party on the last night of the crossing. Little girls would be in bed." That foggy night, the ship sent out a message that sounds like poetry, like a line of compelling blank verse:

"We have collided with another ship. Please. Ship in collision."

On the front page of *My Sister Life* is a newspaper photograph of the Stockholm's crumpled prow, where another young girl was found alive in the twisted wreckage; the first twenty feet of the boat is missing. They called her the "Miracle Girl." But the girl's sister had been swept to sea. If my father hadn't changed the tickets, instead of those other two girls, it would have been *my* sister and me.

As survivors, our eyes have been opened. We foresee that our lifetimes will rack up further disasters. When the *Doria* sinks without us, that's when our wakeful journey begins.

"No Penetration"

I n my first intimate encounter with River-rat, I had given him a blow job, but he had not even touched me. We had to arrange a deflowering date for our virgin love affair to be consummated. I was coming back to the city to be on a panel of writers with Starling Lawrence, then the editor-in-chief at Norton, to be held at the National Arts Club in Gramercy Park. Random was putting me up at the Fitzpatrick Hotel, and River-rat and I discussed a tryst. Packing my suitcase, my son interrupts me. "Take me with you," he says. He wants to go to New York. He looks up bookings of his favorite bands, finding the dates posted on the Internet. He wants to search record stores in the village to find rare seven-inch vinyls. I keep promising to take him.

"You think New York belongs to you?" he says.

"No. Not really." I'm relieved that he doesn't see how little I have. How nothing belongs to me now, not even him.

Feeling an insecurity that cheaters have before enacting their plans, I followed him downstairs to listen to him play guitar. The basement room has a single casement window like a tiny black notebook at one end. The notebook deepens as night is written on it. But the room is filled to brimming with music gear and clutter. There are rock 'n' roll magazines printed on pulp paper, empty ice cream cartons glued to the top of the VCR, Powerade Sports Drink and water bottles crushed down to plastic monocles. The trashed room suggests a child still exists here, but my son has found adult authority as a guitarist. He scruffs the strings, expertly stabs notes, crunching chords, and raking the edge of his pick backward up the neck in an electric glissando effect. He crams bar chords and toes the fuzz box that makes his guitar morph into a sonic smear larger than the room can hold.

"Sid Vicious died trying to do that," I tell him.

"Sid Vicious played bass, so that's how little you know." He stares at me with an expressionless rapport that I find annoying and attractive at once. He chops into "Anarchy in the UK" with a smirk. Then he stops indulging me.

His punk venue has subsets called "straight edge," "crust," "thrash," and "power violence," but they all sound luscious to me. As he plays, his eyes lock onto the nothing right before his face.

His ethereal mask and taciturn aloofness are not unlike Versace runway models, I'm thinking. He plays a tune he learned right off a vinyl, something by the "Unseen" or "Toxic Narcotic." We share an appreciation because I had my own obsession with punk music twenty years before. He likes the story about the time I went to the Registry of Motor Vehicles in Iowa to get my Rhode Island license plates changed. Standing in line, I listened to a woman spell out what she wanted

for a vanity plate. The clerk said, "That's seven letters.
It's limited to six."

The woman didn't miss a beat and told the clerk,
"Ok. Just drop the 'e.'"

"Are you sure?" the clerk asked.

"Are you questioning my belief?" the woman said.

I was amused to learn that the woman was so
deeply entrenched in her doctrine that she had
chosen "Pro Lif" without the "e" for her vanity plate.
In direct response to the goings on, I decided to pay
twenty dollars for my own vanity plate. I didn't choose
"Choice" or "Roe V Wade," but for three years in the
Corn Belt I drove around with "Clash" on my car. The
license plate said "Iowa" and in smaller print "Johnson County" but having the band's name in four-inch
print above the Midwestern ID was one way I soothed
my brittle feelings about living so far from my roots
in the Northeast. Of course as soon as I got back east
someone unscrewed my license plates and stole them.

I ask Giovanni to play Hendrix, just a smidgeon for
me, and he begrudgingly plays the spooky intro to "All
Along the Watchtower." Then he playfully insults me
with another mainstream tune from way back then,
and plucks the teasing entry into "Don't Fear the
Reaper." He knows I like the eerie high-neck changes,
subtle inventions of hard-core melancholy, that always
take their toll on me.

He says, "Well, can't I come to New York with you?"

"Not this time."

His eyes are wounded and hot. He nips his plastic
pick between his incisors and tears his amp cord out
of the box. It lashes my ankles by accident, its chrome
plug pinging my instep.

I TAKE a cab from LaGuardia as I had many times before. There's construction and nothing moves. The river of traffic is solid silver, not flowing, but edging slowly into the city over the Fifty-Ninth Street Bridge. I see the real waterway below, golden and veined in the noon sun. I open my compact and look at my face. My blue eyes have tiny threads of topaz; no it's more like fine shreds of tobacco or rusty shale as if my eyes reflect the dirty world I occupy. I study the skyline to find the Random House tower in the East Fifties. Some rooftops have bulbous tips, others have spiky nozzles, vent hoods, gargoyles, electronic fringe. Water towers erupt all over, rusty-sided party hats or swollen-topped mushrooms, like some sort of urban fungi. The Random building on East Fiftieth has something deliciously phallic about it, although it was only one building in hundreds of gorgeous towers. The most impressive granite phallus is the Pilgrim Monument in Provincetown. It is the tallest all-granite structure in the United States, an exact reproduction of the Torre del Mangia in Siena, Italy. Theodore Roosevelt laid the cornerstone in 1907. I first fell in love with the tower in 1980 when I came to Provincetown as one of the mail-order brides ordered by the writing chair of the Fine Arts Work Center in Provincetown. The monument never loses its beauty or its eroticism, even when clouded in fog. At Christmas they string 300-foot cables from the pinnacle to the ground that when lit create a giant Christmas tree effect that can be seen upon takeoff from Logan airport in Boston. And although New York City has famous and beloved buildings: the Chrysler, the Woolworth, Rockefeller Center, and the Empire State Building—the Pilgrim Monument in Provincetown is my favorite tower.

Knowing River-rat would meet me, I was jittery. All the high-rise buildings seemed to stare down at me with slivered eyes, only a few of them seemed to give me a hats off, as my courage flickered back and forth. Other towers seemed to chant, "You left your son behind!"

Arriving at the Fitzpatrick Hotel I rode the mirrored elevator. The glimmering cage multiplied one intention, *it, it, it.* The same message I had seen in my compact mirror. In the hotel room, I rested my small case on the bed, tearing open its red zippers. I dialed his office. "It's me," I said.

He knows my voice has one meaning.

To have me he need not hold his breath, nor take out his pen, nor tell his assistant a lie. He just has to leave his desk and walk five blocks uptown.

There had been many "firsts" in our relationship those early years, but this arranged meeting was momentous. This time I expected him to fuck me. But before our scheduled tryst, I had had to participate in lengthy discussions at a writers' panel at the National Arts Club. The place is a kind of highbrow or hoity-toit organization, and many of its members were wealthy dilettantes. I was amused to learn that one of its former presidents, Dianne Bernard, had once visited Monet's gardens at Giverny and after smelling its jasmine and roses, she contracted with Cartier to create a scent from Monet's garden that would be distinctly manufactured just for her. A "bespoke perfume" inspired by Monet's gardens was hers alone, and she's been wearing it for thirty years. "It was just something that 'became me,'" she said. Ah, the wealthy have such grand delusions, I thought. Veronica would have loved to have had her own "bespoke perfume" if she had had the same resources.

Sitting on the dais at the National Arts Club, next to Starling Lawrence, my mind wandered a lot. I imagined my scheduled tryst with River-rat. In our first time in bed together there had been *no penetration*. Then I remembered years earlier, when I had attended a meeting with Random House publisher Steve Yardley, before the publication of my first novel *The Arrow Collar Man* in 1992. "*No* penetration" had been the topic of discussion. River-rat had arranged a meeting with Yardley and he also had scheduled to meet with media personnel at the Arrow Shirt Company's headquarters at 530 Fifth Avenue in Manhattan. Random was concerned about copyright issues regarding Arrow's company trademark. They wanted me to change the title of the novel.

"Who wants me to change my title? Arrow or Random?" I asked.

He said, "We don't want any legal backlash from the shirt company. Do we?"

I didn't want to lose my title. I couldn't imagine a different one. I said, "Let me talk to these people. I'll be very sweet. Maybe they will back off."

I wasn't making it easy for River-rat. But he told me that before the Arrow Shirt appointment, we had to have a three-way with his boss, Steve Yardley. Yardley was concerned about a different issue. The publisher wanted to know how closely autobiographical my novel was. Of course the book was autobiographical in one way or another. I told him that my mother had once been married to an Arrow Shirt model, and that her son had never met his father. The novel was about the grown son's search for his patriarch. He takes his sister along.

I sat with River-rat and his boss in a tight office at Random. Steve Yardley looked like a youthful high school wrestling coach, fresh-faced and brimming with team spirit, of a sort. After a few moments of friendly chitchat, and platitudes about the literary strengths of my novel, Yardley asked me, "So, we really have to know the answer to one question."

I waited to hear what he was talking about.

He looked at me with his chin tucked in. "In the novel, your character 'Cam'? He's a handsome bloke—"

"Dreamy," I said.

"He has sex with his sister. Did you ever have sex with your brother?"

"Sex with my brother?"

"In real life, I mean."

I saw River-rat leaning forward in his chair, as if he was frightened I'd say the wrong thing. But I didn't know the right answer or the wrong one. I tried to imagine what I was supposed to say.

Yardley said, "As in the novel? The brother and sister, you know, have those intimate scenes?"

"Intimate scenes?"

"He does the deed with her? Is that autobiographical?"

"Not exactly," I said.

"Did you have a physical relationship with your own brother?"

"Or not?" River-rat said.

"Sex with my brother? Well, yes, I guess I did."

The two men looked at the floor, their shoulders frozen, with their elbows pulled back in an identical cringing mannerism.

"But there was no penetration," I said.

"No penetration?" Yardley said. The men laughed. Their cackling was distinctly heterogeneous, as if the two men had wholly opposite reactions to what I had just said. Relief or bemused disappointment? Jealousy or a more closeted disquiet?

"My brother kissed me. We made out. He just felt me up," I said.

"But no penetration?" Yardley asked. "Phew. That's good to hear."

That little word "phew" seemed antiquated, and even false, in such a contemporary setting. And although he said he was relieved that there had been no penetration, he seemed to be a little let down by my admission.

"No penetration," I announced with more confidence. I didn't understand if his concerns were about legal issues or moral questions. Confucius had said, "I have never seen anyone whose desire to build up his moral power was as strong as sexual desire." There I was, in my very first executive meeting at Random House, sitting beside River-rat, and sex had been placed on the table in a very straightforward examination. The interrogation foreshadowed a vivid confusion that only would escalate in the months to come.

Later that afternoon at the Arrow Shirt offices on Fifth Avenue, I wanted to fight to keep the original title of my novel. We met the shirt company's spokesperson. A woman suit. She introduced herself and said, "So, you are the writer of the novel called *The Arrow*

Collar Man? We're very excited, but we are a little curious too."

"He was my mother's first husband," I explained. "He was one of the last models who posed for Leyendecker for those Arrow Collar ads."

"It's a true story?"

"Not really. In the book, the characters take a car trip to find this guy. It's kind of a road novel. In real life, my brother never searched for or confronted his father."

In the novel, the characters get into a swiped Plymouth Duster and ride off together in their quest to find the Arrow Collar Man. I had done my research and had contacted the Chrysler Historical Society to learn everything about the maiden Plymouth Duster 340. The company's ad agency had invented an awkward ad line for the model; they said the Duster was "Big enough but small enough." The company's slogan that year was "Plymouth Makes It!" They sent me several eight-by-ten glossies, and I had all the specs. The high-performance model was a V-8 with four-barrel carburetion. It had a three-spoked steering wheel with a horn ring thin as a wrist bangle. My character Cam says, "Today it's horn *pads*. They don't make chrome horn rings like this anymore. This is gorgeous."

When the novel was published, River-rat sent me my first copy. I cut through the Jiffy Bag. I was thrilled to leaf through the book, carefully stretching open its tight binding. To my surprise, on the face page of each new chapter River-rat had permitted the book designer to reproduce an image of the beautiful Duster 340. The sedan floated above the first paragraph as if peeling by at one hundred miles an hour, racing to the very edge of the page. Every new chapter has the image of the mythic midsize roadster, reminding the reader that he's a passenger on the exciting road trip of the novel.

The illustration felt like a secret love tap. To have gone through the trouble and added expense of an illustrated face page, my editor was in love with the novel I had written, and maybe he was in love with *me*.

My friend Judith said, "Well, it turns the book into an artifact, doesn't it?"

"The floating car on every chapter?"

"It's a fossil. But such oddball relics are sometimes precious."

At Arrow, the woman suit asked us about the novel. "They take the car trip, but do they find the Arrow model?"

"That's right. They find him, and how!"

River-rat didn't want me to explain any more X-rated details. He told the Arrow hostess that he was happy to be able to show me the original Leyendecker illustrations that lined the walls of the offices and he steered me away to go look at them.

If I was being forced to change my title, looking at the Arrow illustrations seemed stinging. A salt-on-the-wound experience. But I was interested in the Leyendecker paintings. Arrow made collars before they started making shirts with attached collars. Leyendecker's depictions of the Arrow Collar Man were used for Cluett Peabody ads in *Saturday Evening Post*, *Collier's*, and *Esquire*, and quarter-page ads in the *New York Times*. The Arrow Collar Man competed directly with ads depicting the Hathaway Man, who always wore an eye patch. Leyendecker's work came to define the fashionable American male in the early decades of the twentieth century, with famous ad campaigns with titles like 'Versatility in white.' The images were crisp, almost too severe. Leyendecker revealed a subject overwhelmed, almost harried by a masculine vigor beneath a polished, halting refinement. It was a study in extremes. The model's eyes were electric, deep, his nose straight but not too narrow or snively, his hairline a firm black, sideburns trimmed level at the first crest of the ear. Most exciting was the mouth: full and yet seemingly reserved, blank. Waiting for an erotic imprint. Then there was the cleft of the chin, so deeply notched, the left plane plunged into shadow before surfacing again on the right.

River-rat and I walked around the offices looking at these dated portraits of hetero magnetism. I looked back and forth, from the gorgeous illustrations to River-rat's face in profile. There was a definite resemblance somehow, the thrust-out chin, and the hungry expression. I found it interesting how men's faces can express both their hunger and their power at the same time. It's as if *hunger* is what gives men their allure and also their muscle. Most of the portraits were of Leyendecker's live-in lover, Charles Beach, who was the original model for the famous Arrow Collar Man. The title character of my novel was straight. One of Leyendecker's last Arrow Shirt models, the youngest man in his select list of Arrow Collar subjects, was my mother's heartache and was nowhere to be seen.

When we finally left the Arrow building, River-rat seemed to sense my disequilibrium and he leaned in to peck me on the cheek. It wasn't a real kiss. If I had sensed it coming, I would have turned my face to get the kiss centered where I wanted it. Back then I felt his shyness. He hovered at my elbow, steering me away from snarls of pedestrians, as we walked back to Fiftieth Street. I had suffered two insults that day. The publisher's queer interrogation about "penetration" wasn't as upsetting as the threat to my book title. I knew that book titles have some sort of importance. Fitzgerald had felt notorious angst about his title, *The Great Gatsby*. He had wanted to call the novel, "Trimalchio," or "Trimalchio in West Egg," among several other titles he had scribbled, but his editor, Maxwell Perkins, convinced him to stay with *The Great Gatsby*. Like Fitzgerald, I still felt strongly about my title; a title can become what they call a writer's particular "brand." Without it, I felt vulnerable. I would stick to my guns, and I would not agree to let it go.

That night River-rat took me to a restaurant. I was again not true to myself, and I didn't get what I wanted. The waiter came to take our orders and he recited a list of special entrees. He told us, "Tonight we have 'baby pig.'" He described a succulent, spit-roasted piglet. He explained that the piglets were "newborns" and therefore the meat would be very tender! The baby pig option would have been my first choice. But I felt a little intimidated knowing that River-rat was Jewish, so I didn't order the pork. I later realized that this was very unsophisticated of me. I should have ordered what I wanted to have. But at that time, we were not yet lovers, and we had not yet dined at a restaurant on Second Avenue after having had sex in my hotel room. At that later meal, River-rat had ordered a lot of extra bacon. It was as if he was acting out in defiance of not only his Jewish background but in defiance of his long marriage and of all other moral obligations that he had cast to the wind after being with me that afternoon.

At the baby pig bistro, I ordered the salmon instead. I was actually very disappointed not to have the baby pig special. I have often thought about the many disappointments of that day: "No penetration." No book title. No piglet.

I had once asked River-rat, "What's your favorite dinner? What does Weensie cook for you?"

Since my mother was French, I had had a very organic introduction to the art of French cooking. My mother cooked everything the French way. I learned no other method. There wasn't a copy of *Joy of Cooking* anywhere in the house. And I didn't need Julia Child or Simone Beck to teach me how to make a perfect roux. I watched my mother take a saucer out of the cupboard. She carved a hunk of soft butter from its block and plopped it onto a little hill of fresh flour. With expert dexterity she worked the tines of a fork to create a sublime partnership, smearing the butter and starch together until they formed a mass of yellow paste. She raked the fork tines through it many times until it was smooth as silk. Then she whisked the buttery amalgam into the bubbling broth or the stewpot or whatever sauce she wanted to thicken. I learned how to make a roux like that, and I also started almost every dinner procedure with homemade stock, made with beef bones or a chicken carcass, adding wine and "aromatic" vegetables. My most important pantry staple is butter. I never buy only one pound of butter. I always get at least three pounds. It's "cuisine au beurre" in my kitchen; butter doesn't just get smeared on bread, butter goes into everything.

So I was surprised when he answered my question, "What does Weensie cook for you?" and he said, "Oh, I don't know. She makes a lot of rice dishes."

"Rice dishes" was an unfamiliar term to me. It sounded very noncommittal. It wasn't just its blandness, but it seemed "anticulinary, antisavory," almost too Mormon, or Amish, or like those bland Pennsylvania Dutch recipes for apple butter, or potato rolls.

"She gives you rice dishes? That's all she makes?"

He looked back at me with a wounded expression, as if saying, "At home, I get no French cooking. No blow jobs. Don't rub it in."

PRINCESS MARIE BONAPARTE

At the Fitzpatrick Hotel I unpacked my carry-on to find my silky underwear. River-rat was arriving just after noon. Edna O'Brien writes, "Married men are lunchtime callers."

I would be ready for him.

I got undressed and looked at myself in the mirror. I wasn't a stranger to myself, and yet I didn't recognize the face above the familiar body. Her eyes were huge like a Walter Keane painting. The room was lit by bright daylight, and then a cloud devoured the sun. The room instantly dimmed and my skin color was suddenly cold silver. The sun returned and my skin turned gold again.

I slipped into my Italian black lace bra and panties that I'd recently purchased at a shop on Madison. The store displayed the tiniest little wrappings, bras and garter belts and panties clipped to mini hangers, little winged items like basking butterflies at the Museum of Natural History. I knew my husband would like my lingerie, so my investment was secure. My husband was my real lover. At that instant I thought of him.

My husband recently had purchased a small knife, an illegal switchblade made by knife maker David Boye. Its blade is "dendritic steel," an amalgam that has its molecules packed tighter than regular knife steel. The blade pops open faster than the speed of an eyeblink. In other words, you can't see it before its threat is released. The manufacturer says: *These knives are an investment in your security.*

My Siamese cat always likes to get into my suitcase as I am packing for a trip to New York. Taking my mother's advice about how to use perfume, I had spritzed Samsara on the lining of the suitcase, and the cat didn't like it. He stopped his usual inspection and didn't jump into my suitcase. He left the bedroom, flipping his tail left and right in angry swipes. That's his "I feel insulted" act.

With thoughts of my polymath cat, I buried my spasms of guilt. Then River-rat arrived. He kissed me in the doorway, finding my lips with tentative, aggressive nibbles or let's say *clumsy* passion. But he found my mouth with real hunger.

"Mmm. You remembered how to do it," I said. "Who have you been practicing with?"

In answer to my question, he kissed me again, seeking more compliments. I nibbled the little sapphire on his bottom lip with genuine affection.

Within minutes I was sitting on top of him. He reached up to cup my bare breasts. "I own them," he said.

He had such little control, I was careful to slow down to minus-time. I leaned forward a little and leaned back, hardly moving my hips, so I wouldn't rush him. But he was finished almost instantly. Afterward he gripped my waist to keep me in place. He said, "God, your thighs are tight. All muscle. You're in great shape."

"I run five miles," I said.

I did have strong legs. I imagined that Weensie must have those doughy thighs of the inactive suburban mom who sits on sofas too much or she drives to soccer games in a minivan that has overstuffed captain's chairs. She buys too many Entenmann's crumb cakes.

My mother's trick was working. The Samsara was a gentle breath over everything. He wanted to do it again. But I already understood that sex with River-rat was too explosive, too sudden. We didn't talk about it directly. In fact, I'm very responsive in bed. I quickly reach orgasm, in one or two minutes, but I need a little more than just thirty seconds. And like most women I need some manipulation along with penetration. Princess Marie Bonaparte, the great grandniece of Napoleon, was a French psychoanalyst who discovered that the optimal "C-V distance," or the little bit of space between the clit and the vagina should be no more than 2.5 centimeters if a woman is expected to reach orgasm from penetration alone. She couldn't get there on her own, and Princess Marie Bonaparte underwent two experimental surgeries, attempting to bring her clitoris closer to her vagina. She ended up badly scarred.

I've always used the shocking vernacular, "I have a French clit." It's not just a slang term but it's actually used in medical diction. The first time I'd heard the expression it came from the mouth of a doctor. It's supposed to suggest that the clit is a little too high to

be stimulated by intercourse alone. My husband understands everything. But he has an oversized cock and
has to be aware he might hurt me if he loses himself in
the moment. So he sometimes enters me sideways to
not go too deep, and he fingers my clitoris, or I finger
it. My G spot triggers my orgasms, so my clit and my
G spot work in tandem, and I love how he orchestrates
it, even if he holds back to protect me.

One day he will kill me. He doesn't keep his guns
locked up. And now he has that little switchblade knife.

When River-rat fucked me he apologized each time
he'd shoot too soon. I kissed him to stave off his embarrassment. I never feel I can really let my hair down. I
should tell him everything I want him to know, just as
I always tell my students, "A writer explores a mystery
by offering an accretion of details, not by withholding
information." But if I was too shy to discuss my "C-V
distance," his urgency was always too dramatic, and
it wouldn't make much difference to him. If I really
wanted him to get to know me, we should have talked
about it. It was my fault. I was keeping my distance
about my *C-V distance*, so to speak. I thought I could
help him learn more control, and I tried to slow it down
to elongate the session, but he didn't seem to want my
help. He wanted it fast. Then he wanted it again.

I only encouraged him.

My MD, Marguerite, says, "He doesn't understand
her, he never will, he lacks the power to understand
such perverseness."

FIFTY-FIFTY

After treatment with ICE, Giovanni wasn't improving. His cancer had a mind of its own. I had lost confidence in Giovanni's doctor at Mass General, an old-school physician who took great pride in his collection of bow ties. At appointments he appeared in a constantly changing array of garish, expertly knotted silk, a new one each time we met with him. As he talked to my son, he often stopped to adjust the tie, tugging the opposing wings of the tight little bow at his throat until they were even. But Giovanni was not in remission.

We switched hospitals. Jerome Groopman, the *New Yorker* writer and award-winning physician, had recommended a new doctor to me, a "powerhouse of hematologic oncology" at Dana Farber Cancer Institute. So we had our first meeting with Giovanni's new doctor, a tall drink of water, of French extraction. He joked with us, saying that we might have heard that French doctors are different. He said, "If a patient asks his French doctor, 'Can't I still have at least one cigar?' the French doctor says, 'No, you cannot have one cigar. With everything you are going through, you should have *two* cigars!'"

Giovanni's new doctor had a European ambiance, a straightforwardness and an elegant transparency that were instantly reassuring. He gave Giovanni his e-mail address. "I'm here whenever you want me," he said. "Day or night." His e-mail address was his name at Partners.org. Dana Farber, Brigham's, and Children's hospitals shared the address. But there was something hopeful to me about an e-mail address at "Partners," like we were all in it together. He recommended that Giovanni enter a new clinical trial called a "tandem transplant," two bone marrow transplants, one soon after the other. The first transplant would be "autologous" using Giovanni's own rescued stem cells, and the second, called "allogeneic," would entail obtaining stem cells from a donor.

These terms "auto" and "allo" mean "of the self" and "from the other." The poetry of metaphor was something I could cling to.

For the first transplant Giovanni's stem cells would be mobilized after daily injections of Neupogen, a drug which releases his stem cells into the peripheral bloodstream where they can be collected over a period of days. He had to wait in a banana chair for six hours at a time, hooked up to an "apheresis" machine. The machine harvests his stem cells that are then frozen, just like his sperm had been. After the "auto" transplant, his stem cells would be reintroduced to him at the end of five weeks of high-dose chemo in the hospital. These weeks of poison would almost kill him. Six months later, for the second transplant, he will go back in the hospital for one week of chemo to extinguish his immune system again, before he can be given an IV bag of mushy red goo, a blazing red sack of his donor's newly thawed stem cells.

My son begins a mysterious relationship with this anonymous donor from here on in. He only knows that his donor is a twenty-something male from Western Europe, a close match to him. He tells me that he often imagines the stranger who had volunteered to sit in a banana chair for hours hooked up to the apheresis machine that collected his stem cells. The anonymity of his donor increased Giovanni's sense of gratitude. The donor's immune system will attack Giovanni's cancer, when his own stem cells were indifferent to it. My son was asked to sign several forms that explained the side effects and life-threatening conditions caused by transplant therapy. The doctor told us that even with two transplants, it was fifty-fifty.

"So it's a coin toss, you mean?" Giovanni asked.

"It's your decision. But if you don't do the transplants, you will probably die," the tall drink of water told him matter-of-factly.

So it's not a win-win. And with a tandem transplant, the allogeneic transplant from a donor will cause "graft versus host disease, or GVHD." His donor's immune system will attack not only his cancer but *every* cell in his body, causing different ailments, some with high rates of morbidity. Even if he survived cancer, he faced long-term disability. The doctor went through the list of possibly fatal side effects that required the patient's signature.

Giovanni signed the forms. Giovanni trusted the doctor. When we left the meeting, he told me, "I like him. He's really got that Crispin Glover thing going on."

EGGHEAD WOMEN

Growing up, I kept reading oddities and masterpieces. My oxymoronic reading habits kept pushing me into a literary life. My mother had once dated the famous editor of *Poetry Magazine,* Hank Rago, when they had been students at DePaul University in Chicago. He'd invite her to go rowing with him out on Lake Michigan. She told me that one time their rowboat had taken on water, and they almost sank to the bottom. She became soaking wet when the dinghy almost capsized, and her sweater was clingy. Rago fell in love with her body first, then he fell in love with her, but it was at DePaul that she also had met her first husband, the Arrow Collar Man. She dropped out of college after only one year. She and Rago had parted company, but in her possession, she had saved several early copies of *Poetry Magazine* that he had sent to her when he became editor in the midfifties. The pages had T.S. Eliot, W.H. Auden, Karl Shapiro, Malcolm Cowley, William Meredith, Weldon Kees, Richard Wilbur, and others. Each of these issues had its infamous standard cover illustration of a flying Pegasus. As a young child and a horse lover, I had coveted these editions and I stowed them away in my belongings. But in my teens, I began to read the actual poems in these issues. That my mother had been a love object of a famous editor of *Poetry* has some meaning to me—I was to become a young poet and one of my major accomplishments was when the editor John Frederick Nims accepted my submissions, and my own poems appeared in *Poetry Magazine* forty years after my mother's boat was swamped.

I also pulled another novel down from my mother's bookshelf, *Portrait of Jennie*, a modern fantasy tale of love, art, and time travel by Robert Nathan. The book taught me that you can push reality to a certain breaking point where it might be helpful to leap into another plane of consciousness, into the fantastical, where soulfulness was enough to escape all boundaries of realism.

Nathan was a commercial novelist, mostly forgotten today. In his lifetime he published more than thirty novels. As a young girl I read *Portrait of Jennie* and then a much more disturbing novel he had written, about a woman who had sought an abortion in the late fifties, a time when it wasn't accepted. She was a woman alone. The novel still adhered to a sexist point of view but it presented an unveiled and gritty portrait. It said: Women suffer.

My mother told me that I was reading too much. She said, "Men don't like egghead women." She yelled at me each time I parted my hair with a ballpoint pen. She took it to mean a warning signal. Soon I'd put pen to paper.

In my teens, I started writing poetry. I bought a copy of Frank O'Hara's *Lunch Poems*, Number 19 in

Ferlinghetti's *City Lights Pocket Poets* series. The book was a tiny square volume the size and shape of a cocktail napkin. I found it in the greeting cards at Happy Harry's Discount Drugs where they displayed "Inspirational" books beside a rack of sympathy cards. But in seventh grade English class we were reading Longfellow's endless poem, "Evangeline." I got into trouble when I sat through class crossing out lines of Longfellow's text and writing over it, in colloquial speech, lines from O'Hara. Longfellow starts with, "This is the forest primeval." O'Hara starts, "Mothers of America/ let your kids go to the movies!" and he says, "It's my lunch hour, so I go for a walk." I had inked the whole page with O'Hara's fresh voice and the teacher said that I would have to pay for the textbook, or I wouldn't get my report card. Of course, I didn't *want* my report card sent home.

THE SEA GULL

The *New York Times* said that my novel *Open Water* explored "nervous, shady sorts that come alive as sympathetic human beings struggling to contain the accelerating disorder in their lives." Willis, the protagonist of that novel, tells me, *"Jesus. Don't mention the* New York Times *review! That makes us sound defensive. You don't need to defend me."*

I'm alarmed to hear his criticism sideswiping me, but I'm also touched that my characters are watching over me now as I tell this story.

But by the time we had published four books together in just five years, I believed River-rat was my dream editor. I had faith that he believed in me. Faith is a cool block of lard in the larder of my naïveté.

When reading my first novel on the train during his ride home to West Chester, he is in stitches. He told me, "I was laughing out loud. Your sense of the way men act is spot on. You know all about men's weaknesses. I was laughing so much that people were staring at me."

I thought, of course they were staring at him, because he, too, is a *man*.

But I was pleased that he understood that the novel embraces human foibles. I like to find a humorous plane within the geometry of loneliness and isolation. I have learned this from many fine examples. One of my favorites is in the final scene of Chekov's play *The Seagull*. A gunshot is heard by friends gathered in a parlor, and they become concerned. One character leaves the room to see what caused the abruption in their peaceful afternoon. He returns to say, "It is as I thought. A flask of ether has exploded!" This instant in the play, when the characters are intensely vulnerable to their psychic wounds, is relieved by a comic moment. But the final line of dialogue reveals that all is *not* well. "What I wanted to say was that Konstantin has shot himself." And the curtain falls. How delightful to have a violent act mistaken for a mishap with a medicine bottle and the resonating humor brings a buoyant cynicism to the ending of the play.

River-rat is not always happy with the work in his lap and he is not without judgment or disdain. But I sense a sort of covetousness—he accepts my faults because they give him license. He calls me from his desk. It's after lunch, and he's hungry for something else. I can hear the office girls, a jangle of fem bartering and bitching, their talk vented up the hallway. His young assistant complains about her new belly-button ring; the nickel loop gives her a reaction. She's a fresh coed from Swarthmore, Sarah Lawrence, or maybe it was Colby College, one of those rural academic enclaves that deliver egghead ingénues to Manhattan each spring after graduation. He stands up to nudge his door shut. The hallway warble stops and there's silence on the line.

It's dead quiet.

That's his go-no-go decision. His countdown. He says, "Tell me what you want to do when you come to the city this week. Recite the list of chores you have to do, you know, in that excellent progression that I like so much."

"My list of chores?"

"You know."

For these secret dispatches, he uses his cell phone. I scold him, "Why don't you call Weensie for a wireless quickie, why me?" I shift in my seat, crossing my legs. My panty hose makes a silky friction that he can't possibly hear, but he's ready. He sits down at his desk and tugs his belt open. My voice connects. I prowl through a tangle of heat-seeking verbs.

He says, "Go ahead. Tell me the list I want to hear. *Say* it for me."

"Okay. First, you put your cock in my mouth. Remember how that goes?"

"Yes."

"I'll take it slow."

"Right."

"Like this?" I say.

"Keep going."

His voice is a honeyed whisper. His words rising and falling, enforced by a shivering abdomen. He has lost his reserve as he loses his respect for me. He doesn't say my name. He says, "Girl. Yes, that's right. That's it. Girl *this*. Girl *that*."

Who can blame him? He says it was my plan. Now I have to live up to it.

The Pursuit of Literature

My friend Judith Grossman asked me about my relationship with River-rat. "What's in it for you?" she said. Judith's feminism isn't preachy dogma but always very practical. In her novel, *Her Own Terms*, her female character, who had attended Oxford, learned how sex was both a bridge and a barrier in her rise to academic success. She described her deflowering at college, and how she had learned how sex can complicate our intellectual endeavors. The pursuit of literature and the pursuit of sex work in tandem, but one must choose between them. She wrote ". . . anyone is entitled to buy condoms—anyone was entitled to a few fucks once in a while . . . but not everyone was entitled to belong to the company of poets. There was no forcing of that issue. My Romantic training made me adamant on that: either the call came of itself, or not."

I had a few other women friends who advised me about River-rat early on. At Bennington College, where I was teaching in the Graduate Writing Seminars, I talked to my colleague Susan Cheever after an AA meeting. I greatly admired the stories of her father,

John Cheever. In his story, "The Cure," his character, in a mire of marital trouble, says "I don't sleep well in an empty bed." In the next scene he follows a woman down Madison Avenue. "It was a very hot day but she looked cool, as if she had been able to preserve . . . the freshness of her bath . . . A voice inside my head was pleading, 'Please let me put my hand around your ankle. It will save my life.'" In another scene, he gets down on his hands and knees to touch the handprints of his children smeared on the baseboard. He had lost everything.

Susan was an accomplished writer, too, and having grown up in a literary household with her father, she was attuned to the publishing world. I admired her memoirs *Treetops* and *Home Before Dark*. But when I told her, "I think I'm in love with my editor," she burst out laughing.

Susan has exactly what it takes to render quite a belly laugh.

I was embarrassed that she considered my problems with River-rat hilarious. She told me, "Everyone falls in love with an editor. A publisher. An agent. It's that kind of business. So what?"

"You mean it's an incestuous business?"

"No. It's just stupid. The way people try to get on top."

It's true; men like us on top. A sex manual suggests that men should have women sit astride, because for some men, that's the only way they can get it deep enough to reach the cervical crown. But I told Susan that I didn't sleep with my editor to advance my career. Sleeping with my editor was no different from when I was very young and I went to bed with my college

professor, who had published a collection of poems.
When I slept with my professor, I wasn't trying to get
an 'A' grade. I just wanted to sleep with a poet!

Susan shook her head and looked at me in disbe-
lief, and maybe with a little pity. She had once met my
husband and had really liked him. She had said, "How
did you find him?"

"I was lucky," I said.

"Well, hell-o. You are more than lucky. *Fortune has
shined on you.*"

I was pleased by her admiration of my husband,
which I hoped might also be an acknowledgment of
me.

I told Susan that I loved River-rat because he had
shared so many books with me. Other than the texts
he gave me, I hardly knew much about him. He was
a stranger to me, except for the charms he exhibits,
both awkward and straightforward, when he walks into
my hotel room. Any other impressions of him came
wholly from literature titles he handed over, starting
with Joseph Mitchell's *Bottom of the Harbor*. He introduced me to some of the most distinguished authors in
contemporary American literature. To be included in
that company was a source of pride to me, and a reas-
surance. I was fascinated by Julia Blackburn's nonfiction, which read *like* fiction, *Daisy Bates in the Desert*,
and *The Emperor's Last Island*. And I was impressed
by Sherwin Nuland who wrote about the end of life
with pragmatic candor, instead of back peddling, in
his book called *How We Die*. Oliver Sacks's books were
transformative until his later years when he became
so self-satisfied. He recently wrote an Op-Ed piece for
the *New York Times*. Diagnosed with terminal cancer,

he accepted his prognosis as if butter wouldn't melt in his mouth.

I fell in love with William Langewiesche and his book *Inside the Sky: A Meditation on Flight*. In the second chapter of that book, Langewiesche introduces us to essayist John Jackson who describes something called "the landscape vernacular," and how we see the world "with clarity and sympathy and yet with a certain detachment" when looking from the cockpit of an airplane. Jackson wrote, "It is from the air that the true relationship between the natural and the human landscape is truly revealed." Reading that, I wondered if I would better understand my feelings for River-rat if I could look down on him from 3,000 feet up.

But I showed River-rat a text by Langewiesche's own father, Wolfgang Langewiesche, that became a favorite of mine. The book, *Stick and Rudder, An Explanation of the Art of Flying,* combines straight fact instructions about learning to fly an airplane with a genuine lyric voice. In his chapter, "The Airplane's Gaits," he describes the various ways an airplane stays aloft. He tells us about the "Mushing Glide," the "Stumble," the "Power-on Stall," and even the "Dive." One of the first lessons a pilot must master when learning to fly an airplane is how to control his "Angle of Attack." That's how the wing meets the air. That is the whole shebang—how the wing lofts above, or sips into, or slides *below* the air. Then you've got "Attitude." That's where you point the nose of the plane. "Attitude" is, in fact, different from "angle of attack." The book has a whole chapter on "The Turn." I read this volume enjoying all its metaphoric layers of information. The book seemed to be cowritten by Keats and Damon Runyon.

I tried to get River-rat to read Thomas Hardy. I told him about a scene in *Jude* when Sue Brideshead jumps out a second-story window to escape her betrothed. I said, "That's a comedic scene in a very bleak novel where, in fact, little children hang themselves!" River-rat didn't try Hardy, but he introduced me to a writer I was lucky to become friends with. Marie Winn was famous for her book called *The Plug-In Drug,* an examination of the dangers presented to kids from watching television. She later wrote *Red-Tails in Love,* about the Central Park red-tail hawks, Lola and Pale Male, famous for nesting on the ledges of New York skyscrapers, sometimes on the balconies of Hollywood icons like Woody Allen and Mary Tyler Moore. Marie came to Cape Cod in the summer and we got to know one another. We bonded because of a mutual immersion in naturalist ideals and issues, but we also talked about our relationship with River-rat. She had a love-hate thing going on with him, just as I did, and we often shared our secrets. Marie has a deep connection to Joseph Mitchell, and her war with River-rat had something to do with their differences about him. She became my confidante. Our shared loyalty to the Cape Cod National Seashore is a binding ingredient in our long friendship. She often calls me to ask about my "GHO." That's a "great horned owl," also known as the "tiger owl." She likes to hear my reports about the birds that roost nearby, and that hunt prey on my land, often claiming my chimney top as a vantage point for their easy pickings.

River-rat had given me books and introductions to new friends. These book connections worked both as inspiration and example to me. I wanted to tell Susan

Cheever that I slept with my editor out of a joy "in the pursuit of literature." It was the same absorption I had felt with my first poetry teacher who had published a collection of poems. There was a pattern emerging: men got into my pants because of my love of literature. My conversation with Susan Cheever made me stop to examine how I might have arrived at my perch as a writer and lover—how I had become one or the other. I wondered if I became a writer by going page to page, desk to desk, or bed to bed?

Perhaps I was always looking for those gloved arms that reached in through the incubator glass. Or like my fever dream, moving one blade of grass at a time, I was collecting snips of my identity both from the pages of the canon and from the motel sheets.

One of my colleagues at Bennington College had had her own troubles with her editor whom she had been sleeping with for years. We had often compared notes about our disappointments and our trysts. But I noticed that in her first book she has an epigraph from the poet William Matthews. I didn't ask her about her relationship with Matthews, but Matthews had, in fact, been my very first "literary" boyfriend. He had come to Roger Williams College to give a poetry reading in 1975. I didn't know he had a reputation. Matthews kept standing reservations at every motel honeymoon suite in each college town he visited. He was ready for any coed he might meet in the classroom or who might show up in the front row of the auditorium.

After Matthews gave a reading we went out to a bar in Bristol, a working class village dating back to before the Revolutionary War. I was wearing a new pair of velvet bell bottoms. All the male patrons wanted to pet my knee just to sample the softness of the fabric. Sitting at the bar rail, alongside local clam diggers and lobster boat captains, Matthews took charge of me. He monitored the proceedings. Each time a man stepped up to me, he had to ask Matthews for permission to touch my soft jeans. He was William *Proctor* Matthews from Proctor and Gamble family wealth, but he fit in with the local crowd, finding rapport with the dragger fishermen. He was buying shots of tequila for everyone. I didn't think I liked tequila. He asked for the bottle and he poured me a spot using his own glass. There was something intimate about sharing the single glass, so I picked it up. He watched me with twinkling eyes, then with burning eyes. I passed the glass back and forth under my chin examining its fumes. It scorched my sinuses.

"Just do it," he said.

I threw it back. I winced. "Tastes like a porcupine's asshole!" I said, much to the joy of the fishermen.

"That's when I knew I loved you," Matthews later told me at the Bristol Motel.

One thing I recall about Matthews was that his cum yelp was very dramatic. It started with a song-like moaning, like a complicated voice exercise; he sounded like a tenor practicing an eight-note octave scale, its ascending notes rising up and rolling down again, more than three times, until his crescendo at climax.

That was the start of a two-year romantic entanglement where he wrote me letters and sent drafts of new poems. He mailed several new poems from his book *Rising and Falling* with lines like, "It takes 75,000 crocus blossoms to make a pound of saffron." Strange red circles intersected along the margins of his pages where he had put down his glass of wine, leaving imprints of long nights spent writing letters to me or to all of his poetry fans, who knows how many? This was the time of handwritten letters or typewritten notes. I liked the wine stains on his stationery; it gave organic proof to our long-distance affair. And with envelopes and paper, I, too, could spritz my return letters to him with my bottle of White Shoulders. White Shoulders, by Evyan, was a scent that evoked sex. Its overpowering gardenia perfume was so erotic that men could not inhale it without bending at the knees. That scent was worn by femme fatales of the forties and fifties but it has long since been discontinued, except for a very inferior imitation. Being able to send perfume-soaked letters is lost forever to today's texting generation. When I started seeing River-rat, Guerlain's Samsara took its place. White Shoulders might date my Matthews affair, but no other perfume can beat it.

I wrote long, emotional notes to Matthews closing with, "I hope we can get together soon." He wrote back, "Why hope we can get together? Why not plan it? I'm wonderfully Amurrican, as LBJ used to slur it out proud; I believe problems are made to be solved."

When I left my first husband, taking my two-year-old daughter, I complained about being a single mom. Bill wrote, "Being a parent prepares you for death; one grows more philosophical, moved, and powerless by the year. I have to remember that such a love—parent for child—isn't necessarily (or even appropriately) the paradigm for all love." And of course, he always signed his letters, "*Love*, Bill."

In his poem, "Yes," he says, "in love as *in a well I am the water of.*"

Matthews made love to me several times when he breezed through Rhode Island. He was teaching in Colorado, but soon he was hired to teach at the Iowa Writers' Workshop. I learned that Matthews had many little wannabe writer trollops in different towns where he gave poetry readings. He often read from his poem, "Old Girlfriends": *I thrust my impudent cock into them like a hand raised in class.* He was known for his friendly outreach campaign to lonely heart poetesses. I wondered if my Bennington colleague had been one too; I had never asked her why she used his poem as an epigraph in her book. But I owe a big debt to Matthews because he had encouraged me to go to graduate school.

We were in a bar in Newport. He had just brought two scotches over to a table. When I set my purse down I knocked my glass over. He winced in pain. But he didn't get up to buy me another. He told me to have a sip of his drink.

Again we were sharing one glass.

He told me that I should attend graduate school. He insisted that I should apply to the same program where he would be teaching, the University of Iowa's Writers' Workshop.

At the time, I had my two-year-old daughter and I had thought it was impossible to apply to graduate school.

He said, "Bring the baby with you!"

My daughter came with me to the University of Iowa in 1977. She had the misfortune of being the child of a poet, with all its inherent dangers and threats, but thank goodness children are made of rubber.

REMISSION IMPOSSIBLE

On admission to the hospital for his first stem cell transplant, and five weeks of chemo, that might almost kill him, Giovanni started a blog. He chronicles his cancer therapy and offers a rolling critique of punk bands across more than three decades, giving examples with downloads of tracks and videos of everything hardcore.

Remissionimpossible.blogspot.com

About me: 26 years old, fighting 4th Stage Hodgkins Lymphoma, lover of music. Hardcore for life.

Ok, you're going to have to bear with me. I am typing on my iPad and my wireless keyboard's not working. The only fix is to drop a tiny tinfoil ball into the battery compartment because apple products suck. They are overpriced pieces of garbage. It's hard to embed videos on the iPad, but I will do my best. Tonight is my first night in the hospital for my first bone marrow transplant. And I'm sitting in bed in this crazy room with a magnum air filter machine that is humming. Everyone who comes in here is wearing a space suit, masks and rubber gloves.

The summer before I was diagnosed (summer '11) Sandrine and I were walking down Mass Ave in Porter Square. I had to stop and lean against a wall. I was feeling so fatigued, I had to take a break. Suddenly my nose started bleeding. Sandrine had to run across the street to an Indian market to get some tissues. I watch each tissue get soaked with blood. I watch blood hit the sidewalk. In the bright sun it was the most vivid color red I'd ever seen. It was perhaps the ultimate red. There is no comparison to the color of blood. I remembered a poem my father showed me, when Neruda said, *"and the blood of children ran through the streets without fuss, like children's blood."*

My nosebleed foretold the alienation I would feel. People stared at me in ways I have never been stared at. When I got sick my life became the busy street and my bloody nose was all you could know about me. You can't join the cancer club quietly.

Well, they aren't wasting any time, are they? A nurse has come back in here to flush my IV port and start my first poison infusion. In here, they count the days backward, so I'm on day "38." With five weeks to go. I wonder if I'll make it to day "0." I might just want to die. Fortunately, I have no shortage of songs relating to whatever anger or negativity I am feeling. But as much as I can identify with lyrics, I don't want my soundtrack to become a self-fulfilling prophecy of endless misery. There are two songs in particular that I listen to that inspire me to accept pain as a part of life, not to dwell on it, but to see beyond it. This one's going out to all the Jersey kids—you can take a guess what's coming . . .

Learn to live with pain and you won't complain

E-Town Concrete fucking rules. I listened to this album constantly for practically the first year I was sick and I revisit it often. I've uploaded the entire Time 2 Shine record onto MediaFire for any ETC fans who might be looking for it.

Before I go I will leave you with another beautiful song that should close this post nicely. Some funky late 70s soul. Like "Sunshine and Rain." Listen to that goddamn guitar. Take it easy everyone.

How come the things that make us happy make us sad?
Well it seems to me that joy and pain are like
sunshine and rain.

"Audacity with Caution"

My candor is alarming to some people. My father used to say, "Shoot from the hip, but expect them to shoot back." My husband says that, all too often, I "*speak* from the hip!" Straightforwardness puts a toll on the listener, I know. Duras said it's an "instinct to unearth." I seek meaning in my mistakes, and try to understand them backward and forward. Lucidity comes with close inspection. Even with my first book, *Reckless Wedding,* the *New York Times* said it was chock-full of "individual perceptions and authentic feelings."

"*There she goes again,*" Willis says. "*The* New York Times, *blah, blah, blah.*"

And about my first novel, the *New York Times* said, "She makes us understand these people, and the sad tumbling row of emotional dominoes that has brought them to this place in their lives . . ."

"*More Michiko apple sauce,*" Willis says. "*I give up.*"

I remind Willis what River-rat had told me. "That's a bankable review." "Bankable" was baldly business-oriented and sounded tinny to me. But because I had agreed to cut the first chapter of my first novel, against my will, a section in which the female protagonist had stood her ground and had escaped her rapist, the same *New York Times* critic accused the female character of being a "high-strung but strangely passive woman . . . one of those victims who let themselves slide into trouble."

It was as if she was talking about me.

"The background should be evoked by the figure . . . it is the sensation of all space around the girl . . . don't let the background smother the figure."

In *My Sister Life,* I created a layered mural of a shattered American family. The *New York Times* said I had fit together "a jigsaw-puzzle picture burned free of bitterness and sentimentality." In this book, I'm attempting a straightforward portrait of *him* with the same lack of churlishness or romanticism. The closer I look, the portrait becomes a diptych, of course. A portrait of him is a portrait of me. When talking about making his paintings, Edward Hopper said, "I'm after ME." Mark Strand said, "For the artist, the painting exists, in part, as a mode of encountering himself," and, "The point of arrival or the point when the painting is done cannot be known beforehand and yet cannot be totally unknown."

I think River-rat should take some responsibility for the picture. Art critic Martin Gayford writes, "The true subject of a portrait is the interchange between the painter and the subject, what the sitter consciously or unconsciously reveals, and the artist picks up." In his book, *Man with a Blue Scarf,* he writes about sitting for a portrait by Lucian Freud. Reading that book, I started to see how River-rat is my "Man with a Blue Scarf." I must use the same ideological

tools that the painter Lucian Freud incorporates. Gayford calls it Freud's "audacity with caution: an intense
determination to get the thing exactly right." To "get
it right" means that it should be accurate but it must
go beyond concrete details into the more plastic rev-
elations of the sensuous and of the instinctual. These
areas of internal observation present risks. But Lucian
Freud says something that I find very encouraging:
"One always wants to be exceptionally daring."

I remember what the writer Cindy Sue Richards
once said to me. We were having an argument at my
house in Provincetown. It was a hissy-fit catfight. I
lost control of my temper and shoved her off my front
stoop. She was taking back the bottle of wine she had
brought and she dropped it on the sidewalk. When it
shattered, she could have cut herself or been seriously
injured. She stood up and said, "Now you've done it!
I never thought it would come to this. I never thought
I could make you a character in one my stories." She
was calling me a "crazy!" My violent outburst was the
deal breaker. From there on, she had the license to
write about me. She felt free to expose all my faults if
she wanted to in one of her stories, just as I am writing
about her, right here.

River-rat has become a character to me. Everything between us has to be examined by my perceptions as an artist; my responses as a woman are not
enough. Like what had happened with Cindy Sue, the
front-stoop metaphor is somehow the same. River-rat
shoved me off the stoop or I leapt off the stoop myself.
He left me on my own. But I have three things at my
disposal. Arousal. The electric sensation: shame. And
freedom to exaggerate.

In 1908, Sarah Stein, a student of Henri Matisse, kept a little notebook of Matisse's classroom instructions. She wrote down everything Matisse told the studio class. "One must always search for the desire of the line, where it wants to enter and where to die away." One of my favorite moments is when Matisse says that the artist must "exaggerate in the direction of truth." The students ask, "How can one exaggerate the truth?" He shows how the choice of color, and shading, and underlining each mark, are helpful in the delivery of true meaning. An artist gets to the meaning he wants by these exaggerations and inventions. In Jack Flam's book, *Matisse on Art*, a later student, Marguette Bouvier, also tells of her visit with Matisse in 1944 when he helped her with a landscape drawing. Her easel was set up in front of an olive tree that she was drawing. "Matisse took some charcoal and immediately underlined with a heavy line the essential parts, the architecture of the tree." He told her, "You see the empty spaces? They are very meaningful. It's they that will provide your balance." Bouvier said, "He transmitted the essential principles of his drawing to his student; to exaggerate in the direction of truth and to study at length the importance of voids."

In writing my portrait, I try to incorporate this ideal. I make inventions and I shade, underline, and enforce the background or "psychological" tones. The "importance of voids" is also where I concentrate my attention. I think Matisse's directive to "exaggerate in the direction of truth" is quite like Lucian Freud's "audacity with caution."

Nature Wrong Side Out

I have always taken great comfort in the advice of painters. My connections to the visual arts have been important to me. As a fellow at the Fine Arts Work Center in Provincetown, I spent a lot of time in the studios of young painters, sculptors, and installation artists who were tackling the same transformations I was making at my writing desk. Before the work center had the money to offer separate studios for fellows, these artists were mixing paints and noxious chemicals at their kitchen tables, and lead dust got into their food. They were risking their lives to make art. But I loved to sit in a kitchen chair and watch a painter make marks on a new canvas or board. Day after day, the work was altered, reinvented, or painted over again.

I had a very early connection to a painter. My great-uncle, Dodge Macknight, was a noted American impressionist watercolorist, who had in fact spent some time at the Yellow House in Arles with Van Gogh. Macknight's paintings lined the walls of my house. A real painter was part of my family tree. He was a central patriarchal presence, having just about raised my own mother. Each summer her French parents left Chicago to go back to France and they sent her to East Sandwich on Cape Cod to be rid of her. Macknight took charge of her and he even tolerated her teenage years. He taught her to drive, and of course she crashed his car. To teach her a lesson, he left the wreck on a traffic island in the center of Sandwich with a sign explaining that the accident was her fault. But she liked to show me the one-inch scar across her eyelid. Windshields were not made of safety glass back then. It was something she was proud of.

I have long felt an art connection with my uncle the painter. He lived in settings that became my own settings. Born in Providence in 1860, Macknight was the first man to drive a motor car from Hyannis to Provincetown, one hundred years ago. He took the trip with his friend, Charles Ayling, the millionaire founder of Cape Cod Hospital, in Ayling's Model T. That Macknight had driven a car all the way out here, to Land's End at the tip of the Cape where I have made my home, is magical to me, because I, too, took my first baby steps in Macknight's English gardens at his house in East Sandwich. I learned to walk on his soil and I took my first breath of garden air right here on Cape Cod, although today Cape Cod is called "the tailpipe of the nation" because of its bad ozone levels. And Ayling's wife, Alice Ayling, had greatly encouraged me when I was a young poet. Being a board member of the Lamont Library, she gave me copies of every book that won the Lamont Poetry Prize, year after year. When I visited the widow, she had a stack of narrow-spined poetry volumes set aside for me. There is something mysteriously inviting about poetry books, skinny texts

of sixty pages or less. The power in these small packages continues to surprise me.

In 1981 I got a job in the credit card department at
Rhode Island Hospital Trust Bank, when I was trying
to complete my first book of poems. My days were
spent studying microfiche, submitting "chargebacks"
for false purchases, and talking to credit card custom-
ers who were distressed about their MasterCard statements. I advised them, "Just use cash." The days were
long. Each time I looked at the clock, the minute hand
didn't seem to move. It looked like *the photograph of
a clock.* But although I was working a low-level bank
job, I was writing my first book. Macknight was somewhere in the wings, urging me on. I lived only a few
blocks from Macknight's cemetery plot at the historic
North Field burial ground in Providence. I took walks
to visit his stone. This proximity did not seem like an
accident. I've always thought of Macknight as some
sort of guardian art spirit to me.

Although he had died a year before I was born,
Macknight was a well-known American painter in
Boston in the late 1880s through the first two decades
of the twentieth century. He was in a three-man
show in London with John Singer Sargent and Win-
slow Homer. Boston's Museum of Fine Arts and the
Fogg Museum have Macknight collections. And he was
championed by Isabella Stewart Gardner. There is still
a "Macknight Room," named for my uncle, at the Isabella Stewart Gardner Museum in Boston today.

In the late 1880s Van Gogh invited him to the
famous Yellow House in Arles, just before Paul Gauguin
joined Van Gogh there. Van Gogh and Macknight
had studied together at the Atelier Cormon studios,

in Paris, with fellow students Toulouse-Lautrec and Emile Bertrand. The Guggenheim has several letters written by Van Gogh to his brother, Theo, during the late 1880s, that mention my uncle when he and Van Gogh were in Arles. Macknight and Van Gogh painted landscapes in some of the same parts of town. They even painted some of the very same scenes. I have an 1888 river scene in Arles by Macknight that is the very same location with the exact same trees, with knotted limbs and twisted tree trunks, found in a painting of a river scene by Van Gogh called *Orchard in Bloom with view of Arles*. And Van Gogh's *View in the Park in Arles* is the same landscape found in another painting by Macknight. I like to imagine the two men painting twenty feet apart from one another. While spending time with Van Gogh, Macknight met a young French girl, Louise Queyrel, who was my mother's aunt. She was *Tante* Louise to us. Macknight's bride is the French connection in my family. My mother was raised in the same French village of Valserres where Macknight's wife, Louise, had been born.

Van Gogh wasn't impressed with Macknight, partly due to his anger that Macknight had found a patron, Allen W. Swann, who agreed to pay $2,400 for Macknight to spend four years in France, and Van Gogh was penniless. Van Gogh complained about the American and wrote to his brother, Theo, saying that Macknight would "soon be making little landscapes with sheep for chocolate boxes." And Macknight wasn't very fond of Van Gogh either. When Van Gogh "in a moment of frantic need offered him a painting of flowers for a few francs, Macknight gave him the francs, but told him to keep the picture." Macknight remembered Van Gogh as "a queer fellow with pinched features, red hair and beard, given to friendliness and sullenness." In his letters to Theo, Van Gogh mentioned how he and Macknight both frequented the brothels of Arles. Van Gogh wrote to his brother, Theo, with some delight, on July 8, 1888, "Macknight has caught a chancre with a fat woman where quite by chance, I went at the same time."

Macknight was influenced by his meetings with Van Gogh because after his years abroad, his use of color was transformed. The artist Eugène Boch described hearing Macknight quote Van Gogh, when discussing the challenges of painting: "I attack the paper, struggling like a lion."

The wild use of color in Macknight's paintings made an impression on me when I was growing up because my mother had told me stories about how Macknight was criticized for his transformative use of color by staid Boston art critics. Upon his return from France, his new work shocked the public and his collectors turned against him.

I was very surprised to learn that the address of my uncle's art gallery, Doll and Richards, is the very same address as my first publisher, Houghton Mifflin. In 1982, I visited editor-in-chief Robey Macauley at Number 2 Park Street, an antique brownstone building right on Boston Common. I like this weird coincidence— that the famous address "2 Park Street" had had great meaning to my uncle, and one hundred years later, it had the same great importance to me. This coincidence seemed to enforce my secret bond with Macknight.

And from my uncle I had learned that art can ruffle feathers.

Macknight's paintings caused quite a controversy when he had his first show back home. An art critic wrote, "It's a Macknightmare!"

Other critics wrote: "He is turning nature wrong side out." And "Nature in her most brilliant moods never sets the teeth on edge; while Macknight's pictures often do."

Macknight wrote, "I am getting very tired of the criminal stupidity of the human race. It's always the same story. Artists who will not whittle off the corners of their eccentricity to suit the masses have a hard time of it." This statement seems very akin to what I've experienced when writing about my unattractive fringe characters that have no commercial allure.

But others praised Macknight. One critic wrote, "Look at number fourteen. The grass in the foreground is rather bluer than usual, the rail fence is purple, and once again the most noticeable thing is the way in which a little half-inch streak at the horizon suggests miles of distance."

Another wrote, "When a man starts out in a new direction in art—one that is opposed to the methods and traditions of generations—he must expect some adverse criticism."

"Is he doing for painting what Wordsworth did for poetry? Shall we refuse to look at his work because it does not look like Boston Common or a Back Bay sunset?"

Helen Knowlton, in the *Boston Evening Transcript*, wrote: "In color, two M's rule the town—Monet and Macknight! Both these men are discoverers and great as their progress has been, each in his own field, it is impossible to tell where they will finally arrive. Let us bow to honest conviction."

Macknight was at his height when he suddenly stopped painting. Reached in the Grand Canyon where he had been working, he was informed of the death of his son. He didn't paint again after his son unexpectedly perished from blood poisoning due to embedded shrapnel inflicted years before in military service in World War I.

As a very young child, I learned that art causes controversy. The little dustup at the Picasso show at the Philadelphia Museum of Art was minor, compared to what my great-uncle had endured because his use of color was unorthodox, according to his contemporaries. His independent vision was a lesson to me. Macknight's landscape paintings examined our human backgrounds: gardens, meadows, barns, haystacks, fences, bridges. They remind me of Thomas Hardy's settings. Something essentially realist resided in his impressionist paintings; but the more exaggerated his colors, the truer his subjects became. Like Gauguin instructed, "Because your canvas is smaller than nature, you have to use a greener green. That is the falsehood of truth."

Macknight's work and his work ethic greatly influenced my vision as a writer. Veronica always told me, "Art runs in the family. It's your turn now. What are you going to do about it?" Macknight had both scolded and indulged Veronica, and she often used Macknight's very words to instruct or criticize me.

SVT

After Giovanni's diagnosis, I was told I have a condition called SVT. Supraventricular tachycardia makes my heart beat very fast for no reason. The heart's electrical system goes haywire. The upper chambers or "atria" are above the ventricles, and when they beat too fast, over a hundred beats a minute, this makes the ventricles, the heart's big pumps, pause and miss heartbeats. It makes you light-headed, dizzy, and some people might faint. You can drop right where you're standing. I have a mild form of it and I have not yet passed out. But sometimes I stop in my tracks until waves of irregular heart pounding have finished their histrionics.

I was surprised to learn that the bundle of heart muscle cells that involve electrical conduction are called "His" cells, named after the Swiss cardiologist Wilhelm His Jr. who discovered them in 1893. These fibers cause the cardiac muscle of the ventricles to contract at a paced interval. With my abnormal heartbeat I believed that my affair with River-rat is parodied by these illicit heart cells with their comic eponym "*His*." My heart beats too fast. My heart wants to stop.

Miss Van Tassel

One summer I was working at Bennington College at the low-residency MFA writing seminars. I was team-teaching a fiction workshop with a colleague, a pleasant arrangement, but I wanted to get away for a day to see River-rat. My teaching partner was involved in a long-term love quarrel with *her* editor and we often compared our problems with the logistics in these affairs. She told me that if I went to Albany, I could catch Amtrak to the city. Amtrak's Empire Service had many trains running each day from the capital to Manhattan. River-rat was expecting me. She was kind enough to take over the class, a big load for her, without me. She was very generous to let me go, because those classes were all uphill.

Amtrak follows the Hudson River from upstate all the way to Penn Station. I sat on the right side of the car, so I could follow the river and watch its changing swash of water. Starting out crystal clear from its origin at its highest source at Lake Tear of the Clouds and down the arm of the Opalescent River, the Hudson was a formidable presence, always shifting from sun glare to shadow as the train rumbled alongside of her.

The surface was sometimes smooth and sometimes choppy, its reflection always changing colors like a mood ring. Inlets are bronze, sometimes foamy, and beneath the shadowed bank opposite, its pools are inky black. Its central current reflects blue skies with blinding slashes of sunshine. The river's churning temperament mirrored my anxiety and prickling hungers as the train followed the river. I felt its powerful swell pulling me along, as if the river, surging in the same direction I was going, was coursing southward with alacrity and in a devious coercion with me. It was tugging me closer and closer to him, him, him. I felt the river's power throughout every part of my body, as if the wet, wet river were gliding me to the hotel king bed where he would lie beside me.

I had brought a book to read, William Trevor's *Two Lives*, but before I got into it, I watched the river go by. The train was an express and didn't stop very often, but I read the station signs whipping past, and when I recognized the names of several towns, my life flooded back to me. As a child, my father had brought me with him to New York on a business trip. In-between his sales meetings we visited West Point and Tarrytown. He was impressed by the military reservation that had been established by his favorite president, Thomas Jefferson. He told me that the encampment was situated at a treacherous S-curve in the Hudson for extra protection. My father explained that they had laid a huge chain across the water to foul British Navy ships, but that General Benedict Arnold had tried to offer the installation to the British as a bribe when planning to desert to the other side. My father liked military history but he also was a fan of Washington Irving, and he had, of course, read me the stories, "Rip Van Winkle" and "The Legend of Sleepy Hollow." I didn't care for the story about an old man waking up after a long sleep, but I was fascinated by Irving's descriptions of Sleepy Hollow: "A drowsy, dreamy influence seems to hang over the land, and to pervade the very atmosphere." My father liked the story of Sleepy Hollow because of its basis in a Revolutionary War legend. Hessian horsemen battled with Patriot militias, and after a skirmish, residents of Sleepy Hollow found a headless corpse that they later buried in the Old Dutch Burying Ground. The "Headless Horseman" had been an actual historical abomination, and not just Irving's invention. On that trip, my father called me by a nickname each time I complained about being dragged along to these tourist traps. During our sightseeing he said, "Keep your pants on Miss Van Tassel," and "Does Miss Van Tassel need the toilet?" and "If she just sits tight, I'll buy Miss Van Tassel an ice cream cone." In the "Sleepy Hollow" story, Miss Van Tassel was the love interest of Ichabod Crane, and my father enjoyed teasing me with her ridiculous name. Thinking of my father addressing me by the name of Ichabod's beloved while on my way to meet my secret lover was a complicated reverie.

So I took out my book, and I soon became immersed in Trevor's *Two Lives*, which includes *Reading Turgenev* and *My House in Umbria*, novellas about two different middle-aged women embroiled in the surprises and mishaps they faced when redefining their lives. Reading Trevor's words I feel instantly safe; his portraits of the female predicament hinted at my own mistakes, as when one character says, "I will not deny that men have offered me gifts, probably all of which

I have accepted." As I read Trevor, the train peeled away from the Hudson, and sank into the tunnels that brought me into Manhattan.

I checked in at a Midtown hotel. In the room, I unpacked my suitcase. I put my slinky pink shift on a hanger and turned on a hot shower to steam the one or two unsightly folds on its short skirt. I had decided that this was the dress I would wear that evening when River-rat took me to dinner.

But he was arriving at any minute for a lunchtime quickie.

The elevators were under repair, and hotel guests were required to use the stairs. I answered the telephone when River-rat told me that he couldn't find the room. "It's 605," I told him. "You're going to have to take the stairs."

"Climb all the way up there?"

"Miss Van Tassel is waiting for you."

"Excuse me?"

At midday, hotels have a preternatural quiet. He was lying stretched out in bed after sex, and the noontime sun filled the room, making his chin whiskers look extra blond. Our sex had been very open and warm in the very bright room. But River-rat was a little distracted. He seemed to look "guilty" as in making love in broad daylight he had had to remember his wife, Weensie. I thought of her too. Her name was a problem to me. I was surprised to feel an affinity with her; she was named "Weensie" for being the little one in her family. I, too, had been the premie.

River-rat had to go back to the office but he took his time getting dressed. I told him I had shirked my responsibilities at Bennington, and he could thank my academic associate for that. It amused him to think that it had required *two* women to negotiate his little respite from his pencil-pushing duties. I wanted to say, "Yes, it sometimes requires two Miss Van Tassels." But I had a whole afternoon to fill before we would meet again that evening. I thought I might head uptown with him and go on to the Whitney Museum, but I was still undressed.

"Stay like that, till I come back," he said.

I didn't go to the Whitney Museum that afternoon but had remained undressed at the hotel, waiting for him. I got deeper into Trevor's *Two Lives*. Trevor writes, "He was a little mean in some ways . . . she'd seen him taking a lump of coal off the fire." At around five o'clock River-rat telephoned me to beg off our dinner date. It was just like him, to disappoint me. "Taking a lump of coal off the fire." He said that his wife had had some sort of problem. "It turns out that my mother-in-law might have had a 'mini stroke,'" he told me.

"A mini stroke?"

"I have to accompany Weensie through this emergency."

He could have made up a more convincing story. Saying that it *turns out* that it *might have* been a *mini* stroke provided him with several loopholes in his little white lie. I guess his lunchtime diversion with me, in the sunny bed, had left him with a walloping guilt, and meeting me twice in less than four hours was out of the question, even if the sun went down. It wasn't worth the squabble with the missus that he always faced each time he took a later train.

A cheeky Miss Van Tassel might have said, "So you're not going to fuck me *or* feed me?"

I was alone in the city. I decided to check out of the hotel and get back on the train. I'd be back in time to make my class the next day. I had to pay a twenty-five-dollar penalty for changing the departure time on my ticket, but I was glad to hop on another Empire Express, heading in the opposite direction. My teaching colleague will appreciate this story, I was thinking. She had just as many anecdotes about times she'd suffered similar insults of enforced "isolation" from her longtime lover/editor. Writers are never just spurned but are energized, keeping a rolling index in meticulous detail. Her story, "She is Waiting," is a beautiful example of her exasperating relationship with her impenetrable object of desire. "Do not imagine him. Do not forget him. Do not pout. Paint your lips, paint your lips! Draw another rosebud on your mouth. Finally, he is here. He's knocking. Keep the door locked. Don't answer it. Be silent. Kiss the hand mirror with your red lips."

I sat down on my Amtrak seat and opened Trevor's *Two Lives*. Trevor is so good at speaking for me. In his novel, a woman stands in her garden. Like me she is not yet a crone, but she feels it coming. She thinks, "Perhaps I'll become old, perhaps *not*. Perhaps something else will happen in my life, but I doubt it. When the season's over I walk among the shrubs myself, making the most of the colors while they last and the fountain while it flows."

THE CANNONBALL BED

For sex I meet my husband in my childhood bed. I could never part with the handsome cannonball four-poster that was a treasured antique left behind by my great-uncle, Dodge Macknight. I slept in the "three-quarter" four-poster from age five to sixteen. It was part of my dowry when I married my first husband, and after I was divorced it came along with me wherever I went. It went from Newport to Iowa City, to Provincetown, and to North Carolina, and in the end it came back home to Massachusetts, where it had originally been built by Boston cabinetmaker and joiner George Bright, in 1792. My daughter used the bed for several years, and when she went to college, the cannonball bed was moved into my husband's studio.

The antique bed has gorgeous turnings on each post, finished off with a cannonball as round as a large grapefruit. Its headboard has a bullet hole. Over the years, the splintered bullet hole triggers pillow talk of a certain kind. And scattered on the bed stand there are stanzas of poems my husband is working on:

Fragrance does not wear fragrance
It owes its breath
To the thin sheen
Perfume brings to the neck
and
I see straight through myself
And into the No mirror
I'm still here
Drinking Gin in a Lawn Chair

The bed was a "rope bed" with six holes in the side rails, where rope was strung to support the original horsehair mattress that I slept on as a child. When the century-old mattress finally gave out, I centered a piece of plywood across the frame to hold a specially made three-quarter Sealy Posturepedic. A three-quarter bed, not a full double, necessitates some 'give and take' between partners but intimacy flowers on its tight plank.

How do I love you?
Let's figure it out.

The cannonball bed is what we call our "sex bed." He never joins me upstairs. On the second floor, it's my private world. It's where I sleep and where I write all my books. He never enters my rooms and he calls it "her Ice Palace" because I prefer to have sex in his quarters.

My husband's rooms are very masculine, walled by books, with new piles of books on the floor, sent to him each week by publishers who want his attention, since he's an editor at a major periodical. Beside towers of books are his shortwave radios, his Zenith Transoceanic and his Grundig Satellit 800 Millennium, on which he listens to Radio Moscow. Or he transmits his own messages, having earned his ham radio license and his own call letters KB1JUJ: Kilo-Bravo-1- Juliette-Uniform-Juliette. There's a forest of weird self-wrought antennas. A "broomstick" antenna wrapped in copper wire, and his dipole antenna, a huge copper T with twin leads, an inner connector, outer braid, transmission line, and insulators. His collection includes scanners that once pulled in open cell phone conversations before cell connections went from analog to digital. After sex in the four-poster, in our dreamy state, he thumbed the tuner to listen to private cell phone conversations. The stories were complicated and novelistic. People reveal so much when trying to squeeze out of situations, or when trying to climb back into wounded relationships. Raymond Carver, Cheever, even Hardy would be enthralled with the conversations he punched up on the radio. In one phone call, a husband sat in his car and dialed his wife before entering his mistress's apartment. In another, a mother talked to her son, explaining that she had just swallowed a whole bottle of barbs. Teen boys dared their sweethearts to undress at the window, as they watched from parked cars outside. This was before Instagram. Then of course, most cell phone callers dialed pizza parlors, to order pies, and we listened to hot arguments about the extra toppings they wanted.

When he lost interest in shortwave, he started collecting fountain pens. I fell in love with fountain pen lingo. His pens included a Namiki "Vanishing Point"; a

Sailor "Sapporo" with its extra fine nib, a point so delicate it makes lines as thin as a chin hair; a Visconti "Opera Master"; the Yard-o-led "Astoria Grand"; and a German Pelikan "Souverän M1000," just to name a few. He collects cartridges and converters, and his favorite pen has to be filled with a specialized piston. He showed me an eighteen-karat *bicolor* gold nib. Even more seductive were his bottles of ink. There's "Lightning Blue," "Summer Tanager," a crimson-orange, and "Firefly," a fluorescent yellow. "Dragons Napalm" is the color of Mercurochrome. "Black Swan in Australian Roses," is deep black with red "reflections." He showed me how the ink gets its name. He spilled a little ink on a sheet of paper. The black pigment collects in the center, like a fluffy black swan, but its red tones emerge in a large pink blot around the swan, like it's sitting in a rose bed. My favorite inks were "Tulipe Noir," and "Poussière De Lune," which translates from the French as moon "powder," or moon "dust," a sooty purple blush.

My husband belongs to the *Fountain Pen Network*, where nerdy fountain pen intellectuals share their obsession. He writes columns about fountain pens for the *New York Times,* the *Boston Globe*, and JetPens. com. River-rat gave me a beautiful fountain pen for my birthday. A silver–barreled Faber-Castell Porsche Design. I gave it to my husband, for his collection.

He's a man entombed in stacks of books, who owns expensive wing tips made of buttery leather, Italian linen shirts, transcontinental radios, and a world-class collection of fountain pens arranged in several glass-lidded boxes.

Then he started buying guns.

I don't have any secrets
Unless she was my secret
A reaching out
Like a summer kiss
A kiss on the porch in summer
And the porch itself
Extends just so far.

Sometimes, when my husband fucks me, I think of
River-rat. Not during my arousal, or with orgasm, but
afterward. My husband is very deep inside me, he's
almost there, and I think of these men. I make comparisons. But there are none.

Remissionimpossible.blogspot.com

There's a house in my neighborhood that stands out to me. Reggae music is blaring and "Afreecan" is written in permanent marker on the front door. On the stoop, a white cat sits fluffed on its haunches. It has one floppy ear, and I think "That's a pretty adorable battle scar." White cats are usually deaf. Google says that deafness is inherent in white cats with a certain eye color. He seemed to be doing okay, deaf or not. I like to stop and pet the cat every time I pass the Afreecan house. Sandrine says he's my "spirit animal." I finally met the guy who lived in the house. He says to me, "Hey, you." He had a thick Haitian accent and reeked of dope.

I say, "Hello." I have to be careful to stay six feet from anyone I meet if I'm not in my mask. I take a few steps back, but I hate to appear standoffish.

"You've got something going on, don't you?" he says.

"What? I just like to pet your cat." I'll pet any cat I see. But he was right. I especially liked the floppy-eared tomcat.

"He knows all about you or he wouldn't let you scratch his ears."

"He's a nice cat."

"You've got courage," he says. "Don't question your instincts. Keep the faith."

I didn't know what he was talking about.

He was preaching some kind of philosophy, but I liked the guy. He seemed to understand I was waiting to hear about my CT scan. They might find new hot spots or they'll finally say I'm in remission. The first transplant was critical but I need to be in remission to undergo the next one from the donor. That's the important one. The allogeneic transplant is my only ticket to freedom. I am not yet "cured" but yesterday they said I had the all-clear to start eating vegetables again. I am being entirely truthful when I say I miss salad more than I miss alcohol. But I can't smoke pot. Grass has fungus all over it. Crispin says antibiotics don't work for fungal pneumonia and we can't risk it.

VELVET

I came of age in the late sixties. My first boyfriend was eight years older than me, and I lost my cherry to him. He owned a business making "gatorized" electric guitars. He resurfaced guitars with his own trademark "gator finish," an acrylic shellac that checkered and blistered significantly upon drying, giving the guitar its scaly alligator appearance. Rock groups were flocking to him to have their Gibsons and Telecasters "gatorized." The psychedelic band Rhinoceros came into his shop and wanted several of their guitars to get the transformation. His favorite band Ten Years After also was interested. One weekend, he made $4,000 taking orders at the Atlantic City Rock Festival. He spent some of the cash on little postage stamps of LSD that he insisted I let dissolve on the roof of my mouth. When the drug was blasting through me, he took me back to the motel for "acid sex." I was surprised to see the lead guitarist of a big name band was waiting for us. He had been invited by my boyfriend for sloppy seconds. They had made some kind of negotiation when the guitarist had ordered his "gatorized" guitar and I had been part of the deal. As the band member fucked me in my LSD confusion, I watched the motel walls sprout hairs. Each little hair had a face, and all the little clown-faced hairs were talking to me in high squeaky voices.

Later that year, with a little help from the dramatic songwriting of Laura Nyro, I decided to break up with the Gatorized Guitar King. Like other egghead girls, I was mesmerized by Laura Nyro's poetic lyrics and her sultry vocals that were half angelic and half vixen, and often very feminist. With her influence I felt the power to dump my boyfriend as a new era of independence swept open before me. I started wearing a long black velvet coat like the kind Laura Nyro had worn on stage at a concert in Philadelphia. The coat was a midcentury style error. The cascading, ankle-length velvet coat was meant to be chic outerwear to be worn over evening gowns, and many women of my mother's age had purchased them back in the forties and fifties. Soon they were stuffed in the backs of their closets. My mother had given me the out-of-date garment as if it was a loathsome horse blanket. I wore the coat everywhere. Seeing me in the full-length velvet coat inspired our next-door neighbor to offer me her version of the same coat. I had two velvet coats to choose between when I got dressed every morning.

I wore my velvet coat on a jet airplane when flying to visit a boy in Connecticut. He had been a waspy prep school neighbor I had met at a cottage colony in East Sandwich on the Cape that previous summer. He took me out on his Sunfish sailing dinghy, with its lateen sail or "Latin rig," to remote beaches where we took off our bathing suits and "experimented." I had two freckles on either side of my belly button and he walked his fingers from my freckles to my nipples, talking about "the logic of geometry." He described it like this: *The three most common ways to change a conditional statement are by taking its inverse, its converse, or its contrapositive. In each case, either the hypothesis and the conclusion switch places, or a statement is replaced by its negation.* He was showing off his private school education. It worked. I thought his gibberish was sexy. That winter, he invited me to his parents' home in Hartford, hoping to get into my pants again.

On the plane trip, I was placed in an aisle seat beside a businessman who was returning home from a working trip to Philadelphia. But as soon as I was seated in my proper row, my seatmate became very fidgety. He twisted around to look at the back seats of the plane, as if to find someone he knew or as if he was hoping to find an empty space. The commuter jet was packed. Soon we were taxiing down the runway, and the man grew more distressed. His face was very pale and sweat was collecting on his forehead. He tried to get the attention of a stewardess, but they were all too busy during takeoff.

Finally, I asked him, "What's wrong with you?"

"I have to apologize," he said. "But you are going to have to take that off."

"Excuse me?"

"That coat. Could you please remove your coat and maybe give it to the stewardess? They'll hold it for you up front. You can get it back when you disembark, I'm sure."

"You want me to take my coat off?" For weeks, the coat and I had been inseparable. His request seemed outlandish to me. The truth was that I was wearing the velvet coat not as an outer layer, but as a "coat dress." I wore nothing underneath but an underwire bra and my panties.

The man had the window seat and he pawed at the little porthole as if hoping it would open. Sweat was dripping from his face and actually pouring from the tips of his ears. He was in terrible trouble.

"It's making my throat close up!" he said.

"My coat?"

"I can't breathe," he said.

The man explained that he had a severe phobia to velvet, but he couldn't go on talking. He started trembling and coughing.

I asked a stewardess to bring him water. He told her that he could not possibly sit next to me. She explained to him that the plane was full. I remembered an episode of the *Three Stooges* when the character named Curly had had a similar attack in reaction to someone wearing "tassels." He had a "tassels" phobia that made him squirm and lose control, as if he wanted to jump out of his skin. I had not yet learned about all the different kinds of phobias people could have, myself included. Several years later I could not get on an elevator or drive on the freeway. I had to take the stairs, no matter how many floors I had to climb, and I would drive on back roads to avoid the speeding traffic on the expressway, taking hours to get to my destination. It wasted a lot of time. A doctor explained that I must have had a "panic attack" in an elevator or when driving on the freeway and I associated these locales with my uncomfortable symptoms. He said I would have to desensitize myself by getting back in the saddle, taking elevators again and driving in rush hour traffic. If I had known about this when I was on the airplane sitting beside the velvet freak, I might have told him that sitting beside my velvet coat might actually *cure* his phobia. But I traded seats with another passenger who wore a wool car coat.

When we arrived at Hartford, I met the man at the taxi stand where I had been told to catch a cab to my friend's house. The man apologized for causing me any inconvenience. I saw how handsome he was, now that he wasn't having a panic attack. His features were smooth and he was no longer sweaty. I wanted to show him why I had refused to remove my coat on the airplane and could not oblige him. I unfastened the two big velvet buttons on my coat, letting it slip from my shoulders. He watched the coat fall in a black lake at my feet. I stood in my bra and panties on the busy sidewalk. With fatherly embarrassment for me, or something, he pushed me into a cab and got in right behind me. I was careful to pull my precious coat into the cab but I folded it inside out, revealing the silk lining, so the man wouldn't have a relapse. The velvet freak said, "Drive!" to the man behind the wheel. He told the driver to "sightsee" and he tipped me onto the back bench, onto its icy vinyl upholstery. He kissed me. He unbuckled his belt. For half an hour he got to know all about me. He learned that I was a junior at Mount Pleasant High School and that I really liked Laura Nyro. He didn't seem to bother with any foreplay or the "logic of geometry," but took his beautiful time. Afterward he offered me his handkerchief so I could line my panties. Years later, I saw the movie *Dressed to Kill*. In that film, Angie Dickenson was undressed by a stranger in the back seat of a cab. Perhaps that connection is why I have always felt a rapport with *Police Woman*. Before dropping me off at my friend's address, the velvet-freak kissed me on the forehead, like an uncle. As I got out of the taxi, he brushed the palm of his hand up and down the velvet sleeve of my coat to prove he had lost his fear of it. "Thanks, baby," he said.

MISS EYES

When I enter the transplant unit, I have to follow a list of rules. I must take off my coat in the ante room. I enter the sterilization pantry to collect my uniform. My purse goes into a large blue bag. I find a fresh smock to wear over my clothes. At the door to his room, I have to scrub my hands with special soap and find a new pair of gloves from the cubby that has stacks of small, medium, and large nitrile mittens. I put on a bonnet and face mask. When I enter his room, I am completely anonymous, but he knows it's me.

In his third week of high-dose chemo for his first stem cell transplant, he's still pissing blood, but a new rash has exploded from head to toe. It's a little worse than a second-degree sunburn, the nurse says, but to me it looks like he's been splashed with sulfuric acid, like acid-attack victim model Katie Piper who was assaulted by her jealous boyfriend. A side effect of Methotrexate causes the skin to redden, blister, and peel. He is given little cups of medicine to sip for relief of mouth sores and blisters on the roof of his mouth. He is given an IV of anti-inflammatory antivenom to soothe his "sunburn" but these side effects won't abate until he is through the current phase of therapy.

We sit in the sealed-off room. An air filter system is purring, exchanging the room air twelve times an hour with filtered air that moves in a parallel, unidirectional flow; the air enters the room from one wall and exits the room on the opposite wall. The death rate of transplant patients in unfiltered rooms is nearly four times higher.

He lies stretched out without a sheet over him. He's wearing boxer shorts, but even the light cotton throw is intolerable to him. He waits for his favorite nurse. "She's so hot," he says. Although his girlfriend, Sandrine, a beauty from working class Fitchburg, enrolled at Harvard, who every day sits beside him in her rubber gloves and space suit, had not yet arrived at the hospital. He describes the nurse and says, "It's those eyes. Her eyes are killing me." The nurse's eyes are all that he can see about her, since she always wears a mask. The fabric pulled tight, ear to ear, hides everything but her big eyes as she tends to my son's extended agony in step-by-step attentions to him.

First she takes his temperature with an electronic thermometer, holding its tiny sensor against his temple for just a few seconds. By this time, a second nurse appears and they both begin to administer his next round of poison drugs. Wearing blue nitrile gloves, one nurse checks his ID bracelet; she enters his "admit weight" on the BSA calculator to verify his "body surface area" to be sure it matches the prescribed dosages. She flushes his IV port and makes sure his IV infusion pump is connected to his primary IV line, a normal saline or dextrose solution to which she adds each medication to his vented IV plastic bag. She shakes the bag, closes off the IV infusion clamp, wipes his port with an alcohol swab, and inserts the syringe needle through his injection port. She lowers the bag from his IV pole and again she turns the bag back and forth to mix the poison, rehangs the bag, jots down its medication label, and attaches it to the bag. She regulates the infusion to achieve the desired rate. She adds a "time strip" to the bag if the infusion will be longer than two hours. The procedure must be performed by two RNs as independent double-checks, and the nurse with the beautiful eyes joins her partner, to initial all the documents.

After his infusion has started, the staff leaves the room. "They are the biggest, deepest eyes," he says. In his itchy, burning skin he wants to dive into the pools of her eyes. "She's the most beautiful woman I have ever seen."

"Which one are you talking about?"

Two names are scrawled on the dry-erase board in his air-filtered room. At every new shift the names change on that board, just as the air is filtered and exchanged. "Is she Greta? Or the one called Sammi?" I say. The board lists both his registered nurses.

"To me she's 'Miss Eyes,'" he says. "But shit. I wish I could see her face."

I'm encouraged that his interest in women is still intact even as the poison floods into him; his hetero powers are indestructible, or might even be magnified by his life and death battle. I think of Herbie Hancock explaining an important moment when life had changed for him. He said he had once been performing with Miles Davis and he struck a wrong chord. He felt shocked by his mistake and feared that he had ruined the whole performance. He said, "It was a house of cards that came down, because I struck the wrong chord. But Miles responded with a new phrase that turned my wrong chord into a right chord. By some kind of miracle, *poison became medicine.*"

I was impressed by my son's ability to transform a wrong chord into a right chord, every day. He would make that poison work for him. But I'm not ready for his next request. He says, "She goes off shift in about an hour. Maybe you can follow her when she leaves the unit. She'll take off that fucking mask on her way to the garage. If you catch up to her, you can tell me what she looks like."

In the cancer hospital, the masked and unmasked intermingle. At every entrance and beside every elevator there's a dispenser with blue face masks. All over the magnificent complex, Dana-Farber and Brigham's are interconnected like one huge octopus; hundreds of people navigate every corridor fully masked. Both patients and staff move in restricted cocoons, covered in nitrile gloves and survivor face masks. Staff that are through for the day, toss their masks in trash receptacles. I see these blue scraps in pedestal ashtrays and in every available waste bin.

"You want me to trail her? Like a spy?"

"Maybe you can get a picture with your phone?"

I followed the nurse with the beautiful eyes when her shift was over. I caught up with her at the end of the hall and I watched her remove her face mask when we took the same elevator. To my surprise, she had a sharp chin and a rather beaked nose. Her skin tone was beautiful, as rich as wood stain, common to women of Indian descent, but in fact she was pretty homely. But my calculations have shifted. The precise criteria I had learned from my narcissistic mother is changed forever. Of course I believed the nurse was attractive. She was lovely. Her everyday job was to save my son.

GIRL WHO TROD ON A LOAF

By 1968 I had wet my feet with the gator king, the boy from Connecticut, and the velvet freak on the airplane. My mother was getting a whiff of it. She recognized I was sexually active. It was time for me to be booted out of the house.

A few years earlier, when my fourteen-year-old sister had disappeared, it became a linchpin event in my early life. (*Linchpin:* "The most important part of a complex situation or system.") I had learned that the "complex system" in my family was that girls had to vanish at their coming of age. Having once been jilted by her first husband, the Arrow Collar model, our mother insisted that she be the sole erotic temptress in our household and she wanted no competition from us. Of course we had little control over our natural metamorphosis from ivory-skinned girlhood to flesh-toned womanhood. Our father made few attempts to protect us. Instead like a subservient court attendant typical to fairy tales, he did our mother's bidding.

I had begun to recognize the "Snow White Syndrome," and I sensed an undercurrent of hostility in things my mother said. She believed that my older sisters were to blame for their own abrupt exodus and that I better watch my step. The first to be pushed from the nest was my older sister Christine. She enrolled at the University of Delaware at sixteen, an awkward prodigy. Her freshman year, a college professor knocked her up and married her unceremoniously. Soon after Christine had left, my fourteen-year-old sister, Karen, took off. The last I saw of her, I was sitting at the kitchen table writing five sheets of detention homework, the same sentence repeated over and over: "I will not be disruptive in class." Karen paused at the door and said, "I'm going to the corner shop, do you want a pack of gum?" I noticed the kitchen clock behind her head; its second hand had become bent. As it circled the numbers, the needle scratched a gouge in the clock's white face. Then my sister went out. She never returned.

In one week's time she became an authentic FBI case. I imagined my sister dead in the beaver pool or in the marsh sedge along the Delaware River. I pictured my sister's motionless body in a grassy trench, but I couldn't accept that she had left me behind with Veronica on purpose.

With my sisters gone, I maintained my neutrality in my mother's kingdom. In my riding boots and dirty jeans, I was still welcomed in her house, but I had to be vigilant. Like my sisters before me, my transformation from girl to sex goddess was quickly approaching and soon I would be cast out.

The icy matriarch or jealous guardian is a common theme in fairy tales, and "Snow White" is its most famous example. Yet a more obscure story had even greater implications for my sisters and me. My first introduction to a fairy tale called "Girl Who Trod on a Loaf" occurred shortly after my sister Karen's disappearance in the winter of 1965. This story became intertwined with events in my household and its pages seemed to spawn *awakenings* in me which would lead to my eventual flight from home.

One night my mother called me onto the sunporch. She presented me with a new book in a faux leather binding, an elaborate edition of Hans Christian Andersen, a volume selection from Book-of-the-Month. My mother asked me to sit down beside her to sample a fairy tale as she read her new Robert Nathan novel. Her invitation was immediately suspect. She didn't often request my company after the yardarm when she had concluded her maternal efforts for the day. Her inclusiveness was highly irregular and I sat down on the edge of a cushioned bamboo chair, ready to pop up again at the slightest wave of her hand.

After dark the sunporch was a nasty parlor; its huge panes of black glass could never be warmed by the interior lighting. As she faced me, the back of my mother's head was reflected in the window. I saw her hair collected in a tight "chignon." It was a disturbing image, perhaps because I had recently seen the taxidermic skull in the movie *Psycho*.

My mother was a gorgeous beauty, but her chiseled features were harshly exaggerated in the glass room. Reflected in the blank panels, her face looked washed-out and frozen, white as an ice queen. I watched her turn the pages of the Robert Nathan romance. Her casual reading hour and even her typical television habits seemed inappropriate when my sister was still lost. How could my mother have her routine entertainments when my sister was still out there in the night, unclaimed?

I recognized how fairy tale characters often flee from their homes to begin unassisted journeys into dark woods or perilous terrain. Fairy tale characters had to decipher antique maps or draw their own itineraries, choosing the "high road" or the "low road"; their decisions were crucial and would alter their roadbook for better or for worse. To reach the safety of new shores, characters might need to ford a river, shimmy over a log, scale a wall, dupe trolls at a magic kiosk, edge across a rope bridge, or teeter on unsecure stepping-stones.

These fairy tales addressed situations like mine. In order for girl children to survive their sexual maturation, they would have to escape from their malevolent matriarchs. My sister Karen had disappeared. From what poison apple had she sampled? What spell had been cast upon her? I imagined benevolent dwarfs or much worse; I pictured witches in domestic disguises luring Karen into their bungalows or even into their condos. In fact, my sister ran off with a pimp in a detailed Chrysler Newport, heading for NoFuck Virginia.

I read the fairy tale book searching for portraits of kind surrogates, good fairies, and tolerant foster parents who might harbor lost children. But my mother had secured one chapter of the fairy tale collection with her glass swizzle stick, marking the story called "The Girl Who Trod on a Loaf."

"Read this one first," she told me, her eyes cold green as a medicine bottle.

I was suspicious of her recommendation and scanned the table of contents, finding more familiar stories: "The Princess and the Pea," "The Little Mermaid," "Thumbelina."

But the title itself, "The Girl Who Trod on a Loaf," with its strange diction, was interesting to me. The verb "trod" was slightly archaic and judging it so provided me with a safety buffer. If the language was old-fashioned, its moral couldn't possibly be appropriate for modern-day children and I wouldn't have to "learn a lesson." The word "loaf" also seemed absurd in that context. Of course, we always had loaves of sliced bread delivered to our house by the Bond Bread truck. I often ran to the front door to greet the driver who, dressed in a starched white jacket, held a wide basket of fresh bakery items crooked on his arm. I could choose a pecan ring or a jelly roll—a delicious sponge cake smeared with raspberry jam.

I didn't believe that the "loaf" of the fairy tale title referred to delicacies in the Bond Bread truck, but rather it evoked slabs of coarse bread I had seen pulled apart by hand in movies like *Heidi* and *Ben-Hur*. This recognition gave me a feeling of superiority and the distance I needed to enter the fairy tale with my feet firmly planted in the present-day world of Wonder Bread.

Sitting beside my mother, I opened the book. The jacket creaked like a saddle pommel as I wrested the covers apart. The work within must be significant to merit the same sturdy binding usually reserved for Bibles or Shakespeare sets. When I turned the pages, I saw that each sheet had a furry nap and was strangely flecked like blotter paper.

"The Girl Who Trod on a Loaf" introduces a young girl with a "bad streak." "Inger" is "proud and vain" and for her own amusement she pulls the wings off flies. Even worse, she impales a "cockchafer" (again an archaic term) on a pin. She holds a leaf up to the insect's feet to watch it try to climb off the skewer, but of course it is doomed. "Now the cockchafer's reading," Inger jokes. "Look how it's turning over the page."

I recognized Inger's macabre sense of humor. Her wicked mirth cast a spell on me. I recognized myself. I had stranded tadpoles on sunny boulders just to watch them struggle, trying to hop back in the water with their half-formed haunches. I collected salamanders, and with my fingertip poked their spotted flesh, tender as pudding skin. I arranged the salamanders on a Limoges dinner plate and examined them under a one-hundred-watt bulb. To my horror their porous bodies dried up in an instant, stranding the creatures in an ornate pattern circling the rim of the dish.

Inger and I were similarly distressed by our emerging adolescence. Our bodies were changing and we had no control of the outcome. So we asserted our power over helpless insects and amphibians. In the story, we are told that Inger is a *beauty*. "She was very pretty and that was her misfortune, for otherwise she would have been slapped a good deal oftener than she was."

Beautiful girls under the age of twelve get away with murder. I knew this.

I was the littlest, the "cute one," still flat chested. My older sisters were banished as soon as their bodies had ripened. At her menarche, Inger is sent to work as a servant for a rich family where she is dressed in finery. Her mistress's generosity only encourages

Inger's vanity and her obsession with fashionable clothes is her sole occupation. Months pass and her thoughtful mistress encourages Inger to finally return home to visit her mother. "Take this loaf home to your mother," she says, and she gives Inger a "fine white loaf." Inger gets dressed in her "best things and her new shoes" and she leaves her employer's place to walk to her mother's house. On her journey she comes to a "marshy place" and worries about soiling her new shoes crossing the water. With no thought of its value to others, she flings the fine loaf of bread into the brook to use it as a stepping-stone to get across the bog.

Here Inger takes her greatest risk, and like the archetypal draw bridge or rope ladder, her use of the loaf of bread as a stepping-stone leads Inger into her transformation, for better or for worse. With a fairy tale's typical swift judgment, Inger is given a lightning-fast sentence. The instant Inger steps on the loaf she sinks to the bottom of the marshy bog into the domain of the "marsh witch." Here we meet Inger's foster mother who will control her metamorphosis.

"'This comes of taking care to keep your shoes clean,' Inger said to herself. 'They should have corrected me more often and cured me of my bad ways if I had any. Now I dare say they have something to talk about up there—ooh, I am tormented!'"

When hungry she tries to break off a piece of the loaf still stuck to her shoe, but she can't bend her back. She's been turned into a statue to decorate the entranceway of hell. Inger is removed from the human world and is forced to reside in the underworld of the marsh-witch and the devil. Snakes entwine in her hair, and she is forced to hear what people say about her. "A whole ballad about her had been brought out— The proud girl who trod on the loaf to save her pretty shoes—and it was sung all over the country."

Just a few years later, on my daily route to my high school, I walked on a secret path through the woods. The forest trail opened upon a wide stream; after heavy rains it was a torrent and at other times it was a smooth sheet of Saran. To cross the stream, I had to navigate a bridge of random stepping-stones. I made strategic hops to get across several boulders that formed a zigzag route in the rushing water. Crossing the stream using the stepping-stones was a daily test. The fairy tale about Inger was in the back of my mind, each time I crossed the stepping-stones on the way to school. I once met a man at the stepping-stone bridge. He was dressed in a suit and tie, and he said he had left his office for a breath of air. He offered me a cigarette. I accepted the Pall Mall, and he lit it for me. After I took a drag, he put his hand on my breast. I didn't protest. I sort of liked it. The man showed up at the stepping-stone bridge more than once, and soon I found him waiting for me at the high school parking lot at the end of the day. We took "scenic drives" along the Brandywine River where he stopped the car on a turnout. He kissed me.

Soon after my sister disappeared from home, I felt the strong undercurrent of my female fate. I began to understand the "stepping-stones" which led to the erotic life that our mother so coveted and to which my sisters had been banished to face on their own. I started to understand that men would be my stepping-stones to the "other side" of childhood.

I left home before I was seventeen. It was time for me to begin a life alone, *alone.* I have learned that we are alone, even before we leave family behind. I started to see aloneness as opportunity. Finding independence comes when searching for the self *of self*, without intruders or busybodies.

I had my first trial run when I was just a junior in high school. We took a class trip to New York City to see a Broadway matinee performance of *Look to the Lilies*, a short-lived musical based on *Lilies of the Field*. I sat with my classmates to watch Shirley Booth whom I recognized from the TV show *Hazel*, but I couldn't endure more than the first act. I escaped my high school entourage and took a subway to Greenwich Village. I kicked around awhile, but was careful to get back on the subway in time to meet the deadline when our chartered bus was supposed to depart for home. On the train I met a man who seemed all too happy to meet a high school girl from Wilmington. We discussed our commitment to the Students for a Democratic Society and he claimed to be an SDS organizer. He also carried a shopping bag of artist supplies, and he explained that he was a "graphic designer." He scribbled his address on the back of a window envelope and handed it to me. "Next time you're in town, you have to look me up."

The envelope had no address on its front side, its window was empty, but I was surprised to see that the return address on the envelope said NBC. This gave me a little confidence in the stranger who was flirting with me. If he was an SDS captain, and NBC was corresponding with him, or perhaps sending him a paycheck of some kind, perhaps for his reportage on the student organization, he must be a legitimate member of the New York City leftist community or an actual TV reporter. That had a glamorous pull on me as so many small town girls often felt New York City was in our future.

The following week I had a mock fistfight with my mother at a local vegetable stand. She was giving me a lot of criticism when she noticed I wasn't wearing a bra under my tank top. Going braless was a late sixties phenomenon; my nipple-tips were jutting out and even worse, you could see the little ridged circles of areola under my tight tank top. My mother found it tasteless. Her yammering annoyed me and I shoved her into a folding table with a pyramid of melons. The table legs collapsed sending the melons bouncing right and left. Green globes rolled through the parking lot. My mother wasn't injured but was alarmed that I had pushed her and that I had used more than my usual verbal assault, which never had much effect in our back and forth. After shoving my mother, I was ashamed of myself, and when we returned home with our bag of vegetables, I went to find the NBC envelope I had carefully tucked away in the same anthology where I hid my Ortho-Novum birth control pills I'd been using when dating the Gator King. I decided to leave town immediately. I put a change of clothes in my backpack, with some Tampax and lip gloss—the bare essentials—and I hitched my way to the Delaware Bridge.

I got a ride with a college boy heading back to Bowdoin in Maine. I had to listen to him rant about Nixon for two hours on the New Jersey Turnpike, and I was relieved when he got off the highway to let me off in

New York. I jumped out of his VW on the west side, far uptown. It was a shabby black neighborhood. Kids and oldsters crowded stoops and the sidewalk, and a woman nickered to me, "Hi, honey. Are you lost?" In just minutes, some kids approached me and lifted my backpack off my shoulders the way a gentleman removes a lady's wrap at a coat check. With elegant reserve and little fanfare, they snatched my possessions and trotted away.

I had no money, but in my pocket I still had the address of the man I had met on the subway. I followed street numbers, block by block. The city was larger than the Grand Canyon. As I entered each new neighborhood, people looked at me as if I were a stray mental patient. Not carrying a purse or book bag, my arms loose at my sides, I tore across the sidewalks like a junior Miss Frankenstein. There weren't any stepping-stones to navigate, but I wasn't used to stopping at DON'T WALK signs, and I climbed up the heels of businessmen and other startled pedestrians who halted at intersections waiting for the signs to change. I searched for the right address until I finally discovered, after disturbing an unsuspecting apartment tenant, that there were *two* Eighty-First streets in New York. "This is West Eighty-First. You want the East Side," she told me. "You have to go through the park to the other side to get where you want."

I entered Central Park and followed a path through green hillocks and across little bridges rimmed with leaded-glass lanterns and occasional statuary. I was in awe of finding so much natural beauty within a great circle of granite high-risers. As I went deeper I became lost in that Eden. Crossing an isthmus between a span of water, I thought of Inger sinking below the surface, and I must have looked disoriented and frightened, like an understudy to the heroine of the movie *The Out of Towners*. In the East Eighties, I hiked many blocks before I found the right building. I saw the name of the NBC reporter on the front door intercom and he buzzed me through the foyer. I walked upstairs to the fourth floor avoiding a scary elevator with its small black porthole.

My SDS compatriot answered the door. But by now, he had become an NBC anchorman in my fantasy, and I wasn't interested in student politics. As he let me in, three orange "tiger-striped" kittens scrambled to get out. He stopped to collect them as they circled our feet and gently tossed them back in the flat.

He wasn't displeased to find me standing on his doormat, a textured square in the design of a commemorative postage stamp. The postage stamp doormat branded me somehow, as if I might be some sort of special-delivery item. Yet on the floor I saw a catnip mouse and a jingle bell tied to a string. Why worry about a man who adopts a houseful of kittens?

In the tight apartment I was surprised to find a clawfoot bathtub in the middle of the one-room studio. He turned on the tap as I entered the room behind him. "You need a bath," he said.

"I need a bath? Well—okay," I said.

His plan was to get my clothes off. I allowed him to unbutton my shirt and then he turned me around to unclip my bra. It didn't go past me that after my mother's complaint about my not wearing a bra, I'd left home wearing my favorite one, a little Warner push-up. After I sat in the warm suds for ten minutes, he pulled me out of the bath and patted me dry with a towel. Next he led me to the opposite wall and he gently pushed me down on the floor facing him. Before I could understand, he tied both my hands to the radiator with two individual tube socks. At first I giggled as I tried to fight him off. I imagined it was a comic maneuver and I'd better find the sophisticated angle that an adult might find to enjoy the humor of it. I grew alarmed when he knotted the socks so tightly I felt the circulation to both my hands impaired. My fingers were turning white.

He found another cat toy, a long stick with a feather tip. He tickled me with the feather cat toy, dancing it lightly over my bare breasts and swiping it across my belly in slow circles. One of the kittens tried to play with us and he slammed it against the wall. If it was some kind of game he was playing, treating me like one of his kittens, I tried to laugh and blow it off easily, at first. But then he got to work; he kneeled before me, finding my slit with his fingers.

"Ouch, ouch!" I said.

Then he pushed his face between my legs. I pinched my knees shut and shifted my hips, shouting at him to stop. He climbed over my naked body to straddle me, and from out of nowhere he found another tube sock and shoved it into my mouth, the wad of cotton depressing my tongue against the back of my palette, closing off my airway. Again he started licking me furiously, completely absorbed in the task. I tried to endure the rising sensations that were tight little jabs of pain tangled with waves of arousal that seemed wholly separate from my own consciousness, sensations I would not claim as my own. Worst of all, I couldn't breathe with the sock in my mouth and when I tried to scream my voice was absorbed at the back of my throat in the cotton wadding. I had to swallow my protests and *taste* them: they tasted familiar, like my own problems, my own faults. He lapped at me for many minutes, as I kept in a frigid state despite his stamina. When he decided to get on top of me to finish his business, it was a relief to no longer feel his busy tongue between my legs.

The next morning, I left New York. The NBC rapist escorted me to the Port Authority and gave me the cash for a bus ticket. Back in Wilmington, I didn't attend another SDS meeting. I had survived the attack, but my trip to New York had a lifelong influence on my burgeoning sexuality. It was the final stepping-stone out of childhood. Like Inger I had been transformed from an innocent to a devil. But I don't carry it on my sleeve like other rape victims, not like the student at Columbia who had claimed she was raped and she carried a mattress around for weeks, from class to class, asking her department to consider it her "thesis project." Because of my experience with the kitten rapist, I have an acquired cynicism, and over the years I am often surprised to learn of women's hysterical reactions to sexual assault. One summer I taught a fiction writing class at the Fine Arts Work Center in Provincetown. I had assigned my students a story to discuss in class, "The Mud Below," by Annie Proulx. I was confused when a student asked me about the "rape scene" in the story.

"What rape scene?" I said. I had not considered the one sex scene in the story to be an encounter of sexual violence. In fact, the sexual moment Proulx had described was overtly comedic. A bull rider named "Diamond Felts" mounts his friend's wife in the back seat of a truck, although she isn't too pleased. "She bucked and shoved and struggled and cursed him, she was dry . . ." The character had gone to a yard sale earlier that day and she had purchased a waffle iron. When Diamond is doing the deed, "something fell off the seat with a hard sound." The woman screams, "My waffle iron!" She doesn't yell, "Help!" or "Rape!" Diamond says, "I've heard it called a lot of things, but never a waffle iron." I thought the little scene was very funny. When my class of female students didn't see the humor of the scene and insisted it was a rape, I was taken aback. Perhaps my particular history had made me cynical and insensitive to "women's issues."

In lovemaking I am very pleased to take a man's cock in my mouth. It excites me. Yet, to this day, I have never desired oral sex from my partners. It's disappointing to them when I decline, but I can't be aroused from it. I freeze up. And I have no apologies. Cunnilingus is a *hate* thing to me. That's always in the back of my head. And whenever I see an orange tiger-striped cat, the kind that has a white throat and maybe a couple of white socks, although orange toms are believed to be the most affectionate and loving of all felines, I never stop to pet them.

THE FLOWER POT

I was nervous to meet with River-rat whenever I had my period. I knew he wasn't an Orthodox Jew, and probably didn't practice Orthodox traditions. But I worried that he still might be squeamish about sleeping with a woman who was bleeding. After all, in Orthodox teachings they make a big to-do about it. The Torah presents the "Niddah" or Laws of Separation that insist a man cannot touch his wife until the evening of the seventh "clean day" after her period has ended. But she cannot begin to count to seven until she sees no more blood, not even a drop "the size of a mustard seed." And only then, can she bathe in the traditional bath called the mikvah. Perhaps River-rat had these rules somewhere engraved in him, and I didn't want to put him to a test. So I was careful to wear my diaphragm. River-rat never talked to me about birth control. He never inquired about what method I might be using. It was as if he felt that I wasn't real. I was a ghost or apparition who could never get knocked up. In my early forties I was still youthful and curvy lying naked on the bed beside him. My belly was smooth and led to the bushy arrow that pointed directly to the fertile glen that he would enter *unprotected*. My mother used to warn me, saying, "Remember: A woman is a brimming flower pot waiting for seed to grow." River-rat never seemed to worry about what might germinate in my flower pot.

With my diaphragm inserted tight, I sat on the edge of the bed as he undressed before me. I was surprised to see that he wore a pair of undershorts with an unusual appliqué. A little scuba diver in full gear and rubber flippers paddled across his thigh with several bubbles drifting above its little air tank. The underpants were not manly. The cartoon appliqué was an insult to my French-cut panties that I wore just for him, a narrow triangle of silk like a black butterfly that alights on my pussy. These lacy items are de rigueur for every femme fatale. Edna O'Brien describes it exactly. In her story, "Quartet," she tells us how her character is not surprised to discover black net stockings in her mother's bureau drawers long after her mother has died. She takes her matriarch's black net stockings for her own. Each woman has the same needs, to get what she wants she must clothe herself in black lace nothingness, to please all men past and present. O'Brien understands how the tradition is passed down from generation to generation. O'Brien knows that Mother Ireland has thousands of bureau drawers filled with our secret stockings.

"Where in the hell did you get those scuba diver underpants?" I asked River-rat.

"From my wife."

"Weensie bought those shorts? No kidding?"

"She's been taking scuba diving lessons with my sons."

"She does that? You mean with air tanks?"

"That's right."

She must be a little more athletic than I had pictured her to be. I had no desire to breathe into an air mask underwater. I am a great swimmer and I hold my breath to be face to face with schools of fish or to check a boat mooring. But the scuba diver underpants were not a turn on. I was thinking, who does he think he's meeting to show up in those cutesy togs, rubber-stamped by his wife, when I am a serious siren? Our trysts must have become so ordinary that he isn't aware of what he chooses to dress in, or maybe he planned this awkward instant to remind me that his wife has ownership of his drawers, at least. After seeing the scuba diver underpants, I questioned the kind of gifts she awards him for whatever occasion: birthdays, Hanukkah, or anniversaries. I imagined all the rote, affectionate, or silly things they exchanged. I too had given gifts to him, now and then. I purchased a framed monoprint by the artist Vicky Tomayko that evoked my relationship with him. It was a print of lovely flora and fauna found in the uplands of the National Seashore, in its varied wilderness understory. The picture included an authentic depiction of a very familiar vermin, with my nickname. The print included an actual "flea" in precise representational detail. It showed its tagma with sclerotic scales and its hairy legs, the coxa, tarsus, and trochanter, in all of its natural grandeur.

ALL SMILES

Giovanni met his new girlfriend, Sandrine, just weeks before we learned he was sick with lymphoma. The girl was from Fitchburg, and her family was French Canadian. She wasn't scared off when he was diagnosed with cancer. But before Sandrine, Giovanni's early twenties were a roller-coaster ride.

Before lymphoma, he had had his share of woman troubles.

At just fourteen he lost his virginity with a girl he still calls "Baltimore." She was a vixen from Maryland whom he had met at Bennington College when attending the "July Program," a month-long summer camp for high school students who were college prospects seeking expanded horizons and course credit for advanced study. The July Program placed the teens in campus housing, and along with every academic opportunity made available to them, it was a Fuck Den.

He usually met all his girlfriends in his music scene. Giovanni has had three punk bands. The first was called Daylight, a subgenre punk category with the humorous subtitle "Cape Cod Power Violence." His next band was All Smiles, a name borrowed from the stern of a dinghy that sank in our neighborhood harbor. All Smiles was my favorite. They wrote tuneful songs with memorable hooks and inventive breakdowns. The best cuts on their seven-inch vinyl are less than sixty seconds long. In "I Hate the State," the sweetness of youth is revealed in their lyrics: "Don't even dream—don't fantasize. It's a bottomless pit of government lies." His current band, Street Sweeper, is full force hardcore punk, very polished, but just too metal. I want him to return to his other influences, like the Misfits, Sunny Day Real Estate, and Ova Looven. But Street Sweeper has a big following and they perform in Boston, at The Democracy Center in Harvard Square, at Elks Club basements, and in back-of-the-way north-shore neighborhoods of working class kids who come to shows and leave bloodied after cracking their heads and breaking their noses in the mosh pit. His friend B-Mac, from a sister band called Abomination, was arrested for killing a rival at a late-night party. His girlfriend was also arrested for assault and battery. She was alleged to have pinched the victim's head between her knees in a headlock as B-Mac stabbed him.

So it's kind of a relief to me that since his tandem bone marrow transplants, Giovanni can't do any more shows in those dangerous settings. His world is restricted. He can't take public transportation, or be in public places, where crowds can breathe in his face, spreading their cash-and-carry germs. A year before he got sick he had met a new girl online at a hardcore punk site where kids follow their favorite bands. Street Sweeper was getting a lot of attention, and the girl was a fan. "Sherry" was moving to Boston to start her freshman year at the Museum School, starting a program in visual art. In their first weeks together, she had made a sculpture out of all of his apartment trash. She was also making doll clothes. I imagined that these items were for a feminist installation at the Museum School. Scattered around his apartment I found tiny little skirts, the size of cocktail napkins, tight jerseys, panties, and even a little bodice of beaded silk. Sherry was a very good seamstress, unusual for American girls these days, and I imagined she had been given tutelage by her Korean mom or auntie. Then I suddenly understood that these tiny items weren't doll clothes, they belonged to the girl herself. They were her very own teensy panties and thongs, mere little ribbons of silk tossed around everywhere. She was a slight, doll-size nymph who came up just past my son's waist. In his bathroom, I found a bottle of olive oil, and wondered why it was left there, imagining something sexual. He told me she used olive oil to remove her eye make-up. "Ancient Chinese secret" or something. But this girl had put a dangerous spell on him, and transformed his life in destructive ways. Sherry was very possessive and she started to stalk him throughout the day; her tiny face appeared in the porthole windows of his classrooms, disrupting seminars, or she waited outside the office of his part-time job when he worked for civil liberties lawyer Harvey Silverglate. She hovered in the hallway of his building, and surprised him each time he got out of the elevator. He said she was sex crazy in direct response to her very strict childhood. When she fucked him she would sometimes scream epithets to an imaginary bystander, probably her father. The craziness accelerated to NASCAR speed until Giovanni finally disengaged from her.

He became wise to her dangers, but he still adored her. When she texted him so furiously, he believed that everything was *his* fault. He became very depressed and talked about suicide. He knew that I hated to hear the "S" word, so he'd often say. "I'm going to *disappear.*" I understood that the word "disappear" was code, and I got him into therapy. His psychiatrist was a looker, named Pamela. Because she was a hottie, he kept his appointments for several months. He seemed to be improving.

Until he found a new fancy named Elizabeth.

The new beauty dangles from her closet pole.

She was my son's second oversexed girlfriend, and she was crazy about him. She followed his band Street Sweeper and they started talking online. She lived in West Palm Beach and she bought airline tickets for him to come visit her. Together they went across the country catching shows with seminal punk bands that he would never have seen without her funding their sojourns. In just a few months, she too exhibited traits of psychosis. She texted him one hundred times a day. He turned off his phone, and when he turned it on again, the apps were all seized-up. I was relieved to hear that he finally broke it off with her.

This happens next:

When he rejects her, the girl hangs herself. In just two days, with the Florida heat, her arms and legs have swollen, bursting the tight skin.

A detective scrolls down the many texts Elizabeth had sent to him. "Please don't break up with me. I'll kill myself," she wrote to him. The detective dials my son's number. Giovanni's working the night shift for Securitas, as a night watchman, chasing junkies from the rooftop of a Marriott Hotel in downtown Boston. He's standing on the rooftop all alone when the detective tells him that she's gone. The detective says, "In her texts, she threatened to end her life? Is that right?"

"She said that a hundred times," he tells them. But he already had sensed that something was wrong. Elizabeth had stopped texting him two days before.

Giovanni had once shown me a cell phone picture of Elizabeth wearing a fanciful hat. I looked at his droid and saw a picture of a pretty girl sporting a crazy cap, a furry beret with white whiskers and slit eyes. A live kitten was nestled in her hair! The girl in the "kitten hat" is a very tragic image. My son can't get it out of his head. His despair over what happened to that girl weakened his immune system and made him vulnerable to cancer. It was the poison kernel that implanted in his lymph gland, the one that would eat him up.

AFTER TRANSPLANT therapy, he wears his "transplant survivor" mask. His handsome face is always covered by a swatch of blue pleated mesh. Behind that mask, he hides his unrelenting guilt about the girl in the kitten hat.

More than twenty years ago, I am talking to River-rat on the telephone in my studio. My young son is outside in the garden tapping the bulkhead with a stick. Above the clanging, I can hear the typical five-year-old monologue, half machismo, half childish sing-song as he stabs ants, or teases a beetle, jacking it over onto its back. He taps a hornet's paper nest, testing its resilience. River-rat is giving me sweet talk. At that time, we had not yet had sex, but we talked on the phone often. When he's making editorial suggestions, it's like he's nibbling my ear. I can feel his blue pencil marks across my skin.

I learned that editors flirt like this. My first editor, who published a Harper & Row anthology of teenagers' poetry, back in '69 when I was just sixteen, told me he liked my name. My name excited him. "Your name is the new 'Grace Slick,'" he told me. She was an icon back then, a sexy goddess-type weirdo, who sang about women's affinity for drugs and sex. I never felt a connection to Grace Slick. But my editor said, "Your name is a love poem." I didn't tell him that I had dropped my middle name, "Celine," trying to uncouple from my French extraction. As a kid, I seemed to already understand that being of French extraction was going to cause me a lot of extra trouble.

On the telephone, River-rat is praising a passage in my first novel, a revision he had requested the week before. Spring sunshine floods the room through the venetian blinds. Blurred slats of gold increase across the walls. June bugs shoot against the window screens and turn around to bump the screen again.

Then I hear screams. Full shrieks of terror or pain, I don't know which. My son tears across the lawn outside my window, a scarf of hornets flowing behind him until he freezes and the golden turban coils around his head.

"I have to get off the phone. My kid is screaming."

"I'll call you back," River-rat says.

I run outside to find my son is safe. The shimmering cape of stingers has lifted into the treetops, undulating like bubble wrap. Two stings make rising welts on Giovanni's cheek, but ice is enough to soothe him.

A few days later, River-rat confides to me that his own son cut his face open falling off a bunk bed. The boy needed stitches. There's a thousand miles between these boys, but they are here with us, in our growing secrets. But who is riding the ghost bike? Elizabeth, the girl in the kitten hat, is on it. Every day she invites my son to climb on the seat beside her.

THE EMPTY GLASS

As a young girl, I had a very idiosyncratic expo-
sure to different kinds of music and recordings. My French mother always was listening to the
latest albums by Yves Montand, the movie star and
crooner, who had been born in Italy but who grew up
in Marseilles. He had both romance languages at his
disposal, and he was the "lover boy" of the European
Continent, after his discovery by Edith Piaf when he
was just a youth. It drove my mother crazy when he
married Simone Signoret, and she had lost her chance
to snatch him. I would come home from school and
from a full block away I would hear the bubbly French
lyrics of Montand's joyful party songs, like his big hit
"La Chanson de Bilbao" or his moody, despairing ballads. His crooning was a palpable river of woe that
sluiced out the open windows. Simone Signoret prede-
ceased Montand, but only after he had had many love
affairs, including a fling with Marilyn Monroe. One of
his dalliances claimed he was the father of her baby
and she wanted a DNA test. The actor had refused
to cooperate, but upon his death the woman won her
case in court and was given the right to get his body
exhumed.

I was interested in my mother's occupation with
Montand, but if it wasn't the French heartthrob, I often
listened to other recordings. I was beginning to notice
the sexual chaos described in many popular recordings, even in Broadway shows. I'm not talking about
vinyls of *West Side Story*; I didn't like that blockbuster
Leonard Bernstein musical, except for the socioeco-
nomic references in lyrics that often had a gritty,
mouth-against-the-asphalt kind of power. I didn't like
the clichéd *Romeo and Juliet* formula in *West Side
Story*. And the song "Maria" has always been a great
annoyance to me.

But my father purchased a 1954 recording of the
musical *Fanny* with Ezio Pinza and Walter Slezak. The
character Fanny, herself, was performed by a very
young Florence Henderson. The show had a wealth of
dramatic plot twists and rising tension. A young girl
like me couldn't resist its larger-than-life characters. I
followed the story's escalating disasters, absorbing its
poignant story despite the fanfare of its orchestration,
with its rising string section, and sharp percussive
punctuation marks at key spikes in the melodramatic
conflicts. The story had true human turmoil. It introduced questions of infidelity and longing. Of choices
between loyalty to self or betrayal to family. A sailor
leaves his pregnant girlfriend behind to pursue a five-
year voyage at sea. She marries a wealthy shop owner
who happily claims her child as his own, but then
of course, the sailor returns and a tortured reunion
unfolds.

I had a favorite song on the *Fanny* recording,
"Welcome Home," written by Harold Rome and sung
by Ezio Pinza. In a period when my family was in

a near-destruction mode, with my sisters disappearing, and my mother's narcissistic personality disorder exhibiting worsening symptoms, the song was very reassuring to me. "Welcome Home" made me hope that one day my own household would evoke the same pastoral reveries.

No matter what I do or see
After turning home again
I get to that corner and then
Sweet voices, I hear sweet voices
Calling to me
Welcome home says the street
As I hurry on my way
Welcome home sings the gate
Like a song
Welcome home says the door
Glad to feel your hand once more
Now you're back where you belong
Welcome home says the chair
Holding out its friendly arms
Welcome home says the bed
Rest on me.
Now you're back where you should be
Close your eyes, close your eyes
And the world will settle down to size

My father had sunk money into a high tech record player before it had become a household item. It had *stereo* speakers. The unit was a high-end piece of furniture, with a highly polished, fine wood mahogany console. A big triangular box, with a flat lid, it had two very large acrylic mesh speaker grills, one on either side of the cabinet. The bass speaker was on the *left* and the treble speaker was on the *right*. The unit came with a forty-five record that had several examples of "stereo sound." There was the tingling trill of a marble rolling across the floor, left to right. A contest of two crickets chirping back and forth. The thunderous acceleration of approaching hoofbeats from a stampede of horses, again galloping from left to right. I liked to curl up on the floor right against the box cabinet to listen to records. My father would be in his recliner with his first Old Fashioned of the night, and he wouldn't shoo me away until my mother came in to sit down with her scotch and water. I sometimes huddled by the bass speaker or I sat against the treble. My father purchased a famous Vanguard boxed set of folk music called "American Folk Singers and Balladeers." Sitting beside the treble speaker was best for listening to guitar pickers like Ramblin' Jack Elliott, and for the thin nasal voices of Hedy West and Jean Ritchie. Joan Baez's ascending octaves made a pinching sound like when opening the tin of a canned ham with the little key that comes with it.

It would be a few years later when I'd sit down beside the bass speaker to listen to the 1967 hit "Expressway to Your Heart" by the Soul Survivors. "I was thinkin' 'bout a shortcut I could take. But it seems like I made a mistake."

With the Vanguard recording of folk singers I learned many important elements of storytelling. I didn't depend on the hokey popular folk groups that sang covers of Pete Seeger's "Where Have all the Flowers Gone?" including the Kingston Trio who had claimed authorship of that title. Upon Seeger's notice of their false songwriting credits on their album cover, the Kingston Trio was forced to have their names removed thereafter. The song was so universally applauded at the time, with the rising surge of antiwar philosophy during the Eisenhower era, I suppose that the Kingston Trio could have somehow imagined that they actually had written the song.

But with the singular Vanguard anthology, I studied true Appalachian songs and original English Child Ballads. These compositions were hundreds of years old and introduced me to betrayals between man and wife, icy jealousies within extended families, and extramarital diversions, sometimes deadly. My favorite Child Ballad, Number 20, is "Down by the Greenwood Side," in which a mother murders her two out-of-wedlock baby sons:

> There was a fair maiden lived in the north
> Fell in love with her father's clerk
> Till her, the young man did betray
> Down by the Greenwood side-e-o
>
> She leaned her back against a thorn
> Oh, the rose and the linsey, oh
> And there two bonny boys she's born
> Down by the Greenwood side-e-o
>
> She took out her wee pen knife
> Oh, the rose and linsey, oh
> And there she took those sweet babes' lives
> Down by the Greenwood side-e-o
> She wiped her pen knife on her shoe
> The more she wiped, the redder it grew

From these Child Ballads, I learned about "rising tension," and I became interested in characterizations that evoked man's inherent weaknesses, hungers, and deceptions. I also admired the same uneasy portraits in contemporary music.

Growing up in Wilmington, Delaware, the "Chemical Capital of the World," I would often wake up in the morning to see the paint on our family car blistered from the caustic clouds pumped from smokestacks at Dupont's paint factory, "Chambers Works." I lived just twenty minutes south of the Philadelphia oil refineries. Misty mornings were in fact not velvet fog, but a blanket of "aerosol oil droplets." But alongside the industrial fallout, we had the Philadelphia airwaves. The radio was drenched in Phil Spector's "Wall of Sound." Ronnie Spector's "Be My Baby" and "Walking in the Rain" were important Top Forty singles that I listened to over and over. The pie-shaped stereo console had a button for "automatic repeat" and the needle would swing back and plop down at the lip of the same record, again and again. I listened to the Ronettes and began to notice the repetitions in their songs. Repetitions of phrases worked to mesmerize me:

Like walking in the rain (*like walking in the rain*)
And wishing on the stars (*and wishing on the stars*)

Repetition is a powerful mechanism. Repetition not only soothes the ear but evokes obsession. Refrains are always tricky. The refrain in the Child Ballad, "Oh, the rose and linsey, oh—" appears to be innocent in its simplicity, but when repeated over and over it becomes directly evil.

I absorbed a lot of information about writing from both pop music and folk music. I attended the Newport Folk Festival each year and in 1965 I was present at the giant milestone when "Dylan went electric!" I was the charge of my eldest sister, Christine, a full-time beat-generation-turned-hippie princess, whose biggest claim to fame was that she was the first person in her neighborhood, in the college town of Ann Arbor, Michigan, to have purchased a "butterfly chair." A midcentury modern contraption, the chair was made of a black canvas sheath tucked onto a wrought iron frame that had the appearance of a butterfly with its wings spread open. She had many pictures taken of her sitting cross-legged in its sling—strumming an autoharp—a true beauty wearing a necklace of "peace cranes" and hippie beads, a pure feminine icon of that era.

Before our last trip to Newport, she had just left her husband. We picked up two hitchhikers from Kent State, less than two years before the shootings. One of the boys, the pretty one, slept with me when we stopped at a house in Providence to spend the night. In the morning he wanted me to take his dick in my mouth, but I said, "Wait a minute. Wait a minute!" I first had to remove my retainer. I inserted the little contraption every night to correct a tiny separation in my front teeth. Its pink plastic disc was molded to fit my palette. I held the retainer in the palm of my hand as the boy fucked my mouth. It was my first time, and I was thrilled to experience the fantastic transformation of a hard-on, and the passion it required from him. I was thrilled that his excitement was attributed to *me*, but I was ashamed of my crooked teeth.

That afternoon I sat beside my sister on the bleachers at Festival Field in Newport, to listen to the newcomer Janis Ian who had recently gained fame with her song "Society's Child." I was just a teen, and when Janis joked about her guitar, saying, "It's just a phallic symbol," I asked my sister, "What's a phallic symbol?"

When my sister explained the word "phallic," describing its derivation from the Greek, I remembered that very morning with the Kent State kid. I didn't need a symbol for it.

And today, when I'm lying in bed beside River-rat, I think of the vacuum of our arrangement. In my head, I hear the lyrics of Peggy Lee's song, "The Empty Glass."

> Close the door
> And pour the wine.
> Fill your glass
> But don't fill mine.
> Here's to you now for the last time
> Here's to me your *sometime* pastime

Child Bride Syndrome

I left home at seventeen. I was a victim of "Child Bride Syndrome" when girls get married at a young age to escape a narcissistic mother and a hostile home environment. My first husband was a waspy rich boy who had a three-piece name. The name was passed down from generation to generation. He was "the third" and his name ended with the Roman lettering "III." I started to call him "Trey" under my breath. He was a Brown University grad and I thought this meant that he was a little above the "Gator King" and the Velvet Freak. At the wedding, guests were told not to throw rice at the bride and groom because little birds can't digest it. Instead they showered us with sunflower seeds. It was so Earth Day '70s! Next we went to a party where I watched a dog gobble up a broken wine glass. A dog eating slivers of broken glass somehow became a harbinger to me about what married life would mean. I married the Brown graduate just to escape from my dangerous mother. At the time, I wasn't conscious of my motives, but I wasn't destined to stay married very long. After all, my new husband wasn't a poet. His favorite reading material was *Lord of the Rings,* which upon finishing the last page he read over again from the beginning, instead of trying new titles. But he encouraged me to go to college. He also fathered my firstborn child, Annabel. I had wanted to ca¹l her "Isabel," but he said he didn't like "ethnic" names.

In my coming of age, some might say I was "oversexed" but I was equally consumed by poetry. As Judith Grossman said, "Anyone was entitled to a few fucks once in a while . . . but not everyone was entitled to belong to the company of poets." I was driven to be a poet.

I had never finished eleventh grade. I left high school two years before graduation. Without a high school degree I applied to Roger Williams College, a liberal arts college in Bristol, Rhode Island. I was admitted solely on a poetry manuscript I had submitted to the chair of the creative writing department. The college was introducing an "Experimental Admissions Criteria" following a model that Brown University had been tooting its horn about. They had opened up admissions to genius candidates who hadn't received the typical rubber stamp with 800 SAT scores or exceptional high school transcripts. They were seeking a certain "fringe" element to energize and add diversity to their stodgy legacy student population. At the smaller private college, I too might fit the bill.

The poetry professor at Roger Williams thought my manuscript was interesting. I had already published poems in a Harper & Row anthology called *It is the Poem Singing into Your Eyes: An Anthology of New Young Poets,* edited by the leftist editor, Arnold Adoff, a second generation Polish-Russian immigrant, who had edited two important anthologies of black writing, *Black on Black* and *Brothers and Sisters*. He was married to the black writer, Virginia Hamilton, a MacArthur genius, who wrote one of my favorite children's books, the National Book Award winning *M.C. Higgins, the Great*. Recognition by Adoff was an important transformative event in my very early life as a young writer. And I was thrilled to speak to his wife, Virginia Hamilton, every time I called his house in Yellow Springs, Ohio. I was only seventeen when seven poems of mine appeared in that book. For my poems I was paid a huge amount of money for a teenager's poetry. Adoff divvied up his whole advance, so that all his teen poets got paid. I got $800. Twice! First, for the hard-cover edition, and because every American high school had ordered copies, I got the same $800 for the paperback. That payment, $800, was the same amount I would get for my first book of poems that won the Houghton Mifflin Poetry Prize twelve years later. My Houghton Mifflin editor had told me that it was a larger advance than what Houghton Mifflin had paid poets Robert Lowell and Elizabeth Bishop when she had won the same prize in 1946. But, in fact, the payment from Houghton Mifflin got me into some hot water. I didn't declare my $800 advance when I filed my taxes. I had been working at Rhode Island Hospital Trust bank in credit card operations, and when I filed my bank job returns I had forgotten about the book. I had to pay a penalty to the IRS.

With no high school diploma, but with the Harper & Row credential and with a new manuscript of poems, I was asked to meet with the creative writing professor, Gus McCannlish. He mentioned a poem of mine that he had liked very much. He read a line from my manuscript out loud, "'Her hair ribboned with rainboas.' That's very nice."

"Rainboas?"

"A good image," he said.

With embarrassment I said, "I think that's a typo. It's supposed to say 'rainbows' in my hair."

He looked at me with great disappointment. In the years to come I would become a better poet and would learn to write stronger images with metaphorical snakes, but I was admitted to the program. I was allowed to attend classes at Roger Williams as an experimental *special student*. But having never graduated from high school, to be admitted as a special student at Roger Williams College, I had to take my GED test. I would sail through sections called "language arts," "reading comprehension," and "literature," but I worried about the math questions. I hoped that if I filled out the multiple choice answers, choosing each little box at random, careful to shade in the tiny circles with my number-two pencil, regardless of the correct answers, I might just squeak by. Either by sheer luck or by mathematical probability, I might get a passing total of correct responses.

I wore my velvet coat to the GED test. I sat down in one of those uncomfortable wraparound desk-chairs, and watched the reactions of the other people assembled to take the exam at the testing center, a huge basement room with cement block walls. In my velvet coat, I must have looked like a B-movie ingenue arriving at a *Dracula* shoot, lost at a back lot somewhere. The group stared at me, with secreted smirks, until they let loose with full-bellied laughter. In my seat, I piled the long velvet skirt of my coat across my knees and I read the first question. It was from the "Science Section."

> **Question 1:** Clay soil forms a fairly effective barrier against the movements of water. It also swells and shrinks significantly as its water content changes.
> Sandy soil, in contrast, allows water to move freely and does not change shape as the water content varies. In which statement is the appropriate soil selected for its intended site?
> A.) Sandy soil would make a good lining for a toxic waste site
> B.) Clay soil would work well in a drain field.
> C.) Clay soil would be a good foundation for a large building.
> D.) Clay soil would form a good liner if a person built a pond.
> E.) A sandy lake bottom would prevent water from seeping out of the lake.

Of course, I was good at science, being an amateur naturalist, and I always read Tuesday's *Science News* section in the *New York Times*. I chose the answer: "Clay soil would be a good foundation for a large building."

I believed a college education would be my foundation.

But my first year at school, I was put on academic probation. I had to prove I was college material. In my first two semesters at Roger Williams College, my grade reports showed a letter "S" for "special student" printed beside my name. I felt this "special student" status also applied to my experimental marriage. I received straight As at Roger Williams. My grades had nothing to do with the reason I went to bed with my poetry professor.

I often visited his office. Or he took me home. He lived in a defunct lighthouse right beneath the Mount Hope Bridge. To live in a lighthouse beneath a gorgeous suspension bridge seemed to be a dreamy ideal for a poet. And he took me for sails on his nineteen-foot Corinthian Sailstar sloop. I lolled on the ship's forward deck when the water was flat and there wasn't enough wind to sail. The boat drifted beneath the suspension bridge; its monumental shadow was dramatic. It was where many had leapt to their deaths.

Together we celebrated the publication of my professor's first book, *Lip Service.* I felt that his poems were not merely written for readers like me, but somehow they seemed to be written *by* me. That's how identical our soul-felt urges seemed to be. Of course that's what poets have been doing for centuries—matching, or awakening a reader's thoughts and feelings. "The streetlight on the corner is not the moon . . . it responds only to the absence of light." His words tingled in my bones! We went to bed at the Bristol Motel. He said he was disappointed that I wore cotton underpants. I told him, "I didn't know we were coming to the Bristol Motel or I would have put on my satin bikinis." But he soon fell in love with my classmate Elizabeth Jensen, whom he was also sleeping with. Like me, Elizabeth was hitched. She had married a local Portuguese boy named Chicky. I liked that she called him "Chicky." My husband's three-piece name was a great embarrassment to me.

Elizabeth and I often discussed our romantic feelings about our creative writing teacher and we invented a nickname for his very distinctive cock. We called it "The Concorde," like the iconic French aircraft. His penis was slightly deformed. The head of it dipped in a dramatic arrow from the rest of the shaft, just like the nose of the supersonic jet.

But he wrote a poem for Elizabeth called "Waiting for Next Semester" that appeared in his first collection. It says, "I think of the long rows of words. Then you, Elizabeth, and the heat of your first female poem."

I was soon to learn that poetry professors were always on alert, hoping to find a "first female poem." I would go on to graduate school, to jobs out in the literary world, at the university, and at the shimmering cloisters of Random; on every plane of recognition for my work, it was because I was female that anyone paid attention.

MY SLUTTY SEVENTIES

As a young woman, I had had literary boyfriends, but I left the Ivory Tower often and had some interesting relationships with everyday people. I was wide open to a wide-ranging economy of hetero wealth all around me. Like many other young women of that time, we just stopped counting, but there are a few moments I can't forget. In my early forays into sex, I felt like Cat Woman with nine lives. With each new seduction, I understood the risks I was taking, and I knew that the next liaison might be my Number Nine.

In 1976 I was unhappily married. I left my toddler with my husband many nights a week to seek some release from my entrapment. I went to local bars where I once met the famous maverick Ted Turner who was in town to scope out his competition for the America's Cup twelve-meter sailboat race that he would win the following year with his boat the *Courageous*. He bought me a few rounds and flirted with me. I found him very charming despite his reputation for arrogance. The *Newport Daily News* had published a few stories about the flamboyant opponents who were in town preparing for the forthcoming boat race. His detractors called

Ted Turner a tyrant, a gadfly, a runaround, a flake. He was "the mouth of south" and "Captain Outrageous" but his Georgia drawl fascinated me. This was before he was famous for starting up TV stations like CNN, Turner Classic Movies, and TNT, and before he gave a billion dollars to the United Nations. Yet he had just purchased a baseball team, the Atlanta Braves, but I had no idea about the pitcher, Phil Niekro, that he was bragging about to all the barflies. I didn't know anything about the Braves. A few years later, I became a Red Sox fan, falling in love with starting pitcher Oil Can Boyd. My husband once told me that Turner, like him, had attended Brown University but he was kicked out of school for having a woman in his dorm room.

At midnight, we left the bar and got into Ted's sedan in the parking lot. He was more than a decade older than I, but I found him very attractive. A word came into my head that I had never really understood until that moment with Ted Turner. "Debonair" is a French word. Veronica would have agreed with me. Ted Turner was suave and charming. He asked me about myself and showered me with compliments about my hometown, Newport. I didn't admit to him that I was a transplant. We had a make-out session for less than a half hour, until one of his crew members off his boat the *Courageous* showed up and opened the passenger door.

But Ted Turner wasn't the only sailor in town. Newport celebrated the bicentennial with a Tall Ships regatta. Hundreds of tall-masted sailboats arrived in the harbor. The city had a celebratory ambiance mingled with a sense of impending flight. I wanted to believe that one of these tall ships might have an extra bunk.

I imagined my elegant departure, leaving town via the harbor, on a ship that had the whitest sails, and a full spinnaker that looked like a bosom of silk. I was ready to leave town.

It was the summer I decided to dump my first husband.

At the Tall Ships celebration in Newport, I met three young French sailors who had set sail from Le Havre in a gorgeous two-masted ketch, what they call a "Blue Water" sailboat because it can be outfitted to sail across great expanses, across open seas and wide oceans, and perhaps might undertake "round the world" expeditions. These young men were suntanned and healthy-looking, as if they had been breathing sea air without any other obligation but to breathe sea air for eight weeks. They were not just partying because of the bicentennial celebration, but in fact when I met them it was July 14th, Bastille Day. Their *own* national holiday. French National Day celebrates the uprising of the "Constitutional Monarchy," and in respect for their country they had found a bottle of brandy onboard ship, and we brought the bottle with us in my Dodge Dart. I wore a sundress with spaghetti straps that kept slipping off my shoulders. One of the sailors kept nudging the little shoulder strings back up my arms as if he feared I'd lose everything too soon, before he had a chance to claim me. They wanted to sightsee and drive past the mansions on Ocean Drive—a magical route south of town. I had had to remove the baby's car seat and put it in the trunk in order for all three Frenchmen to pile in. I gave the one called Bastien my car keys, Gaston piled in next to him, and Didier sat in the back seat with me. Bastien was delighted to steer my bulky midsize car. He said he loved the Dodge and was tired of "tout petit" Citroens and Fiats in Bandol where he came from.

Didier kept reciting Leonard Cohen poetry, much to my annoyance. I didn't like Leonard Cohen, and hearing it recited in a French accent made the cloying poetry sound even more ridiculous.

We tooled past the famous summer cottages of the Vanderbilts and other robber barons, and I recited the famous names of each mansion: The Breakers, Château-sur-Mer, The Elms, Marble House, Rosecliff, Kingscote. It was a beautiful night. Driving parallel to the crashing surf alongside the famous seaside cliffs, a mist lifted above the road and the headlights became golden tubes of water particles. We kept going farther along the rocky shoreline until we pulled over in a wooded patch. I wasn't alarmed we had stopped. I expected some sort of four-way snuggle, but first I wanted a sip of the brandy. Gaston handed me the delicious orangey elixir that reminded me of my mother. The French brandy reminded me to tell the sailors with pride, "I'm French, too, you know. Half French."

"Which half?" one of the sailors asked. I was used to this question. Of course I'm supposed to say that I'm French below the waist.

"I'm just saying, my mother was born in France," I told them.

"Where was that?" Didier asked.

"A tiny village called Valserres. That's in the sticks somewhere, right?" We had relatives in Paris, Marseille, and Nice, but my mother was born in a rural enclave. The house was above the barn, and she had told me that they kept orphaned lambs and baby pigs

in the house, in pens on the kitchen floor beside the
cast iron stove to keep them warm.

Half French or not, in a car with three French sailors, a girl was going to get her share of something. I
had had several beers in town, and drinking brandy
wasn't a good idea. In the back seat, Didier started
kissing my nipples. I still had a little milk, since my
daughter had just been weaned. I was about to warn
him, but he shushed me and said, "Lait du bébé est
sucre."

"French men have seen everything," Veronica would
say.

This one didn't mind a little "sweet milk" and he
went first. The other two would have sloppy seconds,
but it was all very democratic. I didn't appreciate the
Leonard Cohen poetry that Didier babbled in my ear,
but he had a remarkable dick. Having sex with three
French sailors is what some people might say was a
"low moment," for a young girl, but I was very happy.
I was curious about men, and I liked to compare each
one's girth, not just the length of their cocks, when
fucking three guys one right after the other.

Years later writer friends listened to my stories
over coffee or taking nips of whiskey in faculty apartments at two different low-residency programs, Warren
Wilson and Bennington, and I wasn't surprised when
details I had told them soon appeared in their own fiction. I had told the Bastille Day story to the novelist
Lynn Freed when we were colleagues at Bennington
College, teaching at the graduate seminars in Vermont.
Lynn had a pleasingly dry humor about men. She said
she liked the part of the story where I had valued "cir-
cumference" above the length of a cock. Lynn once

had told me that a woman's neck is her most important feature. "She's got to have a *long, white* neck."
I joked with her about my experience as a young girl
having had sex with three French men on the French
holiday. She thought the coincidence was very funny.
She had liked it so much that she used the details I
had told her about Bastille Day in Newport in her novel
The Mirror. It wasn't the first time a writer used "my
material." Years before, Francine Prose had published
a story in the *New Yorker* in which she had incorpo-
rated information she had learned from me. She had
liked a story I had told her about my daughter, Annabel, being tested at the University of Iowa for her ability to "read minds." Researchers had tested both of us,
my daughter and me, to see if Annabel could either
"send" or "receive" information. At a very young age,
my daughter exhibited traits where she described
events of which she had had no foreknowledge. She
forecasted inconveniences or accidents that had not
yet happened, like mentioning a locked door, before
I discovered I'd lost my keys, and warning me not to
cut myself on a broken glass before I had dropped it.
She second-guessed thoughts I was having. She said,
"He's not home yet," before I had dialed my boyfriend.
It was as if she was inside my mind. Yes, we were born
on the same birthday, and researchers considered that
to be of no real importance, but the connections we
presented were fascinating to them. The research team
at the University of Iowa put us in separate rooms and
asked us to arrange colored blocks. We created identical pyramids and towers, of our own fancy, with an
identical sequence of shaped blocks, and in the exact
same colors. My daughter somehow visualized imagery

without any clues, and when tested with a battery of flash cards she guessed each hidden subject and was correct 99 percent of the time. Next I was asked to draw images of my own invention on eight–by-ten paper: a cat, a tree, a wheel, a house. My daughter, in another room, sketched the same objects in tandem with me, without any prods or cues. Together we were examined for our uncanny mother-daughter simultaneous thought sequences that had attracted researchers' attention. Francine Prose had found the story interesting enough to write about it.

I don't own my stories. If I tell someone a story, it's up for grabs. Any writer is welcome to it. In the blockbuster movie *Basic Instinct*, the character Catherine Trammel, played by Sharon Stone, tells the detective played by Michael Douglas, "I'm a writer. I use people for what I write. Let the world beware. Do you want me to take a lie detector test?"

Radiation

Yesterday I was with my son, walking the long halls at the hospital. We were looking for the radiation oncology unit. Giovanni was starting weeks of daily radiation. First he had to have a "patient immobilization cradle" modeled to fit him exactly. He was asked to lie on a blue pallet as uncured chemical foam expanded, cinching tight to his body, and then he had to wait, stone still, as the foam hardened in an exact cast around his broad chest. He will slide into the preformed foam hammock each time he is positioned to lie dead still for radiation. His specialized form is tucked away in a closet, and pulled out again at his next appointment. This blue "immobilization cradle," in the shape of his manly chest, is an upsetting image in my mind, a premature sarcophagus that haunts me every day.

In the hallway of the hospital, I must have looked disoriented because a security officer asked me, "Where are you supposed to be?"

I said, "I'm with him."

From behind his blue face mask, Giovanni said to the guard, "Can't you see the resemblance?"

LA GRENOUILLE

A month before the publication of my memoir, *My Sister Life,* just weeks before he showed up at my hotel room, River-rat met me at a party. Random House had decided to host a luncheon to celebrate the book. The party was a publicity event, to encourage some print media "buzz," and all the guests were writers from magazines and newspapers. Two company publicists and River-rat hosted, but I was the guest of honor. I was expected to "talk up" the book. The luncheon was held at a famous midtown restaurant and it was specifically chosen to glorify my French extraction, and to acknowledge my French femme fatale mother, a major character in the book. The party was held at La Grenouille, a beloved forty-year-old establishment known for its French cuisine and for its rooms that were filled with floral arrangements so grand that *New York Times* food critic Mimi Sheraton once said, "A stranger in town might get the idea that La Grenouille is a high-end flower shop."

I was first to arrive, careful to be punctual. I was ushered into a private dining room that was filled from floor to ceiling, and wall to wall, with towering flower displays. Hot house lilies, hawthorn, chrysanthemums, gold oak leaves, quivers of rosebuds, flowering quince, late season hydrangea of a velvety mauve. The flower arrangements climbed higher and higher, their blooms just opening, as if they had waited for me to arrive to begin their unconscious progression to perfection, their petals shivering open.

Alone with thousands of blossoms, I had time to think of him.

I was no different from one of these tight little florets cascading behind my seat, ready to be plucked.

Soon the guests arrived. All the newspaper reporters and magazine writers were women. They were dressed in fine couture, with expensive handbags, and many had with them little leather notebooks where they could jot down their impressions of me. I, too, had dressed carefully in a midnight blue skirt and jacket of fine wool gabardine, with a white silk blouse that had a prim Peter Pan collar. To appear refined, I had buttoned the collar at my throat with an invisible pearl button. Indeed, I looked elegant, yet my skirt was very tight and its hem was high above the knee, almost a mini. Of course I wore nude hose, knowing that my legs were my most powerful weapon. Riverrat arrived in a huddle of newspaper grand dames. He glanced at me once, approvingly, but he didn't come to speak to me. Earlier that morning, he had called me at my hotel and had said, "Are you dressed yet?" His voice revealed that he imagined me still *un*dressed.

At La Grenouille, he was the only man in the place, other than the maître d' and the busy waiters. He chatted with all the magazine girls, who surrounded him as if he were a movie star. In fact he did have a slight resemblance to the Hollywood actor Guy Pearce, who had starred in *L.A. Confidential,* but River-rat lacked the attractive rawness of that Anglo beefcake.

During lunch, the guests asked me questions about the memoir. Writers from *Publisher's Weekly, Newsweek, Elle* magazine, the *Wall Street Journal,* and the *New York Times Book Review* praised me for my startling candor, and for the sympathy and tenderness I had employed to tell the story about my missing sister. One reporter said, "The French mother in the book is unforgettable."

Another said, "But look at the author. She's so French. Isn't she?"

Everyone at the large table turned in their chairs to appraise me.

"It's her mouth. Her smile is crooked on one side."

"No, it's her hair. Cut straight. That's very French, the way it falls above the shoulder." It embarrassed me to hear them address me in the third person. I sensed that they suspected my secret. They saw the unspoken sexual fire that I couldn't conceal—with River-rat's legs under the table, just inches from me. But next they wanted to know how difficult it must have been for me to reveal so much about my "dysfunctional" family. My sister was a child prostitute. My mother was a "narcissistic lunatic with cruel and sadistic tendencies aimed at her daughters." Yes, it was true, but I didn't like to hear their blithe summaries. In their table chatter, in their giddy voices.

"Dysfunctional" was a trendy word in the nineties, often used by literary critics for books that explored psychological depravity in unseemly "edgy" characters.

The reporters tried to decide if the guest of honor, herself, was just as "unseemly" as the troubled souls she wrote about. Perhaps I, too, was narcissistic like Veronica. Perhaps like my sister, I had whored, and stolen, and lied.

Across the table, River-rat, too, was curious about my personal history. He wanted to know how cheap, how depraved his author was, and how he might navigate the dirty river I walked on, so at home with Mitchell's sludge bubbles in *The Bottom of the Harbor*.

I had been hoping to see *New York Times* writer Michiko Kakutani who had been invited to the luncheon. She didn't attend. Michiko had praised my earlier books, and when the luncheon guests asked about a section in the memoir when my sister performed a crude sexual act as the "prize" in a raffle at an event called "Shriner Night," I wanted to quote what Michiko had once said: "Given the way things tend to snowball in Ms. Flook's novels . . ."

A book editor from the *New York Times Book Review* asked me, "Do you know Susan Cheever?"

"We have some of the same students," I said. This was before I had had intimate conversations with Susan about sleeping with my editor. The *Book Review* editor had asked Susan to review the memoir and because we were colleagues at Bennington, Susan had had to decline. The review was assigned to a newbie, Kaitlin Weaver, a sex columnist for Salon, (her NYU classmates and coworkers at Salon had nicknamed her Kaitlin *Beaver*) and the sister book was way over her head. After she trashed the memoir, the *Book Review* editor Bob Harris knew he had made a mistake. To try to make it up to me, he asked me to write a review

for them. So I wrote a rave of Jenny Diski's complicated book *Skating to Antarctica*. They put it on the
front page. Harris said, "Thank you for doing such a
lovely review for us, especially after what we did to
your book!"

After lunch at The Frog, River-rat walked with me
to the Random building on Fiftieth Street. I didn't go
back to the offices with him. I had to get to Penn Station to take a train to Wilmington to visit Veronica.
"My mother will be jealous that your shindig was held
at La Grenouille," I told him.

"Tell her that her presence was felt, even if she
didn't attend."

He had once told me in his editorial notes that *My
Sister Life* was "harrowing—its power unmitigated, at
once gothic and mythic. Your mother's fingerprints are
all over who you are."

On the sidewalk, before Random's glass doors, we
said good-bye. He took my elbows and pulled me closer.
He looked me in the eyes, as if seeing Veronica's green
irises, not mine.

Just blocks away, victimized displays of flowers at
La Grenouille were shrieking. The open throats of the
shredded, wounded, and tortured blossoms, stapled to
the wall, expressed emergency. I heard their outcry,
their melting mood, and I should have listened to their
warnings.

Two Mike Pratts

I n the last months of my first marriage, before I left
for Iowa City, I went to see a psychiatrist at Newport Hospital at my husband's request to address what
he called uncontrollable "promiscuity." The doctor was
named "Dr. Poseur." His name was suspicious to me;
the name seemed to suggest an impersonator, actor, or
copyist. I wondered if a man with such a name could
help me find my own identity. And in fact, a few weeks
later, I saw Dr. Poseur, a married father, walking out of
the Venetian Room, the one gay bar in town. I realized
that he must have his own two worlds to juggle. This
made me change my mind. I thought he might understand the conflicting emotions I presented to him.

These were the months I was unconsciously preen-
ing, getting ready to flee my first husband. I had a dalliance with a young poetry student at my alma mater.
Lou wrote a manuscript of poems called "Matinees,"
greatly influenced by Walker Percy's The Moviegoer.
His poems were honest and ethereal, but he was more
famous for bringing Bruce Springsteen to campus. The
band arrived late at night in a beat-up van after security
had closed down the venue, but we found extension

cords and they set up in the parking lot and played a full set for stragglers who had hung on.

Then I met a young man who became my fixation. (Fixation: "A neurotic behavior that persists.") He was a Cuban American kid, who had been born and raised in Newport, a New England town. His father was Anglo, with a very British surname, but his mother had once been awarded the title "Miss Cuba," and she had competed in the Miss Universe contest. Because of her beauty he, too, was a looker. I would later describe my character Willis, in my novel *Open Water*, with similar seductive attributes: "He was ethereal, erotic, peppery." Nights, my husband would stay at home with our toddler, spending hours looking at porn. These were the days of no Internet and he had a whole trunk of retro stroke magazines. So I was free to gad about town.

I met the beautiful Cuban boy in a local bar. It's funny how they say that men have "charm" but women have "allure." Because in just ten minutes, the young man walked across the room to sit beside me. I slept with him a few times, but he became cautious when I told him I had a baby at home. When I drove him to his house he asked me to drop him off two blocks from his front door. If I had a kid at home, he explained, then he had just banged someone's mother! He didn't want anyone to see him getting out of my car.

The kid became the catalyst for the central character in my novel *Open Water,* a book about Newport's underbelly that River-rat would publish years later. But when the kid started to avoid me, I saw his older brother, Mike Pratt, at the YMCA. The two brothers were almost identically handsome, and I was

immediately attracted to the next one. He was the
owner of a car repair shop called "Metric Masters" for
British cars like Aston Martins, MGs, Morgans, Austin-
Healeys, and Hillmans. Soon we were lovers and I was
calling *him* the Metric Master. He was a motocross
champion, and he'd take me into the back of a huge
bus he used for traveling to bike events. We fucked on
a mattress cramped against rows of dirt bikes, their
handlebars still caked in mud. He owned Yamahas,
Suzukis, and Kawasaki crotch rockets. Since he was
the Metric Master he also had British bikes, a BSA, a
Greeves 250, and a Triumph Trophy Trail.

Each night I went to swim at the YMCA. I asked at
the front desk, "Did Mike Pratt sign in yet?"

"Which one?"

"Excuse me?"

"Which Mike Pratt are you talking about?" the
clerk asked.

"Are you saying that there's more than one Mike
Pratt?"

"That's right. There's *two* Mike Pratts. You want the
dark-haired one or the blond? The blond one is swimming laps."

The Metric Master had raven black locks, but I was
curious to meet the other Mike Pratt. The blond one.

I got into my suit and I decided to swim a few
laps. In the pool there were some serious swim team
members who wore tight plastic caps, so I couldn't see
if these men had blond hair or not. But when I was
climbing out of the water, tugging down the elastic of
my French cut swim suit, a man approached me. He
said, "I hear you're looking for me?"

"So you're the other Mike Pratt?"

"That's right. We get this a lot."

"What do you get?"

"*You* tell me what I can get."

He wasn't as handsome as the Metric Master, but he was sweet-talking me. Unlike the Metric Master, he had a college education, and in the car on the way to his place, he quoted lines of poetry. "I am not in love, but I'm open to persuasion. With a friend I can smile, but with a lover I can hold my head back and really laugh." I recognized that it wasn't real poetry but that he was wooing me with song lyrics from a new record album by Joan Armatrading. He took me home with him after driving past the courthouse to make sure that his girlfriend was still at work. He found her car in the parking lot. With the world tumbling ahead of me, meeting *two* Mike Pratts, in close proximity, seemed like a wealth of possibilities rather than asking for more complications. But if that car didn't stay at the courthouse there would be potholes on my joy ride.

His place was in one of the older Newport mansions that had been remodeled with Sheetrock and jerry-rigged front doors to make twelve separate apartments. He showed me his bathroom where the tub still had the mansion's original *six* faucets: for salt water, fresh water, and steamed milk. He took me into his bedroom without even offering me a drink. I understood that there was a time component to our impromptu tryst. As we sat down on his neatly made bed, I noticed a sewing box left on the bedspread. The box was chock-full of "notions," with every sewing accessory—bright spools of thread, needles jammed into puffy pin cushions, little silver snippers and seam rippers, and full-size pinking shears. The term "notions" has a peculiar resonance of unfiltered sexism. It was as if men thought that all of a woman's thoughts and desires could be kept in a tiny box like this. His girlfriend was a woman who could mend and darn; she could sew a button back on or even repair a buttonhole, or perhaps she could even make *new* buttonholes. Mike Pratt Number Two made love to me without removing the sewing box from the covers. Lying right beside it, her sewing box was exactly parallel to *my* treasure box. But I didn't analyze the absurdity unfolding, making love to two Mike Pratts.

It was part of my transformative agenda. I could not explain it—and even if sex with veritable strangers wasn't satisfying, it was deeper than sex. It was a footprint I had to fill, night after night, to stand up on my own two feet. Without sex with strangers, there was no me.

The next time I saw Dr. Poseur, I talked about the Metric Master and Mike Pratt Number Two. He said, "You're having relations with *two* Mike Pratts?"

"It's ridiculous, I know."

"When under duress, our actions don't come with a how-to manual."

We both thought that my dalliance with two men, with the exact same name, was very amusing, but the doctor asked me what more statistical proof did I need to recognize my promiscuity? He said that with my indiscretions I might be acting out my hostilities to my husband or perhaps I was rebelling against the constrictive tradition of marriage itself. He said, "You are trying to escape. Some animals find freedom by releasing an appendage, like a starfish losing one arm, or lizards that can shed their tails. You're giving away your body *piece by piece*."

Analyzing my behavior, understanding how I had hopscotched from one brother to the other brother and from one Mike Pratt to another Mike Pratt, the doctor came forward with a wonderful observation. He said, "It sounds to me like you should be thinking about getting a divorce."

I had separated from my first husband, but I had not yet found a lawyer. I was frightened of that course of action, because I had a two-year-old child. But I said, "You're right. I'll have to find a lawyer." But I remembered seeing my therapist at the gay bar. I said, "What about you, Dr. Poseur? Aren't you ready to jump ship too?"

ELEVEN KINDS OF LONELINESS

The summer before I went to the Writers' Workshop I got divorced from my first husband. He didn't attend the divorce hearing, but Gus McCannlish, my poetry professor from Roger Williams, took an active role in the proceedings. I needed to have two witnesses accompany me to the court session. They would be asked to stand up to testify to the fact that I had "irreconcilable differences" with my husband. My second witness was my friend Priscilla Fennessey, a beautiful blonde, whom we had nicknamed Priscilla *Fantasy,* because of her lusciousness. She had been a movie extra in *The Great Gatsby* when it was filmed at a mansion in Newport, with Robert Redford, Bruce Dern, and Mia Farrow. Priscilla Fantasy was a top tier extra, and wore a yellow ribbon on her wrist, so that the director could identify that she was on the A-list and he used her in several scenes. She was filmed dancing on the terrace at parties, and once in a fountain, her wet dress clinging to her body.

At the hearing, the sun was streaming into the antique courthouse windows. It was midsummer, and my birthday. My witness-friends stood up at the side podium, one after the other, to list examples of my unhappy years with my husband. "They had exceedingly different interests," Gus said, and "I guess you could say it was poetry that came between them."

I was beaming. How wonderful to believe that poetry could have such an important imprint on me, and could be proof that I deserved my freedom!

But then Priscilla Fantasy said, "Her house was a wreck. Because why should she bother to keep it clean?"

That was an embarrassment, but worse I was awarded child support in the paltry amount of only $275 a month. Soon we were released to the sunny afternoon where we went to Newport Harbor to get lunch and to get drunk. We sat at a deck-side restaurant beneath a bright umbrella that tilted in the wind like a spinnaker. I thought of the three French sailors. I was released from my bonds and looking forward to going to graduate school, although I couldn't imagine living in the Midwest, so far away from the seaside.

Gus McCannlish, a Midwesterner himself, said, "Iowa City is the Athens of the Corn Belt."

"No kidding?"

"The university there has great minds," he said.

I imagined these "great minds" standing in rows of corn.

The next day, I was at the Plough and Stars bar in Cambridge, with my friend Robin Boyd who had attended Roger Williams College a few years after me. She was a good poet, but she was into booze and snow and got into lots of little jams. For instance, earlier that afternoon we were sitting at a Newport Creamery in Providence eating grilled cheese sandwiches, minding our own business, when Robin jumped out of the booth saying, "My car! My car!" It was the second time that year that repo men had been sneaky. They had hitched her old VW to their tow truck and had pulled it out of its parking space. She was always late on her college loan payments, and her car was towed away every few months. So we boarded a Peter Pan bus to get to Boston, and in no time we were getting "ploughed" at the Plough and Stars.

The beer glasses were very large, like big flower vases, and they were easy to slosh if we didn't sip the surface suds away. We were always grabbing the bar rag to mop up. When I leaned over to put the rag back in the sink, I saw a handsome man sitting at one corner of the sticky wood plinth. I thought I recognized him. I said to Robin, "Look, isn't that Dick Yates?"

Richard Yates had once visited Roger Williams College, and I had broken my eyeeteeth on his books *Revolutionary Road* and *Eleven Kinds of Loneliness*. I was reading his story "Glutton for Punishment" when I had decided to divorce my first husband. Yates understood a woman's predicament and he had hit the nail on the head when he wrote: "The orderly rotation of many careful moods was her life, or rather, what her life had become. She managed it well, and it was only rarely, looking very closely at her face, that he could see how much the effort was costing her." At the end of the bar, Yates smiled at me but in the next instant he sneezed violently. He wiped his nose with his cuff, and again he sneezed with such force I saw celery leaves flutter in the bartender's bins of cocktail veggies. Dick Yates had a whopping cold to be sure. He said, "It's got to be something tropical. Like nothing I've ever had before."

He was drinking house scotch but when he asked for a refill he told the bartender, "I'll have another dose of sulfa, if you please." Yates had once had TB and he did look pretty sick. But Robin and I moved down four barstools to sit beside him. "Do I know you?" he said. "If I don't, should I want to?"

"That's a pretty good line," I was thinking, but I said, "I met you at a reading, I think."

"Good grief."

"No, no, Mr. Yates, I'm a great admirer of your work."

"You don't say."

"No, really."

"Don't tell me. I guess you're a writer yourself?"

I explained that I was accepted to the Writers' Workshop and that I'd be leaving for Iowa at the end of the summer.

"Fiction or poetry?"

"They admitted me in poetry, but I write short stories too."

He shrugged. He blew his nose into an insubstantial cocktail napkin. "Poets have something going for them. They don't have expectations."

"I have big expectations," I said.

"I mean fortune and fame. You poets can't expect much of that." He was telling his mind, but in fact, he was quite genial, and he entertained Robin and me for an hour, complaining about the struggles he'd been having with his forthcoming novel, *A Good School*, his third novel in four years. He was having a comeback, after some bumps and potholes. Critics had hated his novel *A Special Providence*. But he persevered and had published *Disturbing the Peace* and *The Easter Parade*. Like Hardy he was a writer who worked through dark consequences and reemerged again and again, despite no real popularity.

I couldn't tell if he was flirting with me, or if his kindness was fraternal. But despite his runny nose, I thought he was attractive. He teased me relentlessly about my plans to attend the Writers' Workshop. "A girl like you should find something better to do," he said.

"Something better?"

"If I weren't under the weather, I'd show you."

This sounded like an invitation, but his face was ashen. He seemed to be saying that writing was not a tenable occupation, and his concern was genuine. He said, "There are ways you can ruin your life that are much more fun."

Robin had to work in the morning and she had to run to catch a bus back to Providence, but I stayed behind. Yates bought me another round. Finally, he said, "I should go home and nurse this cold."

I wanted to leave with him, imagining my candy-striper mode (I had once dressed in a sexy white uniform to care for a boyfriend who had had his wisdom teeth removed), but I didn't have the courage to suggest it to Dick Yates. If he had asked me directly, I would have gone willingly. When he stood up, he pulled me off my barstool to face him. He kissed me. "That's what you wanted, isn't it?" he said.

His kiss was sensual and dismissive at the same time. It was erotic and mournful, as if he understood both how much I had to offer and how much I had to learn. I told him, "Yeah, you really know women."

He buttoned his coat as if to face the winter cold, but it was July. He said, "When you go out to Iowa, give them hell."

"This Poem is too Female"

I packed up my car to leave for the Midwest, and buckled my daughter into the baby's car seat. I noticed I had left a novel on the back dash of my Dodge Dart. I had left the book there all summer, as a kind of talisman or something, fully aware it was visible to anyone who walked by my car on the street. It was Gail Godwin's *The Odd Woman*. The book had particular meaning to me. I almost *flaunted* the book, daring anyone to question me about my plans to go off on my own and become a real writer. Like Godwin's character, I was a woman trying to find my independence. An "odd woman."

When heading off to graduate school in Iowa City, I thought of the woman in Godwin's story. Her character had had some fears about what it takes for a woman to be on her own—there were threats everywhere. The novel was set in a Midwestern town where a local scoundrel known to everyone as "The Enema Bandit" was breaking into houses and assaulting women. Godwin had based the character on a real criminal in Champaign, Illinois, Michael Hubert Kenyon, who had pleaded guilty to a decade-long series of armed robberies and sexual assaults in which he would administer enemas to his female victims.

Arriving in Iowa City, I thought of the Enema Bandit. I wondered what kinds of people I might meet in a small town that was known to be the "Athens of the Corn Belt." The way I gauged individuals was often not until some sort of sexual moment was broached. Famous sexual harassment cases involving writing faculty at the university had not yet emerged, not until the early eighties, when Nobel Prize winner Derek Walcott got into trouble when teaching at Harvard. The *Harvard Crimson* reported that a sophomore had complained that Walcott said he "did not want to discuss poetry with her and began to discuss sex, asking the student, 'Would you make love to me?'" When she declined him, she claimed to be the only student in his class to receive a "C" grade. More than a decade later Walcott was in trouble again when teaching at Boston University. A graduate student in BU's playwriting program claimed that Walcott threatened to prevent a play she had written from being produced if she didn't have sex with him.

Two poets who I knew personally had hit rough patches also. In 1981, the poet Paul O'Donnell was in trouble at Princeton for sleeping with a student. A decade later, at Syracuse University, the poet Jim de la Mare tossed a drink into a girl's face when she accused him of commenting about her breasts, using "salty language." Both teachers got into trouble for their actions with female students.

But in fact, years before the Syracuse disruption, de la Mare would be *my* lover when I was his student at Iowa. He was my teacher. *And* my lover. And with a little sheepishness, I have to admit that I also once had sex with the poet Paul O'Donnell at my house in Newport when he had come to give a reading at my alma mater, Roger Williams College. O'Donnell had just won an important prize; his collection was the selection in the prestigious Yale Series of Younger Poets. That had impressed me, but an uncanny coincidence emerged. The very first time I heard the name of my future husband was when O'Donnell tried to have anal intercourse with me. I declined. But when trying to get me to acquiesce, he said that he had been instructed on the proper method of doing it for a *woman's pleasure* by his good friend—the man I would marry eight years later. (The man who will probably kill me.)

In the seventies, liaisons between student and faculty were all too common. My undergraduate college had invited many writers to campus, and from my freshman year all the way through graduate school many of us were involved in that all-too-common sex ruckus at the university during those pivotal years before sex with students became more unacceptable. Acceptable and unacceptable had once been a matter between the two participants. I had wanted to have sex with de la Mare; I liked him a lot. He introduced me to the mysteries of Anglo Saxon riddles. These riddles were questions in poetry, and in life, and were not just magic tricks. There are always *two* correct answers to the riddles. One answer is seemingly innocent, while the other answer is overtly obscene. In these English riddles the reader must recognize double meanings or "hinge" words in order to discover the answer to the riddle. There are five distinct types of riddles: the true riddle, the arithmetic puzzle, the clever question, the conundrum, and the neck-riddle. The answer to a neck-riddle is only known by the author of the riddle. Its purpose is to "save a person's neck if the situation ever arises." De la Mare assigned a riddle to the class:

Swings by his thigh a thing most magical!
Below the belt, beneath the folds
Of his clothes it hangs, a hole in its front end,
Stiff-set and stout, but swivels about.
It is his will to fill a well-known hole
That it fits fully when at full length
He has often filled it before. Now he fills it again.

"It's a key," I said, knowing that there was a different, and very obscene answer on everyone's lips.

De la Mare was my only true teacher at Iowa. I didn't learn a speck from the other instructors. But one Writers' Workshop instructor once asked me to get into his car after class. "Let's go for a ride," he said.

I told him, "You've got to be kidding."

Needless to say, I wasn't awarded any financial aid when I was a student at Iowa although I was the only single parent in that program, and was in great need. De la Mare laughed at me. He told me that I had to learn to be more politic. He told me, "Don't say, 'You've got to be kidding.' Just say you have to pick up your daughter from the day care center."

In the decades before the new awareness or transparency about the power struggle between female students and their teachers, visiting novelists and poets often removed their wedding rings when they came to campus to give readings or to sit in on seminars, expecting to snag a little pussy before their ride to the airport the following day. When novelist Rick Chrysler visited the Fine Arts Work Center in Provincetown, in the spring of '81, I noticed the white ring of puckered skin on his third finger, where he had taken off his wedding band. As he went bar-hopping with several female fellows, at one point in the evening, he was heard to say, "Let's ditch the ugly one," pointing to a girl who was a little frumpy, and who didn't interest him. The next day, his wife was joining him, and he made sure to twist his tight wedding ring back on his ring finger at the breakfast table that morning.

I lost three wedding rings with my first husband, even a precious one that had once belonged to my French great-grandmother. The ring was passed down, wife after wife, until it came to me. It was yellow gold with a fleur-de-lis pattern imprinted on the band. The stylized lily or lotus blossom has been used to represent French royalty. Legend has it that an angel presented Clovis, the Merovingian king of the Franks, with a golden lily as a symbol of his purification upon his conversion to Christianity. Others claim that Clovis adopted the symbol himself when water lilies showed him how to safely cross a river and thus succeed in battle.

I soon came to learn that marriage is the same as any clash, military campaign, war of words, contest of minds, or life-and-death struggle. So I left my wedding bands on the sinks in public restrooms; that's how much I wanted to wash my hands of them. I don't believe in tokens of resolve. I never wore a wedding ring again.

As Susan Cheever said, "Everyone sleeps with editors. Publishers. Agents. It's that kind of business." To her list we should add our teachers, visiting literary super stars, or resident poets, novelists, and professors. Our work on the page, even poems with titles like "Environmental Impact Statement," seemed to evoke a belief that our poems were invitations. Many novelists and poets came to Roger Williams College as visiting writers: William Styron. Richard Yates. Donald Justice. Robert Bly. Tom Wolfe. Sometimes these guests tried to spoon with coeds, removing wedding rings, or giving students instant pet names. My classmate, Lynne Wentford, a beautiful southern blonde who looked like Kim Basinger's little sister, became involved with the poet Kenneth Koch. Lynne was a knockout, something I could vouch for, because once, after a long party, we had had bathtub sex in our drunkenness. When Koch visited the college, he took Lynne back to Long Island with him, where he fucked her all weekend. She called me from the hospital where she had been rushed for a bruised bladder wall that had bled a great deal, creating clots that she couldn't pass. "It's not too bad," she told me. "But the doctor said I was too tight for Kenneth. They told me I should go easy from now on. But you know Kenneth—"

Lynne's little hospital trip was an eye-opener. But I never got injured from any of my visiting poet action. In those years, I had had many one-night stands with surprisingly renowned literary bigwigs, each of them all too willing to read my poems.

When my undergraduate teacher Gus McCannlish wrote about his student lover Elizabeth's "first female poem," it foreshadowed what I would later experience at the University of Iowa Writers' Workshop. The professor who had invited me to get in his car with him once told the class that he couldn't possibly critique my entry on the worksheet. He said, "I can't discuss this poem. This poem is too *female*." My classmate in the workshop, the poet Jorie Graham, who would later win the Pulitzer Prize for her poetry collection *The Dream of the Unified Field*, jumped to my defense. She told the teacher that of course we should talk about the poem I had written for class. Jorie volunteered to lead the discussion. She said, "Your problem is not with the poem's subject. It's the author herself who is much too female. That's what scares you."

This prejudice happened to me often. I was vulnerable to others who believed me to be "too female." This wasn't just in academia, but it surfaced in my work-a-day world.

When I was a single mom living in Iowa City with my three-year-old daughter, I was hired at a motel just outside of town, right off of an exit ramp on Interstate 80. It wasn't my first motel job, but this one had a strict policy. All dayshift maids were told to clean guest bathrooms without using any water! "Water leaves drops on the tile and on the glass shower door!" the manager said. "Do not turn on the tap! Use your cloth with your disinfectant spray. Wipe everything down. That's all! Be sure to collect all the pubic hair, especially in corners and behind the toilet. I don't want to see one hair left behind!"

In my previous motel jobs, I could rinse these random pubic hairs right down the drain, by turning on the shower. But for my new manager I had to use a rag and reckon with each stray hair, face-to-face. Sometimes the manager popped in to make sure I wasn't turning on the tap. When I was on my knees chasing down the pubic hairs, the manager stood behind me to make sure I didn't miss any. I was surprised when he grabbed me by the hips and pumped against me. When I stood up, I stumbled into the towel rack, spilling the fresh towels. He led me to the motel bed that I had just remade, with hospital corners. He told me to be careful to flip the stained coverlet over to its clean side, another in-house regulation we were supposed to follow. I told him, "I already flipped it."

"Looks good. Let's try it out."

I had to make a quick decision to save my job. Or look for another.

So I found a new position as a corrections officer, trying to make ends meet while living in Iowa with my young daughter, and being "too female" cropped up again. I worked second shift at Iowa Security Medical Facility, a maximum-security setting that housed inmates for pretrial evaluations, and it also kept under lockup every kind of mental case inmate that the state prison system couldn't handle at its other maximum-security facilities: Anamosa State Penitentiary, Luster Heights, or Mount Pleasant. These inmates often were given Electric Shock Therapy, and I had to assist the doctor by holding an inmate's ankles, so when he jerked his legs in response to the electric current he wouldn't fall off the table.

I was only one of a few women who had been hired into the "old boys" system of male corrections officers. Male corrections officers didn't want to work shoulder to shoulder with women, but the state was trying to abolish gender boundaries and wanted more women woven into the payrolls of the correctional system. I was snapped up right out of grad school, and was

promised I could teach inmates "composition." I soon
learned that the few women who were already on the
payroll were of only two specific types. There were a
few girlie nurses who came to work dressed in frilly
attire, pink shirtwaist dresses, and with hairdos that
looked very 1950s. There were also a couple of very
masculine-looking types, women who arrived at work
dressed in khaki shorts and men's golf shirts. The
women who were acceptable to work at the prison
were either foo-foo types or they were very butch.
I was the only female CO who looked like a regular
woman.

My first weeks at the prison, I worked in a small icy
room in the "tower." The tiny suite was called Master
Control. A wall of video monitors showed the hallways,
the intersections, and the external gates. The room
was flanked by cabinets of gleaming weaponry: rifles,
pistols, sawed-offs, stun guns (this was before tasers),
tear gas grenades, hand and ankle cuffs, belly chains,
flares, and prodders. The air-conditioning was up so
high that I had to ask my supervisor for his jacket. I
knew this was a dangerous request. He might mistake
it for flirtation or for physical weakness typical of the
female. He told me it was cold to keep the ammunition dry. "And the cold will keep you on your toes,
sweetheart."

I had been promised I would be teaching composition to inmates since I had a post-graduate degree in
English, but they didn't give me a class to teach. I was
left in charge of a large board of video screens and
blinking lights that controlled the system of electronic
doors throughout the prison complex. Each doorway
was comprised of two glass panels that swept open

when a button was touched. Only one panel could be opened at a time. The person walking through had to be temporarily boxed-in within the glass lockup before the second door could be opened. I had to learn to work the levers that operated both the doors, in progression; the first door had to be closed before the next door could be activated. I sometimes closed the first door too quickly, hitting the occupant upon entry. I jostled a prominent psychiatrist, brushing his shoulder with one door, and then being nervous and out of synchrony, I struck the doctor with the second door as he tried to squeeze out of the compartment. I had lost control of the *controls*! And it wasn't just a vendor trying to squeeze past, or the laundry personnel; it was the top-cheese mind-control expert.

"When can I start teaching composition?" I asked.

"Keep your pants on. We're never going to run out of 'students.'"

After my first couple weeks at Iowa Security Medical Facility I had started sleepwalking. It's not uncommon for people to sleepwalk during the first months working in stressful settings. In a prison, on submarines, on deep-sea oil-rig platforms, or for military personnel during "in country" duty, there's a high incidence of somnambulism. But when I finally started tutoring men in the prison I felt a little better, more like a substitute teacher or a guidance counselor than a corrections officer. Some inmates called me "Teech," and I liked the nickname. But soon I was given a new nickname. Inmates called me "Sidewinder." I was confused by the nickname but an inmate told me that they liked the way I walked. No matter how much I controlled my posture and adjusted my gait, and was careful not to swing my hips, I was just a little too curvy. I was unlike the foo-foo nurses or the mannish female corrections officers. Inmates recognized who I was. I was a twenty-something larger-than-life female.

Several inmates tried to win my attention when we spent time at small card tables in the recreation area on East Unit, playing games of backgammon or dominoes. To begin a game, I had to be taught the correct lingo. In dominoes, when it was time to choose our pieces, the pile had to be stirred around on the table-top the way you might shuffle cards. If it was his turn to shuffle the pile, I had to be sure to give my opponent the correct invitation to begin the game. I had to say, "Shake 'em Jake, my fingers ache." When it was my turn, he had to say, "Shake 'em Jane, my fingers are in pain." If I didn't recite my direct invitation, an inmate stared at me hotly, and wouldn't begin the game.

One inmate showed me an apple tattooed on the inside of his wrist. His name was MacIntosh. He told me, "Teech, I'd give you this apple but you wouldn't want it. It's got worms."

I said, "Worms don't scare me." My comment was misinterpreted. He thought I was saying that if I wasn't disgusted by him that it meant I could "go for him." My supervisors said that fights were erupting between inmates who claimed that I liked one more than another. An inmate had been stabbed in the showers with a shiv made from a plastic scrap removed from a pallet in the kitchen. My supervisor said that I "looked too pretty when I came to work."

"I wear slacks. I try to look nondescript," I said.

A different officer tried to be sympathetic. He told me, "It's not your fault. You're just too hot."

"Too womanly," my supervisor said. "We don't want that."

This was another version of "This poem is too female."

"Maybe you can wear one of those loose-fitting hippie smocks?" the friendly officer suggested.

Working in the prison system is one thing, but as students at the university we were wholly vulnerable to what our male teachers wanted to believe that we, as young female writers, presented to them. And when I had been accepted to the most prestigious graduate writing program, the infamous Writers' Workshop at the University of Iowa, it might have been because of my "female" traits. When waiting to hear about my application, which had somehow been lost in the pack, my undergraduate professor, Gus McCannlish, telephoned the poet Donald Justice, who headed the faculty at Iowa, to ask about my status. Justice had been a visiting writer at Roger Williams a few years before, and I had met him in class. His poems were an influence to me, his rhymes and off-rhymes mesmerized me. In "Women in Love," he says, "It always comes, and when it comes they know. / To will it is enough to bring them there. / The knack is this, to fasten and not let go." And in "A Map of Love," he writes, "Your face more than others' faces / Maps the half-remembered places / I have come to while I slept— / Continents a dream had kept / Secret from all waking folk / Till to your face I awoke, / And remembered then the shore, / And the dark interior."

When Gus asked about my application, Justice said, "Are you talking about that girl with the beautiful long hair? That one?"

"That's her," my professor said. He didn't tell Justice that I had since cut my hair. It was shoulder length.

Justice said, again in a magical off rhyme, "I haven't seen her application, but don't fret. The girl with the silky hair? She's it!"

THE RED-THROATED LOON AND THE DOVEKIE

Living on the National Seashore we often see natural catastrophes. We find harbor seals with shark bites or with wounds from boat propellers. Carcasses of seabirds wash ashore. Black-backed gulls have a wingspan of five feet and finding them on the beach, with their wings stretched open, they look like broken box kites that have plummeted from the sky. Or I'll find a bowl of feathers; a flecked mat is all that's left behind where a Cooper's hawk has pounced on a rock dove. Closer to home, birds often fly into sliders and plate glass windows. I often hear that familiar "thunk" and go outside to see another victim. With glass houses, birds see straight through to the other side, just to hit an invisible wall. Titmouse. Blackbird. Carolina wren. I'm most upset to find a hummer conked out. Cupped in my hand, I blow on its feathers, and sometimes it revives. Right as rain. I might find a bird that isn't injured but that is just exhausted. In migration, songbirds and warblers fly all night and must rest in my privet before they slog on.

Before cancer, Giovanni was driving to school. He called me on his cell phone to say that he had found an injured bird on the street. I went to meet him and together we saw it was a loon entangled in fishing line. Sloppy tourists often leave coils of monofilament fishing line on the beach after they spend their vacation casting for striper. Amateurs. These tourists often leave trash behind, charred wood from their bonfires, beer cans, and the plastic webbing from six packs which endangers all kinds of wildlife. They cause the greatest harm to shorebirds when they don't collect their fishing line.

The loon was enwrapped in monofilament. Tight wire crisscrossed its body, from its red throat to its webbed feet. The line was coiled deep inside its feathers and would be hard to snip, so we wrapped the loon in a towel and drove to Eastham's Wild Care center where rehabilitation experts treat injured or orphaned wildlife. They would know the proper method for removing entangled fishing line.

One week later, Giovanni received a formal letter from Wild Care. They told him that the bird he had rescued was a female red-throated loon. She had survived. He was invited to attend a ceremonial event at which they would release the healthy loon into the natural wild again. They planned to return the loon to a beach close to where Giovanni had found her. This was a professional operation, I thought. Sending the do-gooder nature lover a thank you note, on embossed stationery, and including him in the release of the bird would reward him for his ethical deed and would further their conservation efforts. That the bird had survived was all the gratification Giovanni desired.

A different time, Giovanni and I found another victim. Along a sandy lane in Truro we discovered a very small black-and-white bird in the slush. Cute as a puffin, it was in fact the smallest of the auks, and indeed it was part of the puffin family. Although it didn't look injured, it didn't fly away. Something was amiss. It was so tiny, it could fit in the pocket of a down jacket, and we brought it home that way. Again we delivered the bird to Wild Care.

Giovanni received another letter explaining that the little bird he had rescued was a dovekie, the tiniest of the auks. It breeds along the high-arctic coasts and in winter makes its way southward as far as Cape Cod. Dovekies are explicitly dependent on the sea. They attain flight by paddling across the surface of water. They cannot lift off from dry land. If a dovekie falls to earth it is doomed. Our dovekie had been stranded for hours when we had found it. It was in shock and could not be saved.

Giovanni's bird rescues have resonating vibrations. Since his cancer diagnosis, these episodes have poignancy to me. I tried to imagine what had caused the dovekie to fall out of the sky. A creature that cannot fly without the generous surface of the open sea to launch him seemed metaphoric. In his cancer ordeal, Giovanni must try to soar again from his perch of bare earth at near death. He must find his footing.

"So it's not a win, win?" Giovanni had said when Crispin had told him his chances were fifty-fifty.

These are Wild Care statistics: One bird was saved; one bird didn't make it.

"QUILTY"

fter *My Sister Life,* my fourth book with his blue pencil marks, was published, River-rat showed up at my hotel. I gave him the first 200 pages of my new novel, *Lux.* He later phoned me to say, "This is your best work yet!" I was thrilled to hear his encouragement. But I remembered that he had said these very same words to me once before when I had turned in a manuscript of short stories. We had worked together on my story collection, *Rhode Island Fish Company.* He was happy when I agreed to extract a few stories from the manuscript, and we agreed on the same ones we felt should be left out. At his suggestion, I revised and added scenes to a few of the stories, and I wrote a brand-new story, "Prince of Motown," that Michiko Kakutani would take note of in a *Books of the Times* review.

Oh Christ, you're obsessed with this Michiko shit! Why do you need that validation? It's so phony. I'm surprised to hear that it's not Willis this time, but my protagonist from my novel *Lux* speaking his mind. My characters want me to stand up for them. *Don't give up your authority,* he says. And he's someone I can trust. The protagonist in *Lux* was a dream lover who had learned how to use a can of Dust-Off in foreplay, aiming the pin-hole wand up and down his girl Alden's naked body, scrolling a tight seam of compressed air across her nipples and down to her triangle with icy blasts from the can, like invisible fingertips. Alden couldn't resist it.

But with my book of short stories, River-rat's suggestions were very important to me. He opened doors in the narrative where there had been walls. Or he told me when I was getting locked in my own circles of razor wire, with too many descriptive entanglements, and he helped me get out of the extended metaphors I sometimes get strangled in. When I had finished the manuscript he told me, "This is your very best work!" But, again, we had a little squabble about the title of the book. "Rhode Island Fish Company" was one of the strongest pieces in the manuscript, but he felt the title was too regional or just too colloquial. He proposed a new title for the collection. He wanted to call the book, *You Have the Wrong Man*. I didn't like it at all. It sounded like a chick lit book, or even like a clit lit title. It was so Fay Weldon!

River-rat wouldn't budge.

Forced to accept my new title, *You Have the Wrong Man*, I found an epigraph for the book that would make it clear that book wasn't just a collection of "girl meets boy" fantasy tales. In the movie *Sunset Boulevard*, the character Norma Desmond is set with the task of finding an undertaker to bury her pet chimpanzee. In an early scene, she mistakes a handsome screenwriter named Joe Gillis for the funeral director she had called to the house. She explains to Gillis what she expects him to do:

> NORMA
> *I want the coffin to be white. And I want it*
> *specially lined with satin. White, or deep pink.*
> She picks up the shawl to make up her
> mind about the color. From under the shawl
> flops down a dead arm. . . . It is like a child's
> arm, only black and hairy.

> NORMA
> *How much will it be? I warn you—don't*
> *give me a fancy price just because I'm rich.*

> GILLIS
> *Lady, you've got the wrong man.*

This scene from *Sunset Boulevard* is the kind of black comedy that I strived for in my stories, and I hoped the epigraph would ameliorate or supplant the unfortunate title I was stuck with. River-rat had said that the story collection was "my best work yet." But the *New York Times Book Review* printed an iffy review, citing my typically edgy characters as distressing examples of American society, although it also said, "Ms. Flook is clearly an accomplished stylist. Her writing never succumbs to cliché, and there is a metaphorical opulence to her prose." I asked River-rat if the mixed review would be bad for the memoir that was scheduled to be published the following year. River-rat told me, "The story collection? We just pretend it *doesn't exist!*"

I was startled by his abrupt dismissal of my story collection. So when River-rat told me that my new novel *Lux* was "my best work yet," I remembered how he also had praised the story collection only to abandon it! A strange thing happened just a few weeks later. I received a two-page letter from River-rat on his Random House stationery describing why he would not publish my new novel. I recalled his first "memo" when my agent had said, "He's not ready to get into bed with you yet!" But after four books together, that were well-received but that had made little money, he felt he had met his "liability cap." Money is what a corporate servant has to deliver, and I had to acknowledge the cash nexus, and that there are figures at stake—

His change of heart, after liking the first 200 pages of *Lux,* was confusing to me. But even more peculiar, in his letter describing his issues with the manuscript, he repetitively called my main character by the wrong name. He kept referring to the main character by the name "Quilty."

In his list of concerns about the novel, he said, "Quilty *this*," and "Quilty *that*."

Clare Quilty is the name of the hypersexualized character double or doppelganger in Nabokov's novel *Lolita,* the man who eventually steals Lolita from Humbert Humbert. River-rat referred to my character as "Quilty" and he didn't seem to notice his repetitive error as he wrote his rejection letter. River-rat was so overwhelmed by our secret relationship that the mysterious Nabokov character had emerged in his repressed consciousness about his sexual desire for me. I was nonplussed by the bizarre confusion in his letter to me, but even more, I was disconsolate that he would not publish the novel and, in fact, he refused to work with me. My agent contacted an editor at another major publishing house who was interested in my work. The editor had admired my first novel, *The Arrow Collar Man*, and an offer was made on *Lux*. The following year, the novel was published by a top-tier literary imprint, at a company that competed with Random House books.

A friend of mine once told me about her brother's conference with his rabbi. He went for counseling about an affair he was having with an office mate. His rabbi advised him, "Don't mix business with pleasure. Don't piddle in your bread basket."

If River-rat was concerned about his professional life merging with his erotic life, the only control he still had over me was to reject my new novel. It's shameless, isn't it, girls? A man can turn his back on you, when he won't turn away his front. Each time he kissed me, I'd nibble the little sapphire on his lower lip, believing his heart would melt, and he'd read my pages again. That didn't happen, but he had no power over his secret urge. "Lolita. Light of my life, fire of my loins. My sin. My soul."

Remissionimpossible.blogspot.com

I was crossing the street. A woman came up beside me. She leaned on a cane with a tennis ball on its tip. It gave her more traction, she told me. The image of this woman with the tennis ball on her cane stayed with me all day. That's kind of how I feel going around in my cancer hell. I've got my own kind of tennis ball, although it's a mental thing. I don't know if people notice my tennis ball, but sometimes I see them look at me as if I had an asterisk hovering over me. Death.

We all have these asterisks, don't we?

I'll keep this post short. Any Devo fans out there? Well, "Gates of Steel" is one of their best songs so I'd like to dedicate this post to the various hardcore/punk covers of it. Gotta start with the original to set the stage. The song starts with that opening synth, sort of like a bizarro The Who, before getting into a driving tempo. Simple power chords establish the melody. From the classic Mark Mothersbaugh voice quiver of "twist-and-shou-ou-out" to the spoken declarations that "man is real," this song is virtually perfect for three and a half minutes.

As for the covers, first up and most recent is by Slapshot. This is a very faithful cover, but still sounds like Slapshot. Well, front man Choke is definitely trying to hit those Devo highs, but ultimately this is old school Boston hardcore.

Next up is the Groovie Ghoulies. GG play some pretty damn good Ramones-worship pop punk. This recording comes from *The Island of Pogo* on Lookout! Records. They up the tempo a little bit, but otherwise this is basically Devo done Ghoulies Style with those snotty old-school pop punk vocals.

In Your Face was a Long Island band from around '88– '93. This cover came out on a compilation in 1990. Lots of energy here, and the vocalist really nails it, remaining faithful to many aspects of the original, but it's straightforward hardcore punk.

Well, that about does it. Three good covers of a damn good song. There is a Skankin' Pickle cover as well, but I will let you find that for yourselves.

THE SIOUX CITY SWEDE

The poet Jim de la Mare was very helpful to me as a young poet. He told me, "Your poems are too 'private.'" I asked him, "Do you mean they're too surreal, too secret?" He said my work had too many obscure landmarks and personal references that readers could not bridge. He said that I gave only enough information to engender curiosity, inquiry, and to create agitation. "There was a door/floating on the water/a white door with a glass knob/ All the envelopes swirled after . . ." He said I should make direct observations and must take responsibility for every lyrical proposition I make. It's true that I relied on image as supreme statement. As a young poet, I felt that an image wasn't just a hint or marker, it must be law!

I started to think that a poem is a "half-told" tale, and that sometimes it feels "staged." So I turned to fiction because I wanted to tell a story in a more natural way—with a beginning, a middle, and an end. Fiction has room to catalogue our feral traits and in a larger timeline I could develop characters. But for de la Mare, I got to work trying to open the lockbox of each new poem I wrote.

I met de la Mare at a party at the Mayflower Hotel, an exotic destination in Corn Belt Iowa. The Mayflower was where all the international writing students were housed. At happy hour, the lobby often was filled with women in colorful saris and sometimes men wore turbans. I recently had learned how to wear a "cloche," thinking the tight French cap was very chic. De la Mare came up to me and said, "Get that rag off your head."

He flirted with insults. It was a love-hate relationship from the start. Love-hate relationships are the most interesting kind. He took me dancing in Cedar Rapids, and then we went to bed. Mornings, over coffee, we talked about poetry.

But de la Mare went on to date other grad students and I soon found an authentic Iowan from Sioux City and with him I entered another love-hate relationship. Dag Peterson was a Midwesterner of Swedish descent. He explained to me that Nords are more endowed than other men because of the cold climate. He said that because of the chilly weather, Nordic women have evolved over time to have "deeper vaginas—a good two to four centimeters longer than most women, and therefore their men needed to have extra-large members." He didn't have to give me a dissertation. His sensuality in the bedroom was wholly different from anyone I had slept with. He made love attentively, with reverie for the female form. Veronica would call it *European.* But when de la Mare met him he told me, "This guy isn't a brain bank, so I see you're in it just for the sex."

"Like *you,* he writes poems," I told de la Mare. In fact, Dag Peterson took a course in "Book Arts," taught by bookmaker Kim Merker, in which he produced a little chapbook of his own poetry called *Peace Among the Violets*. I thought it should have been "amidst" the violets, but because the poems were about Vietnam, I excused the awkward title. Peterson was also writing for the *Daily Iowan* newspaper and he wrote a column called "On the Bus." His other daily job was as a bus driver for the campus bus company, called CamBus, a bad pun. I told de la Mare that my relationship with the sensual Swede wasn't wholly for his much longer dick. "He writes a column. He writes poems. Unlike you, he's got a real job." I didn't admit that Dag recently had run a red light and crashed his bus into a mail truck.

The Swede was very attractive. Tall and sharp-featured, with high cheekbones like a Swedish model's; he seemed to hum with an oversexed alertness, an intense carnality that seemed to be my only respite from Iowa City's freezing cold winter, a climate so demanding that I had to have my car battery plugged into an outlet. Peterson was like a battery warmer to me. And I appreciated his acceptance of my daughter. He didn't flinch when we took my three-year-old to a poetry reading and my daughter disrupted the proceedings. The poet Carolyn Forché was reading her poems, typical pseudopolitical hogwash. Her poems about Central American strife made her a rising star in poetry circles. The reading was in a science building auditorium. As in many other university lecture halls there were often two televisions mounted on the wall behind the podium. These screens were used for slides or VCR tapes of class materials, but the televisions were of course turned off during the poetry reading.

Fifteen minutes into the reading, my daughter, Annabel, noticed the big blank screens on the wall. "They've got two TVs!" she shrieked. The audience reacted in a wave, turning in their seats to locate the rude child and the irresponsible parent. Some people chuckled tolerantly, but Forché was annoyed. She turned a page hotly and continued to read.

But the Swede and I had something in common. We had daughters born on the same day. My daughter was, in fact, born on my own birthday, July 9th. Peterson had a daughter named Jade, and she too had a birthday on July 9th. I found this coincidence—that *all three* of us were born on the same date—to have a witchy importance. My daughter, Annabel, and I met Jade when she came to Iowa City to visit her father. We all piled into his car, a rusted Pontiac station wagon. There was a hole in the floor under the passenger seat where I could watch the pavement smearing past. I was forced to ride sitting Indian style with my legs tucked under me. I was surprised to learn that he was taking us to an amusement park. It was the dead of winter!

When we arrived, I said, "Too bad there's all this white stuff, or we could go on something."

"It's great! Everything's buried!" Jade shrieked, as she climbed onto a carousel horse. Dag joked with me about the freezing saddle. Jade jumped down and ran to a big pavilion where bumper cars had been left in their awkward arrangements since the power had been turned off at the end of the summer season. "This is the place!" my daughter cried out. He put her in one of the cars, and Jade climbed into another. The little girls gripped the steering wheels expecting something to happen. Dag removed his gloves and stuffed them in his pockets. "Are you ready, drivers?"

He leaned his weight into Jade's car and smashed it against my daughter's vehicle. He went around to get behind Annabel's car and he pushed it into Jade's. The cars ricocheted left and right. The little girls screamed with glee. For twenty minutes, the little cars moved backward and forward, smashing into one another under his manpower. He claimed it was easy, "like monopoly pieces," but his head was drenched. His sweat dripped in little icicles from his chin.

The scene at the frozen amusement park with our two July 9th daughters lifted us higher than our carnal plateau, at least for that winter afternoon. Dag was the man my daughter called "Daggy" for "Daddy." But Peterson was a sex addict and he wandered into dangerous settings for sex. When I confronted him, outside a bar, we had a raging argument. I decided to leave him behind, but he had unscrewed the distributor cap from my car, and I had to walk home in the freezing cold. When I reached my house I locked all my doors, fearing he'd show up.

I was brushing my teeth, when he smashed my kitchen door. He joined me in the bathroom and grabbed my toothbrush. He tugged my ponytail violently and started scrubbing my teeth. His jabs with the toothbrush cut my mouth, and my gums started to bleed.

In my first book, there are poems about the Sioux City Swede. "In love, keep yourself half dead. / Sleep with one foot on the floor / Let dreams walk away and never come back." And I based my psychopathic character "Tracy," in my novel, *The Arrow Collar Man*, on him too. Dag Peterson, a wholly complex human being with his own vivid *living hell*, was the perfect antagonist for my other male character in that novel. They were excellent "purgatory mates," and they worked together as a driving force.

I was amused to learn that Dag Peterson later went on to become a head writer at Hallmark Cards. It is surprising that someone who was greatly influenced by the French surrealist poet André Breton— "My wife with the hair of a wood fire / With the thoughts of heat lightning / My wife with shoulders of champagne / My wife with the hips of a skiff / With hips of a chandelier / My wife with a sex of mirror / My wife with eyes full of tears—" could find his niche writing greeting card schlock.

The greeting card industry has advanced in recent years regarding what are acceptable criteria for greeting cards in its racks. Dag had to compete with American Greetings who recently produced a thank you note that says on the inside, *"I like having sex with you. Sometimes in this busy world we forget to slow down for the special things that really matter like having sex."* Peterson can't take credit for that particular card, but a testimony like that, about our simple gratitude about good sex, brings my connection to him full circle.

MITTEN

I think of my years in Iowa, at the Writers' Workshop from 1977 to early 1980, as endless night. Winter evenings in the Midwest sink down over a flat seascape of open fields, and by three in the afternoon it's twilight. The snowy streets were never fully cleared but municipal trucks sprinkled sand over the hard-pack snow. Bright yellow aggregate dusted upon the new snowfall looked like streets of cookie crumbs. The winters were so cold, I bought an engine block heater for my car, but I often forgot to plug it in overnight. My first December in Iowa City, I was advised to purchase long underwear for my daughter and me. Wearing leggings under my jeans, I was suddenly in the woebegone realm of Thomas Hardy. The winter cold was relentless. My daughter was attending Melrose Day Care Center, and I sent her off with more than one woolen hat. The kids got snow-drenched when they played outside in the six-foot drifts and she went to school with extra caps to replace the sodden ones. At night she would return with different tasseled hats, none of them the same. Parents didn't care if their kids shared their watch caps; there was a constantly shifting inventory and the tradition seemed to exemplify Iowa's democratic ideology.

When the season changed, it was a long, luxurious awakening of earthy smells. The frozen fields began to thaw, releasing the previous year's tons of fertilizer into the Iowa River, combining with the snowmelt and spring rains. The scent of nitrogen and phosphorous en-cloaked the town reminding us that we resided in a giant bread basket. But I had a wonderful visitor when spring arrived. When the Sioux City Swede had punched a fist-hole right through my kitchen door, it had left a small opening in the door frame. A house wren liked the fist-hole and decided to build a nest. Each time I came and went, she shot out of her hiding place startled by my departure and my return, but soon she was back on her clutch. The song of her mate filled my house. A wren's mating call is a jumbled bubbling with abrupt churrs and scolds followed by twelve to sixteen sweet syllables. Its halting notes, rising and falling, didn't falter even during shouting matches with the Swede.

At Iowa, I met other young writers. Some of my classmates would go on to win Pulitzer Prizes: Jane Smiley, Jorie Graham, Michael Cunningham, and my friend Elliot Winn.

The poet Jorie Graham had a charismatic presence at the workshop. She had learned about the glamour principle from her mother, the sculptor Beverly Pepper, and when I went to a party at Jorie's apartment I was greeted at the door by a large photograph of a little girl splashing in the Trevi Fountain in Rome. In the picture Jorie seemed perfectly aware she was "making a splash." I also was amused to see how Jorie had prepared for her party guests. She had left her unmade bed in disarray. Iconic designer Christian Dior sheets, in a print of bright red lilies, were tousled in a messy, crumpled effect to suggest that she and her lover had just had sex. Even more amusing, she had left her diaphragm and an open tube of spermicidal jelly on the toilet lid in the bathroom. She wanted us to see it. I realized right then that it wasn't just our professors and visiting writers who created the sexual chaos at the university, it was all of us. And with youth, we had our volatile hormones, our sublime innocence, and our arrogance, in equal measure.

In my years at Iowa I became close with three young writers of particular importance to me. I am changing their names here to protect their privacy:

My first semester, I became acquainted with Cindy Sue Richards. She had just published a chapbook of prose poems about her West Virginia childhood, with a wedding photograph of her parents on the cover. The book was a great encouragement to me. The poems presented a "sweet savage" tone, in confessions of a country girl trying out her skills as a wounded, childlike femme fatale. The sweet savage voice worked in the short form but would become a telltale weakness in her later novels. She was soon to get notice for her first collection of stories which made her an overnight sensation. With that book in '79, she got the overblown attention from literary heavyweights who wrote blurbs for the back jacket. Several superstar hetero kingpins added their two cents. One called her "a crooked beauty," another said she was "electric." She was "audacious" and "an exciting new voice." The

book caused a little storm quite similar to what newcomer Mary Gaitskill received a decade later.

Cindy Sue had met her editor at a writers' conference where she had dazzled him. Cindy Sue has a pronounced mannerism. She stands very close to a man
in conversation, placing her heart-shaped face right
beneath *his* face, with her pretty little chin thrust forward, and her lips pursed in a plump pink berry. She
talked with a whispery voice, her under-the-breath
words like little air kisses, to people she wanted attention from. Cindy Sue was very attractive with a wasp
waist and generous hips. In fact, men liked to joke
about her large ass. They called her "Bum Richards,"
the name of a colorful football coach of a famed NFL
team. In Iowa City we became friends after she had
recently broken up with her boyfriend, a philandering
novelist, and I was having problems with the Sioux
City Swede. We talked about our man troubles. We
admitted our defeats and spanked one another with
our critical observations. Once, impatient with my
negativity, she said to me, "What? Lost your mittens?
Then you are a naughty kitten! And you shall have
no pie."

We chastised one another with the "Three Little
Kittens" nursery rhyme quite often. "Oh mother dear,
we greatly fear, our mittens we have soiled. What?
Soiled your mittens! Then you are naughty kittens!"

Soon we were calling one another by the same
pet name. We addressed one another as "Mitten."
We exchanged notes, with the salutation "To Mitten"
and we signed them "Love, Mitten" or "*Your* Mitten."
We recognized our vulnerabilities as women and felt

strengthened by aligning ourselves in this way. Two Mittens against the world.

This nickname appears in two books she had signed for me. In her first collection she wrote, "To Mitten, the only one who came out to California." And she signed her next one, "For you, Maria, in honor of black ice and long distance hearts—love Mitten.

Recently, Cindy Sue sold all of her papers to the University of Texas at Austin. The index lists her correspondence to and from many writers, and includes my name. Perhaps some of these Mitten letters are in that collection.

When she had left Iowa for a teaching job in Arcata, California, I sold some items, a collection of rare antique Quimper bowls and plates, from my French grandmom, a tiny cash pot that I'd never see again, and I flew out to visit her. She was renting a cottage in a little California town called Trinidad. I sent a postcard to Veronica from Trinidad and she thought I had escaped to the Caribbean Islands right off Venezuela, but I told her that I was in hippie-dippie California. I explained that on one street in the small town of Arcata there were seven different shops selling homemade soap made from sheep tallow!

I had great admiration for Cindy Sue's dedication to her craft. She got up in the morning with her cup of coffee and faced her typewriter. She was getting noticed, and it was encouraging to me to watch her hatching out of her self-made egg. And she expressed her admiration for me too. She encouraged me to apply for a fellowship at the Fine Arts Work Center in Provincetown, and her faith in me gave me confidence. But when I showed her my own fiction, she told me, "You should *not* be writing stories. You're a poet." A year later Houghton Mifflin would accept my manuscript of poems, *Reckless Wedding*, but despite Cindy Sue's warnings, I continued to write fiction.

On my visit to California, I saw how her charismatic nature had a destructive effect on other people's lives. We drove north to Portland to see an old friend of hers. She had brought her dog with us, and she let it off its leash without thinking of her host. The dog ran into his house full of cats! The kitties climbed the walls tearing claw marks in the wallpaper and shredding a couple oil painting canvases that were hanging on display. Her friend had recently cut off two fingers with a table saw and his hand was bandaged. His injuries were throbbing when Cindy Sue asked him to look at her radiator which she had filled with only tap water. Temperatures were dropping and she needed him to add antifreeze. I watched her put her pretty face an inch from him as she asked him to do the favor. He struggled to unscrew the cap of the radiator with only one hand. It was rusted tight. She was always very successful at getting what she wanted.

Her cottage in Trinidad was charming. It had a fireplace and she would make fires to warm the chilly nights. But Cindy Sue didn't buy her own cord of wood. She waited until after dark and in her nightgown and bare feet, she ran across the lawn to steal splits from her neighbor's woodpile. "Is this what West Virginians do?" I said. "Steal from your neighbor's woodpile?"

"I don't take too much."

"Not too much at one time. But day after day?"

"He won't miss it," she said.

But after my complaints, the next day she went outside to her neighbor's woodpile with a tray of muffins she had baked just for him.

During my visit, we went to the movies to see the Donald Sutherland version of *Invasion of the Body Snatchers*. We enjoyed the movie but afterward we started to recognize that everyone seemed suspicious. We noticed suspect pedestrians on the street and said, "He's a pod!" Then she and I sensed another paranormal transformation too. There was a sexual component to our friendship that had not yet been ironed out.

And in Trinidad, I was surprised to learn that no one was allowed in the ocean. The waters were too rough. Every beach had warning signs that said NO SWIMMING. My relationship with Cindy Sue had tumultuous whirlpools and breakers. Like the dangerous surf outside, I felt the rising tide of a dangerous attraction and wanted to dive into it. One night, she made a fire and we sat before it. Eventually we went into the bedroom. The rental had a brand-new mattress that she told me was "100 percent foam rubber." I didn't like the idea of a foam-rubber mattress, but I was surprised to find that it was firm but strangely buoyant. The two of us floated on a cloud of foam rubber, at a strange suspended elevation. She started kissing me with that little pointy chin thrust out.

"Don't touch my triggers," I said.

"Your triggers?"

"I mean, don't touch my *on* and *off* buttons, or, you know, we'll have to go through with it," I told her. But she didn't listen to me.

We had sex together only once, engaging in sisterly masturbation. I was surprised to see that she was very shy, with a sexual repression that she blamed on her southern roots. To touch herself she had to lie prone, with her hand between her legs, and her face buried in the pillow so I couldn't watch her in a state of arousal. We both knew we were engaging in some sort of mockery, but I liked it. I liked the smell of her, sweet and yeasty, like rising bread.

The next morning, she was embarrassed and said, "That can't happen again!"

Oh, mother dear, we greatly fear
Our mittens we have soiled

Back east, in Cambridge, we once stopped at a bar on the way to a book-signing party in Brookline. Her appearance in a working-class tavern caused immediate fisticuffs between barflies competing for her attentions. A fight broke out between two young men and Cindy Sue took an elbow. She was bopped in the face. She got a serious shiner. I wrote a poem about the dramatic bar brawl that was published in *Poetry Magazine* later that year.

> The dog has snapped its leash again.
> The dark is sheer
> As a blueprint
> As night plans more nights.
> A woman with a black eye is going to a
>   party . . .
> And
>   At the races, I bet on the horse named
>   Fascination, and it won.
>   I wore your coat. It fit me well. Mirrors
>   flattered me.
>   The wind caressed me with freshness.

Then snow began to fall. All winter I deceived
   you and conspired with snow.
You were gone. Your address was false.
The key would not fit in the door. The key
   was a trick. . . .
And
There is a footprint
Love makes
When it walks out of the body.
An imprint so deep
Snow can't fill it,
Like the darkness in a room
Behind white curtains.

Ray Blake was a brilliant Iowa kid who came to the
University of Iowa as a student and who became a staff
writer at the *Daily Iowan*. He worked at the city desk,
a term I found hilarious out there in a rural hamlet.
Ray Blake wrote investigative stories about municipal catastrophes and the petty crimes that occasion-
ally cropped up in the back alleys of a small town. He
went on to jobs at major newspapers before he became
a novelist. With his first novel, critics compared him
to Sherwood Anderson and William Faulkner. In one
novel he writes about a female ghost who follows him
everywhere, but never gets close. I recognized myself
in her. It was something I was ashamed of.

When Ray's photograph appeared in a glamorous
foldout in the *New Yorker*, he was standing beside my
major influence, Edna O'Brien. The two of them standing shoulder to shoulder made me queasy. The picture
was photoshopped, but I never would have agreed to
appear in a photograph beside Edna—I would never be

so confident. I might kneel down before her to stroke her insteps, and to lick of the soles of her feet, but I could never stand beside her, as if we were equals.

When we first met, Ray was a slightly gawky-looking youth, with features that he was growing into. But in fact, he *would* grow into them, and he soon emerged as very handsome. But as a kid he had walked through a plate-glass door, and he had a dramatic scar running down one side of his face. He was awarded several thousand dollars in insurance money, to save for college, but his folks ended up using it for other expenses, and he never saw a penny. He might have been my boyfriend but I wasn't over the Sioux City Swede. Ray was a few years younger than I was, and he wasn't very tall. He was just my height. For some reason both his youth and his dubious height were obstacles. Being my same height, Ray could look me directly in the eyes. He could *judge* what he saw before him. I avoided his advances, but he gave me rides on the back of his motorcycle, a Triumph Trophy Trail. When I told Ray that I was pregnant with the Swede's baby, he took me for a medicinal ride on his dirt bike. We hoped that the Triumph's bumps and vibrations humming through my pelvis might cause my period to come.

When I was working as a cashier at Iowa Book and Supply, Ray came in to the store to give me a little break from the deadening routine. At that job we had a Nazi manager and we were told to "punch out" each time we used the toilet. For my own entertainment, I had printed the name "Marianne Faithfull" on my ID tag. Baby Boomers who recognized the name would laugh, but most Iowans who came into the store didn't seem to remember her hit song: *It is the evening of the day, I sit and watch the children play, smiling faces I can see, but not for me, I sit and watch as tears go by.* After work one day, Ray invited the faux Marianne, to his apartment, and we made love for the first time. He was very manly and sweet, and for those minutes I couldn't recall the Groucho Marx caveat, "I refuse to join any club that would have me as a member." "Marianne" was happy to be with Ray Blake. Yet I was shocked to hear him say, after rolling off me, "I guess this means we're in love."

I decided to end his fantasy about being in love with me. With my lipstick I scribbled on his apartment door: "Marianne Faithfull R.I.P." I believed the note would end the silly charade, but when he came home and saw my message he thought it was a suicide note. He searched everywhere for me. He was mortified. He really loved me.

On his birthday, we went to a sports bar to celebrate. We sat down at the bar rail and ordered rounds of bourbon, with six-ounce beer chasers. As we got drunker, we stared at our reflections in the mirrored tiles behind the shelves of bottles. We discussed our future options and recognized how far we had to go to achieve what we wanted. I told him about a poem I was writing for him: "Old lovers deny that it was ever serious / Seasoned journalists identify faces at the windows of a burning building / And only the names are saved." Just then, two of the mirrored tiles peeled away from the wall and fell. Another square bent forward, arrested for a second in its gluey caulk, before it flopped to the floor. The rest of the silvery checkerboard came down, each tile popping loose, noisy as a sudden downpour splashing against the stainless steel sinks and rows of bottles. Watching our reflections explode was a comment on our relationship. "That's more than seven years bad luck!" the bartender commiserated.

"Well, Happy Birthday," I said.

Leaving the bar, Ray bent down to pick up a lost mitten on the street. I thought of Cindy Sue and the nickname we had shared. *What? Lost your mittens, then you are very bad kittens.*

With world-weariness or with the pathos of unrequited love, Ray said, "Put this on," handing me the single mitten.

I inserted my hand.

"Fits like a glove," he said. "Too bad we don't have a set."

ELLIOT WINN was one year behind me at Iowa. We liked one another instantly because we sensed our seriousness about our work. He knew I was nothing to sneeze at, and I too sensed he had the savvy required of an emerging "greatness." His critics said, "He has a facility," as if being a fine stylist came easily and it shouldn't be considered much of an accomplishment. He was a Californian, and was just as out of place as I was in the rural flatlands of Iowa. When he brought me back to his apartment in Iowa City, I was amused to see that he kept his vodka shoved across the ice trays. I was very wet-behind-the-ears to have not yet learned to put my booze in the freezer. Elliot was a sophisticate!

A year later, we were both fellows at the Fine Arts Work Center in Provincetown. Elliot wasn't "out" yet. He was sitting on the fence. His sexual orientation was secondary to the driving force that pushed him. He was becoming a powerful writer. At that time he still dated women, and he told me about his affair with Jennie Fields, a very successful creative director of advertising at DDB Needham Worldwide where her credits included the creation of famous McDonald's jingles. She later became a novelist, and her first novel, *Lily Beach,* had scenes where her female character had sex with a man who used kitchen vegetables to stimulate her to orgasm. A rumor circulated that John Irving had named the character of Garp's mother, Jennie Fields, in *The World According to Garp*, after her. She was a girl who got around.

But I was glad when Elliot started dating my boss, a handsome restaurateur at a waterfront café where I was a waitress. When I opened the place in the morning, brewing coffee and chopping strawberries, both men would show up for their caffeine fix in rumpled clothes and with their hair still sharked from long nights of lovemaking.

It took Elliot a few more years to be completely comfortable about admitting his gay lifestyle. In 1991 he appeared on the NPR talk show *Fresh Air,* hosted by Terry Gross, to talk about his new novel. When she asked him directly about being a "gay" writer, he didn't want to be pigeonholed like that. His novel should be judged for its literary merits, not for anything else. I didn't find fault in his inability to come forward. It was like when my teacher had called my poem "too female," and I understood that I was being judged by my sex, and not by what I had written.

In Provincetown Elliot and I had shared the same work ethic. We made a deal that we would work for six hours every day, from eight A.M. to two P.M. and then we'd meet at the Governor Bradford tavern to play a couple rounds of pool. I loved meeting him beside the chalk stand and together we'd chalk our cues and chalk our hands. Slapping our palms to release extra powder was a wonderful feeling. It didn't just mean we were starting a game of eight-ball, but it meant we had completed a whole day of writing. As the clouds of powder drifted over us, our creative energies were released in a big sigh of relief. I had to get my daughter from the grade school at three o'clock, so we kept to our timeline pretty well. Our focus was always our work. But Elliot once told me something that I took as a compliment. He said, "When I'm with you *magical* things happen." Once, at dusk, we had driven out to the Cape Cod Light. The oldest lighthouse on Cape Cod, built in 1797, the gorgeous white brick tower had been authorized by George Washington. When Elliot and I went out, the lighthouse still had its old Fresnel lens, with its romantic, sweeping scarf of light. The Fresnel was soon to be replaced with a high tech VRB-25 LED beacon that flashed in repetitions, without its charming circling arc. At the lighthouse we got out of the car to dance. I had my tape deck pounding "Train in Vain" by the Clash, and Elliot and I danced with abandon, washed by wide pie slices of swirling light. Our youth was at its zenith, and everything was at stake at that very instant. We were powerful, and felt that we could dictate what we wanted for all eternity; we knew that art was beauty with the same repetitive certainty of the Fresnel lens circling around us.

Another time, Elliot came with me to swim at Corn Hill beach, named for the spot where the pilgrims had vandalized the winter stores of the Pamet Indians. When we arrived, there were thousands of swallows sweeping over the dunes, veering to the right and left and skimming above our heads. The swarms dive-bombed us so we had to duck. At the end of summer the swallows collect en masse before they start their migration, but Elliot attributed the spectacle to something magical. He said, "You attract these phenomenons!"

Elliot wrote a story that was highly recognized and that appeared in *Best American Stories* and in several anthologies. His story describes a character who crashes through a sliding glass door and is fatally injured. I can't remember if I had ever mentioned to Elliot my friend Ray's story about walking through a plate glass window, or if Elliot had invented the character on his own. But in Provincetown, I was reading Turgenev, starting with his novel *First Love*. That winter I read all of Turgenev, his novel *Torrents of Spring* was my favorite, and I was also reading Gogol, and more Chekhov. I tried to get Elliot to borrow *First Love*, but he said a very telling remark. He said, "I only want to be reading what's getting published right now!"

He loaned me his brand new copy of Doctorow's *Loon Lake*. Reading the book, I dropped it in the bathtub. I returned the book to Elliot with all its pages swollen so that the covers wouldn't shut! I should have replaced it with a new copy. I made it up to him when

Elliot won the Pulitzer Prize for his new novel that had been inspired by Edith Wharton. We met for drinks to celebrate and I gave him a little gift, a bottle of Elizabeth Arden Green Tea body lotion. It was to repay him for *Loon Lake*. We joked that the emollient concoction would be a defense against aging, but most of all, it would make a great bedside lubricant for jerking off.

THE MAYOR

Before he was diagnosed, Giovanni sent me a selfie. He took the picture as he was lying on his back on the sidewalk outside his building on the first spring day of the year. The sun has warmed the concrete. His black cat, The Mayor, is sitting on his chest, purring. Each time he lifts the cat off, it comes back and crouches at his collar bone. Scientists have discovered that animals can sense illness in their pet owners. They even have cancer-sniffing dogs at oncology clinics across the country. The Mayor won't give up; he kneads Giovanni with his claws retracted, right where his fourth stage tumor would soon be discovered. The cat gives warning. The Mayor seems to know about the ghost-girl in the kitten-hat. She has left behind a dangerous idea, a living fear multiplying in Giovanni.

THE CRIMSON

River-rat came to meet me on my own turf in Cambridge. Once he was in town for a meeting with a writer, Alan Lightman, who worked at MIT. Lightman wrote a book called *Einstein's Dreams,* a novel that seemed to be a hybrid of science talk and fantasy. The book examines what we understand about "time." Time is more often a subjective experience, rather than a literal ticking of the clock. I felt that way often, during my brief interludes with River-rat. Hours were not sharply defined. The world we entered was a timeless ectoplasm of sexual osmosis, of desires that slithered and coiled like amoeba. I'm sure that Alan Lightman's meetings with River-rat were very different from mine.

I sat on the window seat in a top floor suite at the Hyatt Regency, looking down at the Charles River. I was wearing only my panties, a tiny black lisp of silk that Edna O'Brien would approve of. In my nakedness, before the plate glass window that revealed the river view, I thought of Robert Henri. *There are backgrounds so well made that you have no consciousness of them.*

River-rat watched me from an armchair and said, "I could look at that forever."

"It's not much compared to the Hudson," I said. But I told him about the Harvard Bridge, the longest span over the Charles. In 1958 a fraternity pledge named Oliver Smoot lay down repeatedly on the Harvard Bridge between Cambridge and Boston so that his fraternity brothers could use his height to measure the length of the bridge. One "smoot" equaled five feet seven inches. The bridge's length was measured to be 364.4 "smoots."

I often jabbered like this before sex. With direct observations, I tried to find something in common with him.

And right then, on the narrow slice of the Charles, there were a couple of heavyweight crew teams rowing past from the Newell Boathouse, presenting a quaint and often romanticized vision. So I told River-rat how Harvard got its famous school color "crimson." In 1858 a crew member purchased six red handkerchiefs just before a regatta to distinguish the Harvard team from its competitors. During the race, team members wiped the sweat from their brows with the cloths that turned from red to deep *crimson*. News of the colored scarves spread, and the signature Harvard color was born. I said, "This pompous institution got its famous color from jock sweat!"

"I'm not talking about those crew boats. I'm talking about those legs—" he said.

I said, "What are we doing here?"

"Look. We've discussed this before. Our expectations—"

"'Expectation' is desire with a PhD. I don't need a diploma. My dreams dropped out of school—"

"Yeah, yeah."

"Tell me that to my face."

"What?"

"Say, 'Yeah, yeah' to my face."

We had sex. It lasted as long as it took the crew boats to glide past the Salt-and-Pepper Bridge. Afterward we got dressed and took a cab to a restaurant on Brattle Street. I was surprised to see that River-rat was tight when he paid the driver. The trip wasn't very far, but I always tip cabbies extra for the time they spend in bad traffic, and not just for the metered mile. The "metered mile" made me think of the sex—our time together is measured by the distance between us, and by a destination that is never mentioned. I joked with River-rat, "How many 'smoots' from here to there? From me to you?"

Lightman tells us that Einstein believed that time was circular and that people are forced to repeat their conquests or their failures. Einstein also believed that time can "stand still." My visits with River-rat are hourless. One minute or the next makes no difference. Each frozen span of eros an evergreen perpetuity.

Doctrine of Correspondence

At the hospital, we asked to be taken off the list so that preachers and priests would stop "popping in" to Giovanni's room in the Transplant Unit. In his condition, Giovanni couldn't defend himself against Christian chitchat.

I've never had a God. No religion. My pope was Christopher Hitchens. I respected his books *God is Not Great* and *The Portable Atheist*. But when he said that single malt was a fad, and Johnny Walker Black is the only scotch he drinks, I, too, became a believer.

My saints were poets: Blake, Dickinson, Neruda, Cavafy, and a few others. And I found a spiritual connection in the lyrics of the country song, "The Highwayman," that asserts there is an afterlife, even for ne'er-do-wells. "I slipped and fell into the wet concrete below / They buried me in that great tomb that knows no sound / But I am still around." "The bastards hung me in the spring of twenty-five / But I am still alive." "Or I may simply be a single drop of rain / But I will remain / And I'll be back again, and again, and again . . ."

But facing the New Normal of a life within Giovanni's cancer regimen, I needed even more spiritual

guidance. In yesterday's obit pages, I found a denom-
ination I could believe in called "Soupism." Bernard
Mayes invented it. Mayes is famous for having started
the first suicide hotline with one red telephone in 1961.

Once an Anglican priest, Mayes abandoned his
Christian faith and said, "There are no gods, no magic,
no final judgment, and no grand plan. Everything from
planets to humans is composed of tiny particles, energy
and nothing else. All the particles are always moving
and interacting with each other as in a 'soup.'" Our
immortality comes from our interactions with everything. He said, "We are the sheets from the cotton of
the field or the wool of sheep; plastics boiled from min-
erals dug from the Earth, concrete and metal poured
from the rocks of the planet or the oil of ancient vege-
tation; all moving within the endless interchange from
which our bodies are derived and from which others
are already being born. Never does the process cease;
never does it fail us."

Mayes's philosophy is rooted in "scientific materi-
alism." But "Soupism" reminded me of Ralph Waldo
Emerson's doctrine of correspondence. Emerson's tran-
scendentalism is radically humanistic. He believed that
"a correspondent revolution in all things will attend the
influx of the spirit." In this give and take, the "Over-
soul" emerges.

I don't know what River-rat believes in. But Joseph
Mitchell's love of the poison sink of New York harbor,
with its diversity of toxins, sunken wrecks, manhole
covers, sludge bubbles, fish eggs, and wild flowers,
makes me believe he was a Transcendentalist or a
Soupist, and I'm in good company.

THE-RAPIST

In my life, I have once or twice seen a therapist. It's never been very helpful to me except when, years ago, Dr. Poseur suggested I divorce my first husband. Another therapist explained that the complex emotional presentation of "love-hate syndrome" is a common phenomenon. Unhappy partners, long-term spouses, mistresses, or jilted paramours exhibit it. It's often a symptom of a broad spectrum psychiatric condition called "borderline personality disorder." The love-hate response is a powerful entrapment. Hate is fed by unrequited desire, and a strong attachment spikes even higher by each counterstrike of your lover's icy dismissal. Love and hate feed off one another. My mother had lifelong feelings of love-hate for the Arrow Collar Man who had jilted her. After two kids, he took off. He came back only once, and knocked her up again. She called her out-of-wedlock son, "The Immaculate Conception." He was the un-son, and like the character in my novel *The Arrow Collar Man*, his obsession about his missing father ruined his life. And the Arrow Collar Man's departure had lifelong aftereffects for our mother. It threatened her self-image.

His disappearance had made her feel nonexistent. I started to recognize this love-hate pattern with River-rat. I wondered if a preexisting trait for sex obsession is passed down through generations. I see my son's trouble with women, and I fear I have infected him with my DNA, with my own genes that predispose me to "obsessive desire."

I spoke to a therapist about my obsession with my editor.

He said, "Obsession is addiction."

"An addiction?"

"You're an addict. We know that."

It's true that I'm an alcoholic. And I was once addicted to morphine suppositories. Using morphine suppositories creates a heavenly blotter effect; the drug introduced directly to the bowel absorbs all pain and anxiety, as you melt from the waist up. I got my stash from a doctor at the University of Iowa who took me out on "dates." He was an addict too, but he could see his patients and do his rounds at the hospital every day with no telltale sign of his habit. Using suppositories, he didn't have any tracks. He wore short-sleeved shirts in the hot Iowa summer and no one could tell he was singing to the birds.

The therapist said, "This relationship you have is just a fantasy."

"It's a fantasy? But he shows up in the flesh."

"A fantasy is what we create to invent meaning in a suspect relationship. Love. Commitment. Those are *our* inventions."

"If I'm addicted to River-rat, my tolerance keeps going up."

"Tests have shown that obsessive disorder and drug addiction trigger the same electrical synapses in the brain. We call it the 'reward circuit.' It's in the prefrontal cortex and certain parts of the thalamus. It's called the 'pleasure center' of the brain. Desire manifests in very pleasing somatic symptoms. You don't want to satisfy a desire; you want to keep it cooking. Because, you see, the 'reward circuit' can disrupt the 'punishment circuit.' The punishment circuit is a network of neurons that affect your adrenal glands that release hormones that create a self-protective 'fight or flight' response. So in fact, with your 'punishment circuit' disconnected, you can never adequately defend yourself against your obsessive behavior."

The doctor was very well-meaning, but his explanations seemed burdensome instead of palliative. He told me, "You look different today. Less tension around your mouth."

"Really?"

"Therapists have to read faces."

My face is the powdered glass collected with adhesive tape at bomb investigations.

I told him, "You know, 'editor' rhymes with the word 'predator.'"

"When did you realize that?"

"I like word play. I'm a writer, you know."

And the term "therapist" can be deconstructed. Before visiting the shrink, I would say to my friends, "I've got an appointment with 'the-rapist' today. I think I'll cancel it."

River-rat once told me that he had enjoyed the Broadway show *The Lion King*. I was surprised by such an admission. I remembered that Proust, who wrote about obsession and who had once described little biscuits as love objects, once had portrayed a character who suddenly realized that his new paramour was "not even his type." (Likes the *Lion King*?) How could I be smitten with someone who attended blockbuster Broadway shows?

But my therapist kept insisting that my obsession was an "addiction."

I thought about famous examples of this, such as the movie *Play Misty for Me.* In that film, an obsessed woman stalks Clint Eastwood, a radio host. Her love object shirks her advances. But she won't give up. Film critic Roger Ebert said, "She is something like flypaper; the more you struggle against her personality, the more tightly you're held." River-rat is no Eastwood. He never wears cowboy boots, and never speaks in Dirty Harry monosyllables, but he's someone who can dismiss a woman with "cruel efficiency," as Ebert says about Eastwood.

> —*Why don't you see if you can get the fire started?* *she asks him.*
>
> —*All right, he says.*
>
> —*There are some matches right next to it.*
>
> —*All right.*
>
> —*Don't you like me? she asks.*
>
> —*You're a very nice girl, he says.*
>
> —*But who needs nice girls? And you don't want to complicate your life.*

—*That's exactly right.*

—*But that's no reason we shouldn't sleep together tonight if we feel like it, she says.*

—*What happened to that discussion we had last time? You know, the deal about no strings and all that?*

—*There are no strings, but I never said anything . . . about not coming back for seconds, did I?*

—*That's right. You didn't.*

—*When will I see you?*

—*If you want to keep playing these games, okay, but . . .*

—*Do you know your nostrils flare out into little wings when you're mad?*

The woman in *Play Misty for Me* is to be pitied, I guess. But I also remember another example. The Bauhaus textile artist Anni Albers, the widow of abstract painter Josef Albers, famous for his work called *Homage to the Square*, had in her later days become quite attracted to the movie star Maximilian Schell. Although he was thirty years younger than she, he wooed her and encouraged her, expressing great admiration for her husband. His loyalty to the deceased artist impressed her, but most of all she enjoyed the attentions of the handsome actor. She lived for his phone calls and visits, and each time he showed up she gave him gifts of Josef Alber's valuable work. Then Maximilian proposed an idea: He told Anni that if she gave him fifty paintings by her husband, a multimillion-dollar collection, he promised to open a museum in his empty house in Berlin. He got into serious discussions about Anni's will, but it appeared to her closest friends that Schell was trying to steal the paintings. She came to her senses but she didn't blame Maximilian for courting her. She understood how her enrapture with him had been necessary. She said, "You know, I need the obsession to *live*."

I understood her rationale. Obsession is an energizing force. But sometimes I worried that my obsession with River-rat was making me "lose my mind." Yet everything I felt about River-rat only *sharpened* my mind. Every avoidance, every unaddressed longing, didn't dull my thinking. Each of his despairing remarks, each dismissal, awakened my perceptions, and turned over the leaves for me. I adapted.

If we tear the wings from a fly, it crawls.

MOLD FREE

After bone marrow transplant Giovanni has to live a "restricted lifestyle." His new immune system isn't in gear yet. In fact he took drugs to waylay transitioning of his new immune system, because his donor stem cells *attack* every inch and corner of his body, causing graft versus host disease. And he could not yet be vaccinated again with the same vaccines he had had as a baby. Measles. Diphtheria. Mumps. Whooping cough. He was vulnerable to everything. During this transition, he cannot be with people, other than a few designated "family" members who have been trained to wear masks and gloves and to monitor our own sore throats and sniffles, to keep germs at bay. Without a mask, we must keep at least six feet away from the patient, behind an invisible boundary line. He was admitted to grad school but had to defer his enrollment for an indeterminate amount of time. He cannot attend classes, take public transportation, or enter supermarkets or libraries, eat in restaurants, or get takeout food. He cannot go to shows and play with his band. He must avoid a crowd. His sole pastime is to walk *alone* on an open sidewalk, keeping his distance from other pedestrians. Most important, upon discharge after months in the hospital, he could not return to his apartment in Cambridge. His current apartment was a seething mire of fungus and microscopic organisms. After his transplant, he had to reside in a unit "free of mold and contagions." A life with restrictions was life in an aquarium. Cancer PR invented a pithy phrase for it all. They call it the "New Normal."

A colonial town with decrepit triple-decker housing, most of Cambridge has buildings that are more than one hundred years old; some places are even hundreds of years old. Few residences didn't have mold and residual grime as a structural component. Mold was the secret lattice and plaster, a living compound, an all-purpose organic spackle that adhered to the beams and studs and kept these antique structures from collapse. But I had to find a mold-free apartment. It would not be easy.

Giovanni's new girlfriend, Sandrine, accompanied me in my search to find a mold-free apartment. She was pursuing a graduate degree in "brain disorder special education" at Harvard, and we had to synchronize our watches so I could meet her outside of her class schedule. I would do anything to work with her. She was the cure for my son's bouts with yellow fever. When looking for a mold-free apartment, I started to think of this woman as a "mold-free girlfriend"; she was that perfect. She presented no dangers to my son. Sandrine was the Ivory Soap partner who would nurture my son back to health. But even with Sandrine beside me, I sensed the girl on the ghost bike tooling along behind us.

We met a landlord outside a triple decker near
Davis Square. He had a first-floor unit; although first-
floor apartments are not desirable unless there are
bars on the windows. I didn't see any bars. But we
decided to take a look. The apartment had the aura
of a place that was recently vacated by down-and-out
residents. The last tenants had left behind a great deal
of trash. The three rooms were ten by ten, tight as
lockers on the TV show *Storage Wars* where inves-
tors fight over abandoned items. A stained coffee table,
an overstuffed chair, its torn cushions spilling matted
fluff, a kitchen chair with broken spindles, a noxious
futon folded over to make an unsteady sofa, and piles
of kiddy paraphernalia: a high chair without its tray, a
tall blue diaper pail still reeking of bleach. An empty
"baby bouncer" that was left in place in a doorway
gave a crazy poignancy to the picture.

Sandrine wanted to have Giovanni's baby.

A Fitchburg girl believes in traditional things. Marriage and children. It would be an uphill battle for her.
She faced many years of PET scans before Giovanni's
full remission could be ensured. Any future she had
of becoming a mother was cryopreserved in a liquid
nitrogen tank at minus 321 Fahrenheit, with a yearly
bill of $500 from New England Cryogenics.

But first we had to find a home for them. And
there, on every wall of the storage vault apartment
there was a green patina. Aspergillus, Cladosporium,
and Stachybotrys are common in households, but any
black patches could be toxic mold. The ancient wallpaper was stained with pastures of moisture; the base-
boards and wainscoting were edged in suspect grime.
The place was a mold emporium.

I found a local real estate agent named Dez DeSilva, who listened to my problems. An agent with the name "Desiree" was sure to find a love nest for Sandrine and Giovanni. But she said, "You want a mold-free apartment? Then you're talking about a *new* apartment. That's going to require an investment. I think I might have something, but it's way over your budget. And did I say it's in Somerville?"

One town over, Somerville is the new Cambridge, the same way that Brooklyn is the new Manhattan, and Queens is the new Brooklyn. In these big cities, working class communities were morphing into high-end neighborhoods. I met the agent at a renovated condo in Union Square, knowing it was going to cost something. With his restricted life, Giovanni couldn't be employed. Since he could not work, I was paying for almost everything during Giovanni's ordeal with borrowed funds from my second mortgage, and debts were amassing. He was approved to receive disability checks and food stamps because he could not work, but it was less than $700 a month. He was sick when he turned twenty-six and was kicked off health insurance. He had to apply for Obamacare. There was a lot of red tape and the government insurance policy rejected payment for his Neupogen injections that cost thousands of dollars. Neupogen is a growth factor that stimulates the production, maturation, and activation of white blood cells or neutrophils. It is classified as a "colony stimulating factor." It stimulates the release of neutrophils from the bone marrow. Each time I heard words like "neutrophils" they gained a magical, or almost spiritual music. But in his treatment, he was often prescribed drugs with price tags of four and five figures. He's also taking CellCept, a drug used for the prophylaxis of rejection in patients receiving an allogeneic transplant, and it comes with a sticker price of thousands of dollars. Thankfully, most of his medical bills were finally covered. It was up to me to find a mold-free apartment. That means New. That means big bucks. But I turned to Blake's Proverbs of Hell: "You never know what is enough unless you know what is more than enough."

We met Dez, the realtor, at Somerville, and again we entered a unit that had not yet been cleared out. A woman was in the process of packing up her world in the throes of a mean divorce, and her possessions were in waist-high piles. Movers were wrapping her glassware in clean sheets of blank newsprint as she collected her precious bric-a-brac and mementos with tears in her eyes. She told us, "Don't mind me. I'm starting over." We had entered familiar ruins. Someone's marriage had failed. But I was pleased to see that the apartment was brand new. It had big windows facing south, and the place was filled with light. The walls were freshly painted, and every room had perfect wood flooring. There were granite counter tops and high-end appliances, and the apartment's clean surfaces shimmered when juxtaposed to the current tenant's personal tragedy. It was clear that we had arrived at the *end of something* that was, in fact, a new beginning for the victim. The unit felt uplifting to me because it was christened by another's search for independence and self-awareness. "I'm starting over," she had said, claiming victory. And there wasn't a sign of mold.

The Pilot

I met my present husband in Provincetown the same year I published my first story in the "Pilots in the Cockpit" issue of *Playgirl* magazine. The coincidence is important because the attractive man I would one day marry was not only tall and dark-haired, but he wore a blue blazer with an appliqué that said "American Airlines" on the interior pocket of his jacket. The blue blazer was official attire for a captain of a Boeing 737. Of course he wasn't a pilot; he was a poet. He had found the jacket in a thrift store in Greenwich, Connecticut.

In my writing life there have always been "pilots in the cockpit," but with this one, I had met my match. When we first met he was living with a painter, a lithe brunette who looked like Ava Gardner. His many girlfriends often looked like movie stars, and in his first collection of poems, he wrote invectives about them. In diverse lines, he said:

"I put a spell on her by holding back / She
        became another thing I saved myself from."
"We love someone more fragile than ourselves /
        but hurt her as the world hurts us."

"I don't want to hear any more about love /
unless it's a particularly one-sided love /
possessive love / love immobilized by need /
love with no chance of fulfillment."

"It must have been that last drink that made
me think of love as a relief / instead of the
relief of nothing to love."

His poems were misanthropic, even misogynistic,
but his cynicism was a challenge to me. It turned me on.

Before our first date, we talked on the telephone. I
said, "What are you doing tonight?"

"I'm listening to 'Sports Huddle' with Eddie Andelman on WBZ."

I had not yet heard of Boston Badmouth Eddie
Andelman, but a poet who listened to sports radio was
a whole different ball of wax. I liked the hetero aspect
of such an admission and the combo: poet and sports
aficionado was intriguing, as I tried to round it out in
my mind.

"What are *you* doing?" he said.

"Talking to you," I said. We both understood it
was more than just talk. I knew that he lived with a
painter who looked like a movie star, but I invited him
to dinner at my house. (I planned to make authentic French fare, beef bourguignonne with baby carrots
and pearl onions!)

I also invited my neighbor, the poet Stanley Kunitz,
and fiction writer Michael Cunningham. Stanley lived
at 32 Commercial Street, and I lived one door away
at number 34. Stanley often came to my house with
a jar of martinis he already had mixed at his home.

Approaching winter in Provincetown, the streets are empty. My modest, messy, uninsulated house became a salon for a shambling group of artists, fellows from the Fine Arts Work Center like Michael, Denis Johnson, the painter Sam Messer, and others. Poet Alan Dugan was my mentor that year. Kunitz was an imperial presence, but Dugan was my soul mate. I felt a deep connection to his poems and he helped me with my pages. But both these older poets showed me a different sort of attention. Stanley Kunitz acted as a matchmaker and encouraged the "pilot" to pursue me. He said, "Her place will be the 'nerve center' in Provincetown this winter." I didn't understand what he was talking about, but I remembered what Stanley had told me at the end of the summer.

I had been swimming in the bay across the street, when Stanley called to me from his front porch. He waved a silver pitcher back and forth to invite me over. He said, "I've got martinis!" I was still soaking wet in just my swimsuit. He ushered me inside the house and his wife, Elise, asked me to sit down on a velvet settee. After several cocktails, I stood up. I saw that my wet bathing suit had left an imprint on the sofa.

Stanley said with delight, "Look! She left her bottom for us!" I was horrified to see two distinct cheek stains on the velvet cushion. But Stanley had great affection for me *and* my bottom. And Dugan, who advised me on the work I showed him, also paid attention to me in other ways. He noticed a small mole on the back of my neck, right above my collar. I told him I wanted to get it removed and he said, "Are you crazy? Don't do that. It's a beauty mark!"

Both these men encouraged my writing, but they engaged with me on a different plane from my work center peers. The other young writers were men.

But Stanley and I had made a deeper connection that autumn. We both had been caring for my landlord, Fifi Bergman, who was dying of cancer. In the late '40s, Fifi was Richard Avedon's first model and she had appeared in *Junior Bazaar*, and on the covers of *Collier's* and *McCall's*. Avedon said, "She was my first model, and there has never been another like her. An intelligent beauty. She brought wit to every photograph. Irresistible. You just had to love her." In later years, Fifi became a professional cook and was assistant to food critic Michael Field. With him she worked on the Time-Life Books series, *Foods of the World*.

She warned me: "A woman's life begins with glamour, and then we have to start homemaking and cooking!" With his jar of martinis, Stanley came over every night to see Fifi who had refused to return to New York at the end of the season to join her philandering husband, Lewis Bergman, the editor of the *New York Times Sunday Magazine*. She stayed with me. The approaching winter didn't faze her. She told Stanley that it was my "spirit" that kept her alive. Because I was a single mother pursuing a writer's life, I reminded her of her early years as a young model seeking her own independence. In her final months, she told me she was reliving all the dreams she had had in her two-stage career. She liked having me around to listen to her retell it. My importance to her also had impressed Stanley. But he was annoyed when my daughter, Annabel, got a kitten and with affection for our elderly neighbor, she had named the kitten "Stanley." When she played with the kitty, calling it by its name, Stanley came to the backyard fence and said, "Are you talking to me or to that ball of fluff?"

The night of my dinner with the "pilot" and friends, I was surprised to learn that the pilot had brought his oyster knife. He stood at the kitchen sink to do the chore. It requires a refined tenacity, and a good bit of strength. I nestled beside him to watch him unhinge the tight shells of two dozen bivalves, carefully cutting the adductor muscle. I balanced an icy plate as he arranged the briny treasures in a full circle. These delicious prehistoric creatures, sweet dollops in bony teardrops, seemed to represent both the past and future of my every female endeavor!

When Stanley asked for another lemon peel for his martini, and I couldn't find one, Michael secretly searched my trash basket to find a discarded lemon rind. He took it to the sink to rinse the cigarette ashes off it.

My openhearted concern for Fifi or maybe it was my domestic prowess, making French food, adopting stray cats, or something, awakened the pilot's interest in me. The very next day he came back to the house, still wearing his American Airlines blue blazer. We sat on my love seat, two overstuffed sections that kept slipping apart, unless we stood up and pushed them back together. Finally we decided to sit together on one end. I put a record on the phonograph, Brian Eno's *Before and After Science*, and the moody recording was in direct counterpoint to the ethereal foghorn from Long Point Light. Eno was the precursor to Moby, and the mysterious music was haunting and seductive. My six-old-daughter joined us and fell across our tangled legs.

Our little trio seemed promising, but I didn't yet know what the pilot had decided to do about the painter, the Ava Gardner look-alike. I soon realized that she had learned about me when, rejected, she had a show of moody abstract paintings called "Dirge Series." Days passed. Then late one night, walking down Commercial Street, I was ready to confide in the pilot. I wanted to say I was in love with him. I said, "I have to tell you something."

He took my hand and said, "Don't tell me. I know."

That was years before he got his gun license and his Taurus CIA, or "carry it anywhere" .38 Special.

DE-ATH

I recently read a nonfiction book, *One of Us,* about the brutal mass killings of seventy-seven politically conscious teens at a youth camp in Norway in 2011. The killer might have been a terrorist acting out against his nation's immigration laws, or he might have been a solo nutcase. I was surprised to see that the English translation of that book was written by a writer with an unusual name. The translator is Sarah Death.

I asked my friend Judith Grossman if she knew anything about the translator Sarah Death. Judith told me that she once had had a lover at Oxford with the same last name. "It's pronounced 'De-ath'," she said. "It's French."

"You had a boyfriend named 'Death?'"

"He was a bore," she said. "In fact I once fell asleep when he tried to make love to me. He got up and went into my roommate's bedroom instead. But the correct pronunciation of his name was De-ath."

Of course it was a French name. Veronica would be happy to add her two cents about Judith's rejection of Mr. De-ath. But I was impressed by Judith's dismissal of her lover. Whatever he had had to offer, she preferred to take a nap. With River-rat I never allow myself to fall asleep. Sleep is like death, they say. Even if he dozes, I never close my eyes. I wait. I study him from head to foot. I notice any changes in the blue sapphire on his lower lip, and question what these changes might foretell. I must remain awake.

COCONUT CAKE

River-rat calls me at midday to talk dirty. He has put his work aside and he shuts his office door. I answer the phone. He doesn't identify himself. He whispers awkward sex talk and sweet-nothings, and then he says, "Are you wet?"

These interruptions were awkward and unnerving. Like our moralistic fascination with New York mayoral candidate Anthony Weiner it always required that we give our empathy to him, if not admitting our guilt as a second party in the sexual chitchat. But one time I told River-rat, "Hey, I'm kind of busy right now. I'm making a cake."

"You're baking a cake?"

"A coconut cake. Too bad you'll never have one bite of it." I had found a recipe in the *New York Times* for a "Hasbrouck, New York" coconut cake, adapted from *Foods of the Hudson*. Seeing the "Hudson River" reference in a newspaper food column gave me a jangled reaction, a gnawing romantic idea, spawned by my secret connection to River-rat who lived on the Hudson. I decided to make the cake. I took out all of the ingredients and lined them up on the kitchen counter; I found the right bowls and the flour sifter, and I took out two sticks of unsalted butter to soften. I carefully separated six large eggs, yolks in one bowl, and whites in another, requiring an artistry I take pride in for some reason, never permitting the slightest thread of yellow yolk to escape the cup of its shell and spoil the silky albumin of the whites. I felt very charged and excited. It was the pleasure one gets when setting a secret in motion. Baking the cake was an intimate gesture that I refused to interpret too closely. I would savor it in private. The cake would be perfect. But at 300 miles away from where I stood in my kitchen, River-rat would not smell the sweet froth of whipped egg whites or the fruit-laden batter rising in the oven, nor would he see the buttery cake turn golden brown.

But I had a taste tester nearby. Living on the outer cape, I became acquainted with the painter Helen Miranda Wilson, the daughter of Edmund Wilson. She lives in her father's old Victorian house on Money Street in Wellfleet. "Money Street" is amusing to see here in rural Cape Cod. Even the street sign is green. My street sign should be red. "Second Mortgage Lane." But I greatly admire Helen Miranda Wilson's paintings and I respect her work habits. I was initially drawn to her "diary paintings," interior scenes and still life paintings that evoke the psychology of the self. I fell in love with her other representational work. Her landscapes—oceans, dunes, inlets with their sandy banks—with a frieze of green trees. In the delicacy of exact observation, Helen evokes expansive worlds. Art historian Hayden Herrera wrote, "There is a tenderness and respect for the world she paints and for the process of painting that makes her art vivid and lovable." Helen entered an amazing period in the late eighties and early nineties when she did many of her famous "cloud paintings." But after 2001 she turned to abstract work, making her "Calendar Paintings" that are grids, checkerboards, and thin horizontal stripes over stripes in lush, saturated colors, blended and blurred. She says these paintings are influenced by childhood quilts and rugs. Next she tried some optical effects with swirls and concentric circles, uncomplicated repetitions without content.

When I first knew Helen, I was pleased to be invited into her studio to see what she was doing. Helen is very engaging, but she's an exceptionally exasperating person. Being the daughter of a famously cantankerous man of letters, one of the most renowned literary critics of the twentieth century, must not have been easy for a young girl. Her father often sent irascible-sounding postcards to his admirers: *Edmund Wilson regrets that it is impossible for him to: Read manuscripts, write articles or books to order, write forewords or introductions, make statements for publicity purposes, do any kind of editorial work, judge literary contests, give interviews, take part in writers' conferences, answer questionnaires, contribute to or take part in symposiums or "panels" of any kind, contribute manuscripts for sales, donate copies of his books to libraries, autograph works for strangers, allow his name to be used on letterheads, supply personal information about himself, or supply opinions on literary or other subjects.*

Helen, like her dad, has caveats and instructions for us. We are forced to remove our shoes before entering her house. Ladies might agree to kick off their flats, but with resistant men Helen gets down on her knees to unlace their wingtips herself. She's very flirtatious when she tells men, "Take your shoes off. Do it for *me*."

Helen was sociable with River-rat. She had loaned him one of her paintings which he displayed on a wall in his office with a kind of sheepishness because he hadn't paid for it.

When I told Helen I was making a coconut cake, she asked me, "A cake for Giovanni?"

"He's not fond of coconut," I said. I didn't explain that I was making the cake for River-rat. She said she'd come over for a taste test. Macaroons were her favorite treat and a coconut cake would be right up her alley. She said, "I'll give you my opinion."

What I love about Helen is her straightforward approach to problem-solving. Helen had been helpful to me when I had to travel by air to attend publicity events for my memoir *My Sister Life*. I confessed to Helen that I didn't like flying. She said, "You're afraid to fly? Don't be silly. Fear is just a *sensation*."

"Fear is just a sensation?" I said. I was skeptical, but I hoped that Helen's explanation might work the next time I faced my terrors.

Visual artists often give very practical advice. When I told the painter Susan Baker that critics complained that my work was "too dark," she told me, "Go darker!"

I was very grateful to Helen for her sensible advice about "fear." I remembered her words when River-rat comes to my hotel room. As I open the door, the night enters with him from the carpeted hallway, its fleur-de-lis pattern twinkling like stars. But to my surprise, each little star dissolved in a pattern of black dots. The recessed lights in the hotel room flicker and wink out. Table lamps don't work. It's complete darkness. Everything familiar disappears. Everything blacks out. Darkness was my rationalization. *It was just a sensation.*

The coconut cake was actually pretty good, and Helen said, "It's a B+, at least." But we thought the cake was a little too dry. Next time I might add a little milk to the batter, or bake the cake for ten minutes less. These new-fangled convection ovens "save cooking time" but you have to second-guess everything.

I imagined River-rat chewing and swallowing a mouthful of the cake. I like to watch a man's Adam's apple as he swallows. It's a very sexy vision, as his throat cartilage plunges downward, freezes, and surges upward again. That hetero apple distinctly foretells a greater bulge in his lower anatomy. I have watched River-rat swallow his secret thoughts like this, and I stop to imagine him now, his kiss tasting of sweet coconut flakes.

Hasbrouck Coconut Cake
Adapted from "Foods of the Hudson"

Ingredients
- 6 large eggs, separated
- 1 cup unsalted butter, softened
- 2 7-ounce packages sweetened coconut flakes
- 1¾ cups flour

Preparation
1. Preheat the oven to 350 degrees. Using an electric mixer, beat the egg whites until stiff but not dry. Remove from the bowl and set aside.

2. In the same bowl, beat together the butter and coconut. Add one egg yolk at a time, beating well after each addition. Stir in the flour. Fold the egg whites into the butter-and-coconut mixture until the ingredients are just combined.

3. Scrape the batter into a lightly greased 10-inch tube pan and bake until a toothpick inserted into the center of the cake comes out clean, about 25 to 35 minutes. Remove from the oven and cool in the pan for 10 minutes before unmolding and cooling on a wire rack.

YIELD: 10 servings

Remissionimpossible.blogspot.com

Today is the 50th anniversary of the assassination of JFK. It's also the 14th anniversary of when I got in trouble in 8th Grade for wearing the *Dead Kennedys* t-shirt posted above. I wore that t-shirt often, but I didn't realize that November 22nd was a historical date, and I got called to the principal's office when the administration thought I was being disrespectful. The Kennedys are gods, you know, especially on Cape Cod.

"Short, fast and loud" is the cliché description of hardcore punk. With good reason. Virtually every *Misfits* song is 1:20. An ancient review of *Operation Ivy's* "Energy" described each song as "two minutes of perfection." *Minor Threat, Agnostic Front, SSD* (Society System Decontrol) . . . short, short, short. When it comes to '80s punk there are a relative handful of long songs. The Dead Kennedys wrote a good chunk of them. DK really nailed the long punk song sort of thing. I'll rank these "epic" DK songs. The longish "Holiday in Cambodia," "We've got a Bigger Problem Now," and "Cesspools in Eden," I won't include here. I am limiting it to five:

5. Chickens hit Conformist (Bedtime for Democracy, 1986)

This song warns us of problems in the scene. It's a stab at bands like the Cro-Mags and Agnostic Front. They could have stopped after the opening lyrics which sum up the song in a few lines. For this reason, I enjoy this 30-second semi-cover more than the original song:

Punk's not dead it just deserves to die
When it becomes another stale cartoon
A close-minded, self-centered social club
Ideas don't matter, it's who you know

4. Stars and Stripes of Corruption (Franken Christ, 1985)

Jello says "Hello, old friend" to the Capitol Building, only to "piss on it when nobody is looking." Jello's lyrical tendencies began to trade subtlety and suggestion for a more direct approach!

3. Pull My Strings (Live, March 1980)

Is my cock big enough?
Is my brain small enough
For you to make me a star?

Hilarious, biting mockery of what music execs had deemed "new wave. Its utter Fuck You-ness makes it the most important statement DK would make. In the live performance, the band pulls their ties from around their necks to make dollar signs.

2. This could be Anywhere (Frankenchrist, 1985)

If DK peaked on their second album, this song could be considered something of a second peak. The music is on point, with classic East Bay Ray guitar work that is eerie and reverbing. The break at around 2:45 will never stop blowing me away. This is the song where you put your iPod down and pull the vinyl out.

1. Riot (Plastic Surgery Disasters, 1982)

But you get to the place where the real slave drivers live
It's walled off by the riot squad, aiming guns at your head

So you turn around, play into their hands
And set your own neighborhood burning to the ground
instead

Buzz saw guitars slice the song down the middle. Loud parts and quiet parts, fast and slow, dissonant guitar work, and a bassline like a bratty kid yelling "na-na-na-na-na-nah!" I first heard this song as a 7th grader in his post-Rancid punk rock discovery period. I wrote the lyrics in my school notebook, and my English teacher Mrs. Levine said, "I wouldn't be surprised if you turn out to be one of those Columbine kids." Guess what Mrs. Levine, I'm still here, in my spooky mask. Where are you now?

Invisible Eden

I n early January 2002, I was recovering from surgery for a fractured ankle. I had had metal rods and screws implanted in my left leg to realign the shattered bones. The accident happened when I twisted my ankle by stepping on a vacuum cleaner hose. It was my *second* vacuum cleaner injury. Years before, I tore my retina when I yanked the vacuum cleaner cord from the socket and the plug flew across the room to hit me in the eye. I had laser surgery on my retina to coagulate the bloody spot before it drifted into my optic nerve. I have a permanent black spot in my vision. When I read a book, the spot obscures the second line of print.

Not many men suffer injuries from doing banal domestic chores. Yet the husband of a friend of mine has Asperger syndrome and he collects vacuum cleaners. He has hundreds of models that are called "Vintage Vacuums." The Hoover Dustette, Little Queen by Bissell, the Singer Deluxe. Antique uprights, canisters, military shop vacs, tiny hand-held Dustbusters. He has specimens from all eras. But he never actually vacuums the house! Men leave it up to us.

The novelist Arturo Vivante once wrote, "No one thanked her for the miles she swept."

I don't expect to be thanked.

I still had a couple of weeks before the semester started at Emerson, so I didn't have to drive to Boston until then. I would have to borrow my husband's Camry, an automatic, since my own car was a five speed and I couldn't depress the clutch until my broken ankle was stronger.

In my recovery, I was at home listening to the local radio station, WQRC, one day when I heard the news that a Truro resident, single mother and fashion writer Christa Worthington, had been found murdered in her cottage. They found her with her baby daughter clinging to the body. The two-year-old had been left alone for forty-eight hours. I listened intently to the preliminary details of the story. A single woman, a successful fashion writer for *Women's Wear Daily, Elle,* and the *New York Times*, and a summer resident for years, had returned to live full time in our seaside town to raise her out-of-wedlock child. The baby's father was someone I knew well, local shellfish constable Tony Jacket. Tony had taken me out on his dragger the *Josephine G.* when I was doing research for my novel *Open Water*. I've known Tony for years. He's a famous lothario in Provincetown, and is both ridiculed and beloved by everyone who can keep a straight face. Other information surfacing about the murder implicated other characters: the victim's own father, her father's sketchy mistress, a South Shore prossie, Christa's previous boyfriend, a children's book author whom she had rejected, and other Land's End

residents. It was a swirl of tabloid mystery. It was anyone's guess who had killed Christa.

That same week there was a story about Christa's
murder in the *New York Times* with a headline that
said, "Truro Author Murdered."

"We thought it was you!" Doubleday editor Char-
lie Conrad told me, in an unexpected phone call from
New York. Charlie went on to say that the photo of
Christa in the *Times* looked just like me!

Other than our shoulder-length hair, there isn't a
straight resemblance and I was surprised by the mistake. Charlie said, "So what do you think? This story
has your name on it."

He wanted me to write a book about the murder in
my hometown. "This is right up your alley," Charlie said.

Learning about the murder of Christa Worthington,
I had recognized many connections. I, too, had once
been a single mom with a very young daughter. I, too,
was a writer living in the same remote nowheresville
community. I knew some of the people involved, the
father of Christa's out-of-wedlock baby for certain, but
then I recognized that the victim herself had once
been my student in a writing workshop at The Fine
Arts Work Center. She had submitted a rambling section from a book she was writing about her mother,
and of course, I was familiar with a girl's desire to
write about her matriarch. At the time she was my
student, I was, in fact, working on an early draft of
the memoir about my missing sister and our mother,
Veronica. I soon learned that Christa had had family
issues similar to my own. The Worthingtons have a
Boston Brahmin surname, and Christa seemed to have
been born with a silver spoon in her mouth, but in

fact they were "swamp Yankees." My family had had similar contradictions: My mother claimed to be upper class French, but in fact she came from peasant stock. Christa's father took up with a prostitute, and of course my own sister had been a working girl herself.

It was not my idea to write a book about the murder that took place less than a mile from my house, but I recognized familiar patterns in Christa's life and the project was suddenly very appealing to me. I told Charlie Conrad, "Let me think about it."

The next day, I wrote a book proposal for *Invisible Eden*.

Re: The Truro Murder

People are lured to the tip of the Cape for the deepest, most secret reasons. These stragglers are called "washashores," lost souls who come here to find escape, or to find themselves, at last. Some find "heaven on earth"; for others it's a wasteland of their own making.

Henry Miller wrote, "In their dream of love, or lack of it, the lost are ever wandering to the water's edge."

"Land's End," as we know it, is unharvested terrain in contemporary nonfiction. Robert Nathan used this haunted landscape in his best seller, Portrait of Jennie, *and both Denis Johnson and Norman Mailer explore the area in their novels,* Resuscitation of a Hanged Man *and* Tough Guys Don't Dance. *A nonfiction book,* Midnights, *by Alec Wilkinson, took a look at small town cops in Wellfleet—but no one has yet reaped this No Man's Land, or its true drippingly gothic territory, in its realest terms.*

Christa Worthington's story has the aura of a Wuthering Heights romance tainted with a jaded Looking for Mr. Goodbar finality.

For many, Christa is the all too common American baby boomer, a single woman who in midlife finds herself searching for connections she had not yet secured in her previous life in New York City and abroad. She wants roots, a child of her own, a footing that neither career alone, nor her extended, complicated family could provide.

The beauty and violence of the seaside landscape mirrors, even nurtures the battle between its wealthy summer residents, visiting artists, and the wannabes and dilettantes that mingle with the genuinely famous. And its hard scrabble year-round fishing families date back to the eighteenth century.

This is a class story.

Truro is a tiny town with a population of 1,500 in the winter that explodes to 30,000 people in the summer. It is the Shangri-La for wealthy New Yorkers and Bostonians, but its working class year-rounders are frozen in low-paying service industry summer jobs.

This is a love story.

Or more likely, it's a love scandal between two individuals from opposite ranks, the wealthy Vassar-educated Christa, and Tony Jackett, a local fisherman. Tony Jackett's family goes back as far as the Worthington's, but his domain was the leaky draggers of MacMillan Wharf in Provincetown, where the Portuguese fishing fleet once thrived before it died in the early '80s, never to regain its financial seat as a fishing port. Jackett became a shellfish warden.

He was often at Pamet Harbor seeding oyster flats,
where Christa lived a few doors away.

Christa's desire for a baby is familiar to thou-
sands of single women who are losing their chances
to have children and family. Her story has romantic
chords, and recalls Poe's lyrical "Annabel Lee," with
its curdled Yankee tones and violent wind-torn topog-
raphy. "That the wind came out of the cloud by night/
Chilling and killing my Annabel Lee." One recognizes
the planeness of its tragic setting: the image of her
laundry and her baby's bibs still left hanging on the
clothesline after she was murdered.

When I took on the assignment, I had to begin my
work immediately because they wanted a "crash publication" of the book. I attended a memorial service
in Provincetown. I had to go on crutches. There's a
misconception about the physiological dynamics of
crutches. You must learn to gauge your movements
and shift your weight in *reverse* of where you think
you are going. Learning to walk with crutches has an
otherworldly component.

I ascended the church stairs at the UU, the Universal Unitarian church, by sitting on my ass and
going up stair by stair on my buttocks. The people in
attendance appeared to be hippie-dippie outcasts of
all breeds, and I couldn't understand Christa's friendship with such washashore un-fashiony types. Their
eulogies were sophomoric and it gave me a stomach-
turning pity for the victim, if these were the souls who
came to memorialize her.

In the next weeks, I was in New York to do more
research. I had appointments with Christa's editors at

Women's Wear Daily, Chic Simple, and *Elle* magazine. When Christa was writing, it was an era of intellectual liberty at *Elle.* Susan Sontag and Christopher Hitchens were contributing editors. Christa, too, was a very literary writer with animated psychological examinations of style and of the textiles used in fashion: "Tulle—is barely there. It holds all the sexual dynamite of the veil, signaling the control of chastity . . . and its imminent release." And she peppered her texts with excerpts from poets and philosophers, as well as fashion designers: "A suit looks good when the woman who wears it seems to have nothing underneath." —Coco Channel.

"Beware all the enterprises that require new clothes." —Henry David Thoreau.

"A sweet disorder in the dress/kindles in clothes a wantonness."—Robert Herrick.

I thought of Christa's bon mots at the start of my interview with the editor Jeff Stone at *Chic Simple* when he said to me, "You must have been a model? Because you are very fashion-y. And those cheekbones—that's all you need."

I came with ready-to-wear cheekbones, but I had dressed for success in my seasonless wool suit and a tight, deeply cut, sleeveless shell that exposed a lot of my white skin. I was supposed to meet River-rat at the Wyndham Hotel in less than an hour. I was happy to learn that the comedic actor Charles Nelson Reilly was a resident at the Wyndham, and I had hoped to run into him. He was known for his engaging performance in the Broadway hit *How to Succeed in Business without Really Trying* and in my youth I liked his TV role in the *Ghost and Mrs. Muir.* I had hoped he'd get on the elevator with me. Instead River-rat showed up. Meeting him, while I was working on a new book for a different editor, caused me great turmoil. How could River-rat arrive, take off his pants, and not want to look at my pages anymore?

Lying beside him on the overstuffed mattress, I told him what I was learning about the murder victim. "One editor called her 'a fashion anthropologist' because Christa noted how 'scarves are used in many cultures as diapers or slings to carry babies.'"

"Interesting."

He wasn't impressed. So I said, "They also say that I look like a model. How do you like that?"

"I like *this*," he said, pulling the sheet aside and crawling back onto me. I noticed that the Venous Lake on his lower lip looked even darker, more sinister.

That night River-rat took me out to dinner.

"You have to be kidding me," I said, when we entered the place and we were shown to a table. "Are you trying to be ironic or something?"

"What do you mean?"

In the hurricane of hard work I was doing when researching murder victim Christa Worthington, River-rat had chosen to take me to a midtown restaurant called "Christer's."

"Are you kidding?" I said. He was taken aback when he realized the buried joke. But I understood his choice to bring me to "Christer's" was a subconscious covetousness of my subject, of my writing, of my world that wasn't in his hands anymore.

Eight months later I flew to New York to be on the *Today Show* for the publication of *Invisible Eden*. The press junket for *Invisible Eden* took place at the end of June, during a heat wave. I got stuck in a traffic jam coming in from LaGuardia. I had been shuffled into a gypsy cab at the taxi line and it turned out not to have any air-conditioning. We were backed up for almost two hours and the temperature in the back seat was nearing one hundred degrees.

Arriving at last at the Warwick Hotel, my face was bright red, as if I was suffering another bout of Slap Cheek Syndrome. I thought I had heat prostration. I was meeting River-rat in an hour. In my room, I filled the bath to its brim using only the cold tap. I reclined in the tub, dipping my head back until my face was completely submerged beneath the icy water. I soaked there, my hair floating in a fan above my head, until my body temperature returned to normal. But nothing was normal anymore. With publicity for the book, I had become some kind of sacrificial lamb, and I wanted River-rat's sympathy. When he arrived, he picked up a copy of my new best seller from the bedside table.

"Great cover, right?" I said. The jacket showed the pastoral scene of the seaside house where the fashion writer was murdered. On the back flap was a full-sized picture of the victim's pretty face. I had had to put my foot down when they had wanted her picture on the *front* cover.

"It could have used some editing," River-rat said.

"Some editing? Get out of here," I said. River-rat was no longer my editor but he was saying the book had needed his golden touch. He was miffed that the book was making money, so he felt he had to insult it.

He said, "Charlie gets the credit. The thing is, I would never have thought of it."

"You mean you wouldn't have asked me to write the book?"

"I would never have *cooked* it up," River-rat said.

It took me a moment to realize River-rat wasn't giving kudos to my new editor for his genius in putting me together with Christa Worthington, the glamorous murder victim. River-rat was saying that the story was too tabloid for him. It was beneath him.

I protested. I said that it wasn't a true slasher title, although *the knife went all the way through the victim's breast, through her diaphragm and trapezius muscle, to make a nick in the kitchen floor.* The book was very literary, often lyrical, and much of it was about a small town's reaction to the crime. I had true empathy for my characters. Christa, herself, was almost like a sister to me. We had much more in common than I had had with my own missing sister, the subject of my last book with River-rat. I had approached the murder story with my usual connection to the fringes and with my interest in "the human condition." I didn't think he had actually read it! Saying that his tastes were too refined for such a sensational story was how he tried to get over this fact: *Invisible Eden* was an overnight sensation.

I pushed him back onto the pillows. "It needs editing, you say? Edit *this*," I said.

When he fucked me, he was a little rough. He seemed to hate me.

He had no empathy for what I was going through. There was a great deal of negative publicity about the murdered out-of-wedlock fashion mom, and *the writer* who wrote about her misdeeds. Critics were saying that Christa and I were joined at the hip. We were both too promiscuous. "It takes one to know one," they said. The next day on the TV show *The View*, Barbara Walters asked me if the district attorney had had more than a professional relationship with me. "He was a flirt, wasn't he?"

I said, "Well, he took an outdoor shower in front of me." First he had soaped up under the nozzle that had no enclosure! Then he sat down at his kitchen table wrapped only in a towel snugged around his waist as we discussed the murder case. It was true that he had often come on to me. He once plastered campaign stickers on my bare knee, when I sat beside him in his state-subsidized sedan. But I never went to bed with him.

The women hosts of that show chided me, asking, "The DA in a towel, you say? Well, that's crossing a line!" Then, when I had to sit opposite Katie Couric on the *Today Show* and she was surprisingly moralistic when she asked me about single women having sex, the studio lights exploded as if in response to supernatural forces. I knew it was Christa from the beyond telling Katie, "Mind your own business!"

CALIFORNIA DREAMING

My femme fatale mother, Veronica, had no patience for my bookworm sensibility or for my style choices, but once she came to my defense in an unexpected setting.

As a teenager I was arrested twice and went to family court hearings where I was sentenced to six months "probation" each time. To Veronica's list—liar, slut—you can add juvenile delinquent and "offender." At fourteen I kept a coffee can where I stashed away all my money. With a Magic Marker I had written across the Sanka logo, "C. D.," my secret code for "California Dreaming." Opportunity knocked on Mother's Day in 1966 when my friend Colleen and her boyfriend Tony decided to take off together. Destination: Hollywood. They invited me along. Tony had swiped a late model Dodge Monaco, finding the keys in the dash. In a sub-development called Windy Bush, everyone left their keys in the ignition. It was his idea to run away to California in a stolen car. He was getting his girl, at last, and he wanted her to ride in style.

My sister was still missing, and I somehow believed that on this impromptu trip, I would find her. That's how I rationalized my involvement in "Grand Theft Auto" and "High Speed Fleeing and Eluding" which would appear in boldface on my juvie record. We made it as far as Baltimore when we hit traffic. Tony weaved through the congested lanes with a little too much abandon. He chose to drive in the breakdown lane and the speedometer crept up to one hundred miles an hour. When I whipped around in my seat I saw six pulsing cherry-tops in a blistering row behind us. But I was closing in on my sister. From my seat in the stolen car, I felt our lives converging, weaving tighter, like zipper teeth locking. My every reckless act from that minute on was a stepping-stone to our reunion. To ditch the troopers, we left the expressway and plowed down an exit ramp. Tony drove over medians, climbed over curbs, and bisected traffic islands. At an intersection, we shot into a stream of oncoming cars. We were hit on the left. Another car struck our tail, and we were clipped a third time. The hood ripped free and slammed down on the other side of the street. The car was totaled in an instant. We survived (although I got seventeen stitches, and Colleen had bitten through her tongue), but it was lucky that other drivers weren't killed in the smashup. From that episode, I was assigned to see Miss McGonegal, a probation officer with no sense of humor. I reported to her office at the courthouse twice a week.

The next year, I was arrested with a circle of hoods, charged for "spending the night in a condemned building" in Wilmington. We had shared tabs of acid, rolled joints, and tipped back a cumbersome bottle of apple wine, sloshing its sweet contents. We tore through boxes of Tastykake Butterscotch Krimpets, and the cockroaches scrawled over the sticky wrappers. LSD makes roaches seem almost adorable in their circus act. Police had found us because we had lit candles on bare windowsills and the blown-out window frames caught on fire.

At the hearing I was singled out by the family court judge. He implied I had a perverse desire to trespass on private property, perhaps to perform unlawful sexual transactions. I was the only female defendant. The other boys were from parochial school, and I was a notorious dropout from a more nefarious public high school. When he implied I was the ringleader, Veronica rose from her seat and said, "Why are you picking on her? She writes poetry!"

I was thrilled when Veronica stood up for me. Indeed she rose from her chair and "stood up." She had announced to everyone, to the world, that I was a poet! I basked in her fiery protest, which proved her allegiance to me. But Veronica went on to tell the judge that she wasn't responsible for my disheveled appearance or for my obscene school record. "That's her own descent into hell," she told the judge.

Speed Trap

When my first novel, *The Arrow Collar Man,* was awarded a PEN/American Ernest Hemingway Foundation citation, I wanted River-rat to attend the formal ceremony with me. But he didn't arrive. The citation praised my novel, saying, "With the voice and hand of the most hard-bitten traveler, she leads us into a world of desolation, hopelessness, and eternal longing. Her characters are distilled to their essences: pure hunger, pure need, pure compassion, pity, obsession . . . a fine beginning to what will certainly be a long and distinguished career." There was to be a fancy presentation at the Kennedy Library in Boston, and one of the judges, new Pulitzer Prize winner E. Annie Proulx (she still used the "E." back then), had felt the gala important enough to show up. I was jealous that the writers Sherman Alexie, who also received a citation, and Dagoberto Gilb, who had won the cash award, were escorted by their editor Morgan Entrekin from Grove Atlantic. Morgan was incredibly supportive of them. He looked very pleased to be associated with his young authors.

I went to the Kennedy Library alone.

I drove the hundred miles listening to the latest news about OJ Simpson's arrest for the murders of his wife, Nicole, and Ron Goldman. I've always thought it amusing to see literary calendars list the birthdays of famous authors. Some of my writer friends were born on the same day as Emily Dickinson, John Keats, Philip Roth, or James Joyce.

I share the same birthday with OJ Simpson.

When I got to the library after driving one hundred miles, I parked the car and got out of my jeans. I had brought a change of clothes: a tight black skirt and a silk blouse. My new agent, Kim Witherspoon, scolded me for wearing a silk top with a printed design instead of a solid color. "From now on, wear only *solid colors* for public appearances, OK?" she told me. But when I had changed clothes, I had worried that my tight skirt would show my panty lines, so I removed my panties and threw them in the back seat. I'd be bare-bottomed beneath my clothes to get my award. If I worried about "panty lines," you can blame that on my mother, who sometimes decided to remove her bra after putting on a cocktail dress. She'd unsnap her bra and tug it out of an armhole. She believed that a low-cut dress or a bare-backed gown should be worn without any foundation garment, "skin to silk."

The Hemingway ceremony was a little stuffy, but when it was over we decided to pile into Annie Proulx's limousine to have dinner in town. Annie was on tour for her Pulitzer Prize book, *The Shipping News*. It was long before her *Brokeback Mountain* fame, but she had a driver waiting for her in a gleaming stretch parked outside. We couldn't all fit into the one sedan, with Sherman and Dagoberto and some Kennedy

Library blue-hairs, although it was quite roomy. So I volunteered to drive the rest of us into town in my old Volvo. My agent, Kim, Morgan Entrekin, and the writer Francisco Goldman, of *Long Night of White Chickens* fame, said they'd ride with me. I had forgotten that I'd tossed my panties in the back seat when Frank and Morgan climbed into the car and found them. They tossed the undies back and forth teasing me. I wished that River-rat was there to crumple my panties in his hand and shove them in his pocket.

At dinner, Morgan said to me, "You have to show me your next book."

River-rat was publishing *Open Water*, so I told Morgan, "I'm already spoken for." That's an old-fashioned expression that a fiancée, or even a bride, might say with pride after she's tied the knot.

Morgan said, "Are you sure about that?" He'd been around the block, and he seemed to think that what I said was poppycock.

On my drive home, I placed my Hemingway citation on the front seat beside me. At two o'clock in the morning, I was fifteen miles from home when I hit a speed trap.

When the trooper came to my window, he said, "I'm afraid you were going twenty miles over the speed limit. It's forty here—"

"I'm a year-rounder," I said. With local constabulary, being a year-rounder is nothing to sneeze at.

But the trooper said, "Yeah, I know. One of us. But I'm going to have to give you a citation anyway."

I wanted to tell him, "Hey, I have a *citation* right here!" I imagined showing him my PEN/Hemingway citation: "She is a Charon of the highways. There is something both ancient and modern about the journey she takes us on." Then I remembered the day I had just had. OJ under arrest, my panties batted around the back seat in men's hands, and River-rat who had been a no-show at the PEN event. Being stopped for speeding so close to home put everything in perspective.

My PEN award had had no stipend, and suddenly I was out-of-pocket in the amount of $250. If I wanted to contest the ticket I had to show up in district court. I brought my Hemingway citation with me. I mentioned to the judge that the night I had been stopped for speeding, I was coming home from an award ceremony at the Kennedy Library. In the Cape Cod courts, any reference to the name "Kennedy" earns you the key to the city. The judge was quite impressed. He said, "So we have an author here? She likes to go a little too fast, is that right?"

"Yes. I was driving too fast."

"But you're a Kennedy-approved author, is that right?"

I showed him the one-page citation printed on official stationery.

He said, "Ok. Let's reduce the author's fine to fifty dollars."

Remissionimpossible.blogspot.com

I got a "Welcome to eBay!" e-mail for an account I didn't create. I kept an eye out for further e-mails about any transactions. Soon enough eBay sent me a confirmation for the product pictured above. It's a "Boyfriend Arm Throw Pillow." A fluffy pillow in the shape of one arm curving around in a hug. It even has an upholstered hand at the end of its sleeve. You can imagine a girl sitting on her sofa snuggling with it.

I contacted Ebay and they said it was a mix-up. Some dude in England ordered the "Boyfriend Arm Throw Pillow" and his Gmail address got confused with mine. The pillow is puffy, cuddly, but it still looks like an amputated arm. But these days when I'm sitting in a waiting room at Dana Farber I can feel that mysterious arm encircling me. It taps my shoulder, and squeezes tight with death's formal black cashmere sleeve. I know it by heart, but I'll try to shove it away.

DANVILLE

In Iowa City, I came home from work one day to find a book on my doorstep. A former classmate had left it for me. I felt it was a passive-aggressive offering because I had just had an abortion, and the book was filled with photographs of adorable, pudgy babies and toddlers. The book was *Photographs* by Emmet Gowin, a collection of prints from his work in the late sixties and early seventies.

Like other graduate students, I had started to take photographs, myself, enrolling in Intro to Photography to pad my credit requirements for an MFA. I learned to develop my own negatives in a black "changing bag" in my kitchen, feeding the film into the tiny spool of a small developing tank. With my arms inserted into the black bag I couldn't see what I was doing, and had to work by "touch alone." I added developer first, agitating the canister, timing it carefully. I used "stop bath" and "fixer" and finally a rinse solution of liquid detergent. I hung my negatives from the bathroom shower pole to dry, long celluloid ribbons of mystery inches.

Making contact sheets at the university darkroom, I watched my images emerge. Faces surfaced, then pastoral landscapes, corn fields, and the Iowa River, or glorious hand-held shots of the Sioux City Swede's big hard-on; whatever my subject it always surprised me. Yet as exposures revealed contrasts and tones, the images were transformed from their primary existence to a different plane of existence. Photographs attain an otherness, in part by the chemical process they go through, but also by the artist's hand when she captures the image in a particular realm of light, and again in the studio when she chooses how long to expose the negative when making a print. The photograph freezes time, yet it's not just external time but a "time of mind." I watched intently, as my images and personal leanings emerged, but breathing fumes from the pans of poisonous developer and fixer often made me dizzy.

Emmet Gowin's book, *Photographs,* is a collection of pictures of Emmet's wife, Edith, the couple's young sons, and Edith's extended family. Most of the prints are set in Edith's homestead in Danville, Virginia, a magical haven that emerges unencumbered by any world but its own. There were shots of Edith, often frontal nudes, or when she's wearing one of many gauzy nightgowns, as if she were dressed in the atmospheric clouds of her family setting. She is pregnant, shown naked with her bulging belly, and naked again with her fat naked babies, or with young nieces and nephews, gorgeous in their long-boned bodies entangled on grassy lawns, a cortege of healthy souls that seemed to invite me into their family. I was a single mother, but

I also was grieving after my recent abortion, ashamed I had been knocked up by my boyfriend, the Sioux City Swede.

The afternoon I had had the procedure, my teacher Jim de la Mare held a party to celebrate Pablo Neruda's birthday. I went to the party hoping to be distracted. It wasn't *his* baby, but when I confessed my upheaval to de la Mare he told me, "You better toughen up." His advice "to get tough" in fact expressed a great deal of sympathy for me. And he understood that celebrating Neruda's birthday was exactly what I needed to endure my ordeal. He asked me to read one of Neruda's poems out loud, believing it was the curative I needed. I read, "Love is so short, forgetting is so long." It was like an Anglo Saxon neck-riddle of my own. It helped me enter into a sorrowful acceptance of my guilt, especially after the abortionist had told me, "It's twins! That's why your morning sickness has been so severe."

I had been very sick with this pregnancy, and had suffered more than I had with my daughter, Annabel. The doctor said that carrying twins produced more noxious hormones, but I had felt my sickness was psychological. From guilt. I didn't want to terminate the pregnancy.

The doctor was a lefty dermatologist who volunteered to perform abortions at the Emma Goldman women's clinic, for free. When I showed up for my abortion, I was surprised to recognize the dermatologist.

"It's you?" I said.

He said, "Hey, I don't just pop pimples!"

So I had a very strong reaction to Gowin's photographs of babies and children, in the familiar backyard of the rambling house in Danville. The southern light in the photographs was warm and misty as if imbued by the ghost-breath of all others who had come and gone before us. There are photographs of Edith's aged mother, Rennie Booher, sitting beside her daughter on an unmade bed; the older woman is frail, almost skeletal, but very distinguished. Rennie looked more than one generation older than her daughter; she looked like Edith's _great_-grandmother rather than her own mom. This gave a strange savor of mortality to everyone in the photos, and then, in a different photo we see Rennie Booher again, this time in her open casket. There's a photograph of Edith beside a Christmas tree with the wreckage of opened presents strewn across the floor; the crumpled wrappings are piled high as a mountain, enough gifts for a very large or, in fact, for a universal family. The opened gifts belonged to everyone. And there's a photo of Edith urinating while standing erect with her legs spread apart. She lifts the hem of her blousy dress above her waist to release a tight stream, her beauty fully revealed. This too had a sense of our most basic human communality.

The pictures of Edith and her children were like mirrors of my daughter and me. Gowin writes about his subjects, "I entered into a family freshly different from my own." But to me, the photographs were so familiar, and comforting, I felt I had found my ideal family. I spent hours examining each plate, dreaming of taking my three-year-old daughter and escaping to Danville to be with them. I hoped they might adopt us.

YEARS LATER, River-rat invited me to go with him to an Emmet Gowin retrospective in New York at a gallery on Fifty-Seventh Street. I was nervous to have my deep connections to Gowin unearthed. I wanted to see the pictures I had adored, but my own history with them was perilous to me. I hoped that River-rat's interest in the photographer might mean we had something in common, but I was too shy to tell him the story about being a single mother in Iowa, about my trials and desperation when very young, although by this time my baby daughter was full-grown.

Before going to the opening, we had sex at the hotel. He told me that our lovemaking was the most erotic, the hottest-hot hour we had ever had together. Perhaps I was in a vulnerable mood, my tensions about going to the opening made my body softer and more responsive to his touch. I was childlike and less steely. My relapse into virginal receptiveness enlivened his manliness as the darkness of the room enwrapped us in warm velvet.

Afterward I lay curled beside him. If he was taking me to see Gowin's photographs, I felt a new optimism or happiness that I had not yet felt in our secret relationship. Perhaps if we shared an interest in Gowin's Danville oeuvre we had something deeper, a stronger connection than sex.

Arriving at the gallery, I was ready to tell River-rat what Gowin had really meant to me, but when we entered the space I was surprised to see him stride away in a different direction. Instantly men and women approached him; perhaps they were publishing colleagues or literary business folk, but in fact some of them acted like housewives from Hastings who might have asked him if he had attended the last PTA meeting. He chatted with the other revelers, acting like he didn't know me.

So I found Emmet Gowin, himself, and I told him what his work had meant to me. Then I spent a lot of time by myself in front of the Danville photographs. A caption beside one photograph quoted Demonio Azul who said that Gowin expressed a sense of a "family's otherworldliness and the solemnity of the everyday." That was the connection I felt.

But River-rat wasn't looking at Gowin's family photographs. He was across the room examining the photographer's more recent work—aerial photographs of western terrain, man-altered landscapes showing how man's footprint has visibly scarred and altered the earth's surface. These were photographs of missile sites, ammunition disposal heaps, pivot-irrigation systems, and off-road maps where man has left tire trails marring natural lands. These photos were taken from airplanes, and don't have the same intimacy as the Danville plates. They reminded me of John Jackson's remarks, when he described "a certain detachment" that occurs in the "landscape vernacular" when seen from aloft.

I suddenly recognized that River-rat didn't belong with the Danville family. I couldn't imagine him in any of those photographs. Instead he stood before Gowin's aerial photographs, keeping his distance from me, with Jackson's "certain detachment." If he once believed that "Willis is despicable," I didn't think he'd like to see the photograph of Edith pissing, standing with her legs spread apart, and he wouldn't understand how difficult it was for me to see Edith's pudgy babies cavorting on those green lawns without seeing the ghosts of my twins.

BEE BALM

Like Joseph Mitchell's awe of poisonous filth in *The Bottom of the Harbor*, I have an appreciation for the complexities of how dirt is generated both by magic and by natural sources. The top soil in Truro is less than a quarter inch deep, a scant layer of remnant decay from the first forests that were cleared by the Pilgrims almost 400 years ago. Beneath this shallow film of organic dust is pale white sand. It's not the red sand you find elsewhere with clay mixed in. The gritty substrate at Land's End is free of organic matter. It offers nothing nutritive. And it doesn't hold water. Its components are finely crushed rocks, sand that was deposited as an afterthought of the Wisconsin Stage glacier, a monstrous wall of ice 10,000 feet thick that shaped all of New England 25,000 years ago.

To begin a garden in Truro, one must solve the first problem: sand. It's too porous to retain moisture, and it's without a trace of nitrogen that root systems require. In Truro we have to *make* dirt. We must develop our own strategies, whether it's making compost factories, collecting seaweed and manure, or if you are well-heeled, you can buy your dirt retail.

I have learned to collect my own. Native litter, sea-weed, fish skins, leaf fall, crumbling bark, rotten fruit, scabs of lichen, dryer lint, kitchen scraps, *New York Times*, lawn clippings. Mitchell's "sludge bubbles," if one could collect them, would be of good use. These composted piles must be babied, forked, and fluffed, so that air can circulate and rain can percolate through. The piles need to cook for weeks, even months until heterogeneous donations have transformed into fermented black silk. A few pounds of 10-10-10 speeds it up. After twenty-four years, my compost bins have become a little city of organic Dutch ovens, a regenerative system of active decomposition that never stills, even in a deep freeze. Worm nurseries can continue their business in deep steamy pockets where my elegant debris cooks, reaching the temperature of a comfortable hot tub beneath pure white snow banks. In spring the compost is mature and offers nutritive dollops for every corner of the garden. With such a savory blanketing, everything leafs out a deeper green. I've vanquished the original plat of pure sand to early photographs, where my place had looked like a tarmac of desert ground similar to Iraq or Pakistan.

My garden beds are at least eighteen inches deep, sometimes two feet deep filled with rich, recollective particles of loamy black velvet. There are eighteen distinct beds, more than 25,000 square feet or more than a half an acre of English Gardens in a map of serpentine paths, ledges and banks, distinct "garden rooms" and theaters with secret switchbacks and crannies.

In this green world, I hide from *him.*

Some mistresses of the garden waltz through their pathways pointing to specimens. They try to impress visitors by reciting the Latin nomenclature, listing four botanical categories: plant family, genus, species, and cultivar. But I prefer the common names of flowers that mirror simple human joys and fits of pique, moral quandaries, icy judgments, and deceptions. *Mock* orange earned its scold by being counterfeit, and another called *false* indigo suggests a copycat. Old world favorites refer to daily plights, like one called obedience plant and another called loosestrife. I'm amused by flowers with opposing names like bee *balm* and bug*bane*.

Plants can be mimics, like basket-of-gold, goat's beard, and pink turtlehead, a compact bloom with tightly layered snakeskin petals, and a sharp little beak. Pincushion flower is a plump bristly ball, and lamb's ear a wooly flap. Other specimens evoke emotional turmoil. There is love in the mist, forget-me-not, and love-lies-bleeding, an amaranth with brilliant red seed head tassels that dribble at the plant collar like a slit throat. Other plant names suggest domestic oppression like mourning bride and thrift flower.

Bee balm is a team player in late June; rising from a defiant network of crosshatched roots, its squared stems shoot up. My intimacy with garden plants is neverending. I can identify bee balm with my eyes shut. Pinching a single shoot with my fingertips I recognize its four flat sides. Its colors range from deep scarlet to violet, and leach to pale pink. Its blossom has a central disc shooting shaggy bright-hued spinets that attract nectar-hunting insects, imperious hornets, skippers, swallowtails, and clumsy bumblebees. Hummingbirds sip from its tubular florets, and even warblers perch on each bristly sphere to comb it with their beaks, searching for tiny visitors. It gets its name "balm" for satisfying the needy thousands.

Bugbane with its dark chocolate wands and sub-divided leaflets prefers shade. In late summer, it presents an arousal of prong-shaped blooms, each one a snow-white bottlebrush as long as a hot dog bun. I snap one off and hold it in my palm. The ghost of his cock.

THE MIAMI BOOK FAIR

My Miami hotel room is pitch black except for the TV screen—a mesmerizing waffle of blue light. I flip channels and freeze on a familiar face. *Who is that?* I'm thinking. My heart stops the way it might when an old lover shows up on the sidewalk. But this is different. This is weird. It's just some pop singer on MTV, a newcomer named Lisa Loeb—almost the spitting image of my daughter, Annabel. In tortoise-shell glasses, she's geeky-looking, individualistic, bravely motherless. Her image triggers a familiar maternal obsession—the covetousness, the possessiveness—but my daughter is grown up. She's no longer in my domain.

Before the publication of *My Sister Life*, I was attending the Miami Book Fair, a gala of writers, editors, and booksellers. River-rat was supposed to be there, but Weensie had made him beg off. I had to be at a Random House cocktail party at the Delano South Beach Hotel without a plus-one.

Long panels of white chenille hung from the ceiling in the lobby, swishing in the breeze. I had to weave my way through the shifting gauze curtains, and it gave the event a bedroom aura. Across the high ceiling, scores of writers' names were projected in stenciled font, illuminated by gel lights. I found my own name, right next to the names of huge literary stars from Random House lists. The names were repeated often. Some of the writers in attendance were thrilled to find their names on the ceiling, but I thought it off-putting. The illuminated names were like Kmart's Blue Light Specials, when a mobile police light blinks at a specific aisle in the big box store, where shoppers could find marked-down prices.

I recognized James Ellroy whom I had met years before at Sarah Lawrence College where my husband, the pilot, was on the faculty. Walking across campus late at night, we bumped into him. I was surprised to see he was carrying a single golf club. Ellroy had worked as a golf caddy in the years before he became a best-selling novelist. Sarah Lawrence has sweeping grass lawns where he liked to practice his drive. But it was after midnight.

My husband said, "Hi, Jim. This is Maria."

"You don't say," Ellroy said to my husband. He seemed amused that I had suddenly materialized at midnight and was standing right before him. As I reached out to shake hands with Ellroy, he licked his palm, grabbed my hand, and pumped it up and down.

I was surprised to see the flash of his pink tongue, followed by his cool, wet tug. He had tricked me. It was funny. A sexy joke, but slightly crude. I liked it.

Meeting Ellroy again at the book party in Miami, he was standing beside editor-in-chief Sonny Mehta, River-rat's boss. If the bigwig had bothered to show up, I thought that River-rat could have made the effort. But I told Sonny Mehta about Ellroy licking his palm the first time we met. Sonny liked the story. I greatly admired Ellroy's nonfiction book, *My Dark Places,* and he, too, said he had liked my new memoir. He wrote a blurb for the back jacket. He called the book "a box of dark treasures." It was nice to run into him again, but most of the time I roamed the party alone.

The soiree was poolside, the narrow deck crammed with writers, publishing kingpins, and nubile twenty-somethings. There were superstar models and model wannabees, some of whom were employed by the hotel to mingle with us, to add glamour to our four-eyes convention. These girls teetered at the lip of the Windex-blue water. Their skintight gowns adhered to their curves in splashes of color as if they'd just been paintballed. The bartenders were mixing pink cos-mopolitans in oversized martini glasses. Every guest held one of these neon flutes—it was hypnotic. The cocktails were refilled in twinkling progression. I could see the young models getting lit, and I thought of my daughter whose face had surfaced on my TV screen. Years ago, I used to drag her along to local taverns and I plopped her beside me on a barstool. She'd order grenadine and ginger ale for herself, telling the bartender, "I'll have a Shirley, hold the cherry." That night in Miami, men came up to chat with me. I com-mented on all the nymphets at the party. Was it supply and demand? I mentioned to one man that my own daughter could be one of these trophy ingenues just to hear his knee-jerk response. "Your daughter? No way—you're not old enough!" For years I have used my daughter in my arena of flirtations. I'd introduce her and they'd say, "She can't be your daughter. She must be your sister? Is she cloned?"

I try to envision my daughter with these Miami beauties, svelte little glowworms still keening for Versace—but my daughter, in fact, is a grade school teacher in Minneapolis. Dressed in earth-tone Patagonia winter wear, always prepared for that brutal climate, she's leading a string of third graders up a snowy sidewalk. The fact that my daughter is launched and has taken up the role of a modern schoolmarm is a great satisfaction to me. When I was child-mommy in search of myself, I was not the easiest person to live with. But my daughter survived it. Annabel's success resides not only in her grade school job but in her temperate humor. She entered her womanhood in "moderation." Annabel is astonishingly beautiful, with sorrel hair and my mother's fine features; she even has her green eyes, the color of a 1950s 7UP bottle. Perhaps such physical perfection skips a generation. But my daughter is indifferent to style trends and the glamour principle. Her sexuality isn't repressed, but she never vamps, preens, or teases.

Early photographs of my mother still send chills through me. She was a figure under the spell of an intense erotic sorcery. I used to watch her dress for cocktail parties. Before she stepped into her dress, she shivered Chanel powder across her bosom. Next she spritzed Jean Patou on the folds of her dress, pinching the rubber bulb of a cut-crystal glass atomizer. Before the full-length mirror, she adjusted her seamed stockings, making sure that each seam ascended the exact curves of her legs in straight cinnamon lines. To protect against runs, she was careful to put on her white cotton gloves that she wore to church on Sundays, urging the nude silk higher and higher until she snapped the clasps of her garters. My mother's routine suggested that *sex was a highway*. Soon I, too, would enter that busy esplanade and merge with the traffic. The fast lane.

I had fled from childhood almost directly into motherhood. Being so young myself, my daughter and I would grow up together. But like my mother, I sought complete immersion in men. As a single mother, I tried to use discretion. But there were men I couldn't resist, despite their bad habits. One boyfriend took my daughter shoplifting, borrowing her Barbie suitcase to load it up with batteries and cigarettes. I quit him for her sake, if not my own. Annabel was my backbone. She was the ground wire, the curfew, the lullaby sung back to me. Because of her, I threw men out of the house or invited them to stay. She was always in the car between us, on the loveseat, or in the next room. I asked my lovers to whisper pillow talk and smother their screams of release.

Her adolescence was uneventful. She had decent grades, raised tropical fish, and in high school she joined the Latin League and won prizes at Latin competitions. She got braces and eye glasses on the same day. I should have staggered these appointments because she came home that night and burst into tears. She said, "This isn't me. Who is *this*?" The braces are long gone, but she still wears glasses—those swanky little cat's-eye tortoise-shell frames are her one fashion statement. But she was never interested in makeup. Once I had pressed her to try a little mascara for a teen party. She tried to apply it in the car as I drove her to meet her friends at the movie theater, but she dropped the wand and smeared her clothes with black gunk. When I drove her back home to change her clothes, she left all her cash in the pocket of the smeared jeans she took off. She had had to wait in the theater lobby for two hours until her friends came out of the movie. It was my fault she was left out. I should have accepted my daughter's resistance to fashion and glamour. She had somehow escaped the femme fatale DNA that my mother had handed to me, and I should have left it alone.

Annabel's first attraction was a boy who was diabetic. He wore an "insulin infusion pump," a tiny device cinched to his waist. He liked to show her the flashing green light that proved its battery was A-OK; I was surprised to see he was using the medical gizmo as a come-on. When she declined to have sex with him, he accused her of being intolerant of his chronic illness. I heard her say, "It's not because you're sick. It's because you're a jerk."

She maintains her independence, but my daughter is very desirable to men. At Macalester College, one boy tried to get her attention. He cavorted and cat-called to her until he fell from the third tier of a parking garage, breaking both hands. The accident seemed metaphoric to me. Men reached out but could not touch her.

At the urban grammar school where she worked there were a lot of problem kids. A boy stole her car keys and she had to leave her Corolla in the parking garage overnight. When two kids got into a fistfight, one mother came into the school, complaining that her boy's coat had been torn. Annabel took the impatient mom into the Home Ec room, and she sewed the sleeve of the coat back on. My daughter is generous to people, and gorgeous, and whole. These days she sits in the Transplant Unit, in space suit and mask, leaning close to the pillow to encourage Giovanni to keep up his fight. She stands in long lines at the hospital pharmacy when he needs his scripts refilled.

When divorced, I had to arrange my daughter's visits with her father, my ex-husband with the three-piece name. I was very distressed the first time I put Annabel on an airplane on her own. I tried to believe she was old enough to travel unaccompanied. She had dressed up for the plane trip, and carried a pocketbook. She looked old enough to enter the queue at the boarding gate, sort of. But when she opened her pocketbook it was filled to the brim with her collection of model horses, prancing ponies covered in velveteen with silky manes and tails.

Seeing the menagerie, I thought, of course, she was too young to fly alone!

At the same terminal, I met another woman waiting for *her* daughter to arrive. To my surprise, *The Odd Woman* resurfaced in my life. It was Gail Godwin's own mother, Kathleen Cole, standing beside me. She told me that her daughter took the trip a couple of times a year to visit her. The woman was pleased to learn that I was a fan of her daughter's work. Watching Annabel's plane accelerating down the runway at takeoff, I thought of all of us, mothers and daughters, of our bonds and mileposts of independence, and the *Odd Woman* analogy was breathtaking. Two years later, in 1989, I was startled to learn that Kathleen was killed in a car wreck on the way to the same airport to meet her daughter, Gail Godwin.

The poolside party was breaking up. Some of the Delano models had found dinner dates with a few of the writers who didn't have their editors with them, and were just as disheartened as I was. I recognized that my thoughts about my wholesome daughter were often sparked by River-rat's rejections. Then a fellow approached. He seemed interested in a Blue Light Special. I like the way men still talk to me—as if they want more than talk. Like Ellroy's handshake, it's harmless. But I always want them to take a stab at it. Shoot me when it stops.

BALL LIGHTNING

On a summer night, I got a telephone call. It was
Sandrine. She said, "Things are really bad up
here. He's getting violent."

Giovanni's new immune system was attacking his
liver. He was taking methotrexate, adding to a long
list of medications, but Dr. Crispin also had prescribed
high-dose prednisone to further inhibit the rejection
of his transplant and to calm his chronic graft versus
host disease. Giovanni's plastic pill organizer tray had
seven columns, each with four compartments to separate pills: Morning, Noon, Evening, Night. Once a week,
he sat at the kitchen table with Sandrine to count out
an array of hundreds of pills and capsules, snapping
the lids shut on each little box. This was the "New
Normal." But with high-dose prednisone you are con-
spiring with the devil. Giovanni faced each day with
escalating surges of "roid rage."

Sandrine told me, "I talked to the doctor. He said
that if I feel unsafe I should call 911."

Instead she dialed me.

"I'll be there as soon as I can."

My dovekie was in trouble.

I would bring him home for a fortnight, to relieve Sandrine. Driving to Boston I went eighty, twenty miles over the speed limit to get there before Sandrine might need to call the cops. I didn't believe she would do it.

Behind the wheel, I was surprised to see an electric storm on the horizon. Soon I was inside it. As the rain fell in sheets, I saw ball lightning. Planet-shaped explosions popped all around me. Elusive glowing orbs appeared left and right and exploded into veils of bright seeds and glittering sparks. Scientists have various speculations about such a phenomenon, but some have captured it with spectrographs and on video cameras. They call it "atmospheric pressure ball plasmoids." Ball lightning didn't seem ominous but magical, and somehow prophetic. As I raced to my son, the secrets of motherhood, meteorology, and mysteries of the natural world seemed to converge. The exploding spheres were an encouragement or an approbation for our survival. As I followed the expressway, everything was illuminated by halting blasts of beauty.

OVERSIZED BOX

My trysts with River-rat often collided with meaningful events in my life. I stopped in New York on my way home from my mother's funeral in Wilmington where I had read a Robert Frost poem: *Nature's first green is gold / Her hardest hue to hold / Her early leaf's a flower / But only so an hour.*

I had a room at the Intercontinental once again. I hung my black dress in the closet. I understood that a woman returning from her mother's burial shouldn't be so brimming with heat, but my afternoon with River-rat was very charged with an undercurrent of something different. There was a certain breathlessness and arousal that seemed a little more desperate, as if enhanced by the ghostly presence of my femme fatale mother. Her passing wasn't unexpected but it had several prongs of meaning. Her life had been ruled by one mortal desire: to regain the attentions of the Arrow Collar model. At her death, she had passed the baton to me. Like my mother, I would wait a lifetime for River-rat to really love me.

I showed him a final note my mother had written to me. "I bequeath my Chippendale serpentine bureau to Maria Flook." I sold it for $65,000, before learning it was worth four times that! Lying beside River-rat, my unfortunate mistake with the antique dresser seemed to echo my habit of giving things away without thinking about it.

River-rat sensed my transformation after my mother's passing. He told me, "God, I can't resist you." But he said this quite often, unwilling to take responsibility for showing up at the hotel. "It's chemical," he told me. He wasn't in charge of it, he said. Something acid or alkaline was always off balance.

Again I stopped in New York after going to my brother's son's funeral. My nephew had been found deceased in the head of a swordfish boat in New Bedford when tying up after two weeks at sea. Off-loading their catch, the crew gets paid in cash, and he'd often used his pay to buy a bag of heroin from his usual connection at the dock. This time, he had OD'd.

At the funeral ceremony, after a tender eulogy by his wharf-rat girlfriend and prayers with a Catholic priest, the boy's coffin could not be lowered into the ground that had been excavated just that morning.

The coffin was too large for the hole.

My brother's son was six foot four, and he required an "oversized" casket. The cemetery director had not been informed of the exact measurements, and the grave had not been correctly prepared. The work crew would have to come back to remove more earth and enlarge the plot. I had to lead my disconsolate brother away from the halted ceremony and get him in the car. We drove away from the cemetery with the coffin still stranded on its winches.

That very evening, in bed beside River-rat, I couldn't forget my nephew's body left behind in his oversized coffin. I stared at River-rat, from head to foot. As he lounged in post-coital drowsiness, I sized him up. He wasn't six feet tall, he was of ordinary height. He wouldn't need an extra-large box.

THE JUMPER

I was walking to my hotel on East Forty-Eighth Street when I was stopped by a commotion. A woman was clearing the sidewalk. She tore a strip of yellow plastic tape from its saw-tooth dispenser. She tied the serrated edge of the yellow tape to a street sign and hiked down the sidewalk, letting the spool sing. At the next No Parking warning, she cinched the tape to the pole and stretched a new length of stenciled ribbon crosswise, clearing a wide plat of bare sidewalk. The boldface words, POLICE LINE DO NOT CROSS, ran nose to tail in a candy-wrapper effect. She anchored the end of the tape to an arbitrary brass sconce at the entrance to an apartment building. Pedestrians obeyed the barricade and ducked into the street, following the curb in two tight streams, east and west. I stayed behind to watch.

A patrolman materialized. He saw the instant landing strip of empty concrete and asked the young woman, "What's this operation?"

He was holding a supersized coffee from the minimart in his gloved hand. She plucked it out of his leather fist and sipped its froth hem.

"Thanks," she said. "Is this milk or cream? It's got two sugars? Yum."

The officer dipped his face and eyed her from under his hat brim. Was she a bald-faced temptress or something? "You with building security?" he asked her.

She shrugged and said, "We've got a jumper."

He lifted his face to study the zenith of the high-rise building. "What floor?"

Together they searched for an irregularity on the tower's sweeping glass face, a continuous shimmer shooting up twenty stories.

"We need this sidewalk evacuated. We don't want someone to get hurt," she told him. She handed back the supersized cup, still steaming. "So we roped this off."

Life magazine once ran a photograph of a beauty queen who fell from a high-rise to land fully reclined on the roof of a late-model Chrysler. Her satin evening dress swirled like a mermaid's tail across the car roof that spooned her body in its crumpled sink. Her face was perfect. Her taut throat and straight nose looked Hellenic in profile, her berry lips unsmudged, her blonde hair fanned across the bowed windscreen. The award-winning Kodak never suggests that underneath this faultless composition the girl was pulverized.

What was her problem? What had her lover done to *her*?

The patrolman watched the young woman disappear into the building. Her gait had a nervous little flounce, as if she was pleased by the authority that her job awarded her. She wore a stylish suit with a micro mini skirt, short as a file folder. Her long legs were easy on the eyes. The officer was amused by the upstart house detective, but he didn't seem to trust security personnel in street clothes, even if she worked in the private sector.

A building manager came out for an impromptu roundtable with the constabulary. The police and condo personnel split up to patrol rooftop exits and to check the stairwells between floors, just as a precaution.

No one had seen a despondent soul.

Office girls drifted in and out to flirt with the meat rack of law enforcement, but the pretty one never returned for another slug of the patrolman's coffee. A team arrived with a room-sized air cushion like the giant pillows used by stuntmen. First responders debated about where to position the mattress since the subject had not yet been sighted.

A vendor walked through the gathering crowd holding a tray of artsy hand-carved wood puzzles. "For your office desk or coffee table," he said. He demonstrated the universal rubric for connecting the wood pieces. He held a polished dowel and a locust wood block. He screwed the "male" spindle into the "female" collar. "Every puzzle piece has a corresponding receptacle," he explained to an office Jill, who giggled. Then, from the tenth floor or higher, a figure emerged. She edged heel-to-toe across a faux balcony rail, holding her arms above her head.

A chorus of bull horns announced, "Heads up." "Stand back."

I didn't wait any longer, thinking that whatever she decides, I can't be witness to it. I was meeting River-rat in ten minutes. But I recognized the woman on the ledge. She was the same girl who had cleared the sidewalk, concerned that people could be injured. "We don't want someone to get hurt," she had said. She had left a lipstick crescent on the officer's Styrofoam Big Gulp. I saw the abandoned cup on the lid of a newspaper dispenser. The pink smear of her lipstick seemed tragically archeological. Her lip stain belonged to me, to everyone. Whatever her man troubles, she made me think of my own. She was getting under my skin. But I went to the hotel anyway. I refused to watch her fall, her arms and legs outstretched, stiff as a Christmas cookie.

Flying home later that afternoon, unlike that girl, I believed I could escape an escalating mistake. I made it back. But every return is a violent reminder of where I have been. As the plane touched down in Provincetown, I looked out the window of the Cessna nine-seater to see the ragged surf chewing the shore.

DNA

When *Invisible Eden* was published, investigators had not yet made an arrest in the Christa Worthington murder case. Her killer was still on the loose. Two years after her death, investigators made a DNA sweep in the town of Truro, intimidating residents when they came to the town dump or to the post office, asking people to agree to have their cheeks swabbed. The ACLU called the sweep a fascist outrage, and it wasn't until a year later, in 2005, that a suspect finally was arrested. His DNA had sat on a shelf at the State Police Crime Lab for more than a year because of an overworked staff. Massachusetts district attorneys were allowed to submit only four samples a month. Finally a match was made. It was Christopher McCowen, a tall and muscular trash hauler, who had been hired by Christa to collect her garbage once a week.

Again the table talk returned to gossip about Christa's sex life. Some local residents believed that the killer had barged into the house and had raped the victim; others said it was consensual sex. McCowen claimed that Christa had been "friendly" with him. My editor, Charlie Conrad, wanted me to follow the case and write an addendum for a new edition of *Invisible Eden.*

McCowen had a history of violence against women. Before his arrest for murder, he had had four separate restraining orders requested by girlfriends he had beaten, roughed-up, dragged out of cars, and threatened. He told one of them to keep quiet or he would "snap her neck." But when we met, and I interviewed him at the Barnstable County Correctional Facility, he related to me with immediate warmth and smooth talk.

I visited him at the jail. Sometimes catfights erupted in the waiting room, when ladies arrived all at once at security to visit the same boyfriend. Visiting hours were very restricted. Inmates were allowed visitors for only one hour, only two days a week. Lady friends had squabbles about who would be checked through first and last. I was an outsider, a journalist, and was lowest on the pecking order. We had to remove our rings and jewelry, even our earrings. We stored our pocket books, cell phones, and outer layers of clothing in a locker. It cost a quarter to get the key. I had to remember not to wear an underwire bra, because it set off the alarm when we were wanded by security.

My meetings with the suspected killer were difficult. I sat down on one side of the Plexiglas partition and was careful not to react when he said, "What are you wearing under that?"

And he said, "Send me a picture. I want to *rule* on those legs."

I started to wonder, "What is it about me that encourages a man to talk this way?" Of course McCowen might be a sociopathic sex-crazed murderer, but I felt the echo of the refrain I had always heard, "This poem is too female." What inherent weakness did I possess to relentlessly inspire sexual fantasy? It must come from my French mother. It was in my DNA.

Getting to know Christa's killer presented me with interior questions I tried to answer myself. He, of course, was the farthest point on the spectrum of hetero archetypes, but I sensed the universal sadness, or *something*, of all men who came before him.

McCowen often called me collect from jail. I accepted every call to learn everything I could about his experience with Christa. He said they'd been intimate. He said she had once asked him to stay for lunch. It was macaroni and cheese. But he liked to end the phone call with sweet talk and he told me, "When I get out, I'm coming over to your place. And I can go *all night!*"

MOTHERS AND LOVERS

In 2007 I was a recipient of a John Simon Guggenheim Memorial Foundation fellowship in fiction. The *New York Times* ran a full-page ad, announcing the winners in the creative arts, humanities, and sciences. I loved being listed beside engineers and neuroscientists as much as I was pleased to be listed among my brethren poets, novelists, and visual artists. Another fiction writer I admired, Kevin Brockmeier, was on the list, and I was amused to see that a startling personality named Koosil-Ja won her prize for choreography. She created a method called "Live Processing" where dancers become a "flow that operates on the cutting edge of movement, decoding and 'deterritorializing' to achieve a new movement paradigm." I was also pleased to see that someone named Edmund Bertschinger received his fellowship in astrophysics. His work includes an interest in black holes and the mysteries of "dark energy and dark matter."

It was reassuring to me to be recognized for my own "dark energy" and to be listed side by side with Brockmeier and with other remarkable individuals of diverse experience and accomplishment.

River-rat saw the announcement and he asked me, "Who wrote your letters of recommendation for the Guggenheim?" He seemed a little miffed. He was curious about who might have stood up for me, willingly, and who might have offered a glowing summary of my talents. I told him the names of a couple writers who had stuck their necks out for me. Notes written by my betters and my peers. I told him that my letters of recommendation were from *artists*, not from corporate crack shots like him. But his questions implied that he felt I didn't deserve the award if he had nothing to do with it.

With the support of the Guggenheim Foundation, I was able to complete my novel *Mothers and Lovers*, regardless of River-rat's dismissal of it. Every book I write, when I am at my keyboard, fully dressed or in my underwear, I am still sitting in his lap. I didn't strive for his "elite opinion" from his throne at Random, but I wanted the subcutaneous connection I had always felt from his mentorship.

A famous "definition of insanity" has been attributed to Ben Franklin and also to Albert Einstein. No one is exactly sure who was first to come up with the adage: "Insanity is repeating the same mistake over and over again expecting different results!"

The last time we met to make love was the last time we met to make love. Was the last time we met to make love. We met to make love. To make love. Again I told him I wanted him to read my new novel.

He said, "Ok. Send it to me."

"If you decide to read it, just don't call my character 'Quilty,' like when you read *Lux*."

Then he made love to me, his touch was different, full of doubt, as if he were mired in longings that were beyond our grasp. He kissed my lips. The secrecies of regret have a stinging sweetness. I told him, "When are you going to get that thing removed from your lip? What are you afraid of?" His Venous Lake sapphire had become a secret emblem of our unsacred desires, but I encouraged him to get the laser treatment.

Lying naked beside him, I turned from my back to my stomach. I was surprised to feel those blue pencil marks scrawling across my hips, my buttocks, up my spine to the nape of my neck. I tried to transcribe the message being written on my skin. It wasn't River-rat, it was Willis! His instructions said, "*You don't need him. Leave this all behind and come with me.*"

But the next day I e-mailed my new book to River-rat. My loyalty to him was in shreds, but these tatters were silken to me. In a week, he wrote me a two-page rejection letter of my novel. He said, "You are a true descendent of Thomas Hardy in your fierce insistence on showing how your characters' pasts, environments, and natures determine their fates and outlooks. Your unique sense of noir wit and chilly eroticism are on wonderful display in these pages, and in Blaze you have succeeded in creating a complex, unpredictable, and compelling character. His history and his emerging efforts to understand that history and to control his behavior constitute the true drama of the novel. April is far less compelling. Early on we are told that her 'most unsettling character flaw was her organic, her natural to a fault predisposition to be consumed by men.' If one were to give her a clinical diagnosis it would be borderline personality disorder . . ."

He was making a moral judgment of my female character. His response to her was personal. He was talking about *us*. The troubled lives I created in the novel mirrored our own disenfranchised relationship. He wrote, "I've tried to do an edit to the first 135 pages, but you might feel so impatient with my response that you would chuck them." He refused to work on the book, blaming me for my unwillingness to cooperate with him. He feared entering my pages, my world, too nervous to cross its erotic boundaries. His panic was symptomatic of Freud's conclusion that "the sexual life of adult women is a dark continent."

When *Mothers and Lovers* was published, the newspaper reviews of the novel appeared to be examining my long affair with River-rat. The *Los Angeles Times* said, "Fascinating and disturbing. Flook is no stranger to the territory of sexual or romantic ambiguity." Kirkus said, "Sexual tensions compound with sexual secrets until they burst open." Booklist suggested our long-term dalliance: "Flook is drawn to stories about people who have boundary issues . . . she captures the thrill of flouting taboos and has the compassion to reserve judgment about people who give in to foolishness." The *Boston Globe* said that that novel takes "subtly witty, deep dives into forbidden sexual acts and desires."

I sent River-rat a copy of the novel. My note to him said, "I wrote this book for you. That's a laugh, isn't it?"

Willis doesn't slap my wrist. He takes my hand and looks me in the eyes. He says, *"Each book you write for River-rat is Ben Franklin's definition of insanity."*

DIAMOND JAMBOREE

After three years, Giovanni was doing well enough to go back to work. He took a job as an assistant to the director of the housing department at MIT. And he also was accepted to a graduate program at Boston University for a master's in Educational Leadership and Policy Studies. At MIT he was getting a reputation as a "troubleshooter" and was encouraged by the dean of students to pursue a career as an educational administrator. He could keep his job while attending graduate school.

After Giovanni went through two stem cell transplants, I was surprised to hear that one of his projects at MIT was to research policy guidelines for global warming at other major STEM schools. There were expected to be major brownouts and loss of electric power in the years ahead, and the university needed to be prepared.

"What do you mean STEM schools?" I said. "Are you kidding?"

He said, "Where have you been? STEM schools are universities for Science, Technology, Engineering, and Math."

"Oh, yeah, yeah," I said. The word "stem" had come to have only one meaning to me after Giovanni's tandem stem cell transplants. I was happy to know that the word had another context.

He told me that with predictions of major brown-outs in the near future, due to accelerated heat waves, MIT would be in trouble. Giovanni was involved in making plans for the relocation of students and faculty, and especially for laboratory specimens and archival materials that need regulated temperatures and that would be put at risk if MIT lost power. Harvard has its own generator system, but MIT would be in the dark. His duties with the research team included contacting housing administrators at other STEM schools to make policy comparisons, and he was on the telephone with staff at Stanford, Georgia Tech, Worcester Polytech, and Princeton.

It was great to hear him talk about carbon emissions, instead of graft versus host disease.

But every few months, Giovanni has to have a PET scan, or "positron emission tomography," using a radioactive drug or tracer, so that Crispin can make sure that his lymphoma hasn't returned. After the last PET scan, I was relieved to hear that he was still in remission. He must be "in remission" for at least five years before doctors will whisper the secret word "cured." In fact, with double transplant patients, *ten* years is more statistically accurate. But with the last PET scan, although they found no "hot spots" when the tracer illuminates active cancer cells, the film identified another area of potential disaster.

The pictures showed that his right hip was affected—the top of the femoral head, or ball joint, was collapsing and beginning to flatten. They said he had "avascular necrosis," death of bone tissue due to lack of blood flow. The ball joint no longer fit perfectly inside the socket. Living bone is always changing. But without blood flow, like a rusty bridge, bone structures start to collapse. Allogeneic transplant patients can no longer produce bone marrow stromal cells that build new bone. He might need a hip replacement.

High-dose prednisone cuts off blood supply to the bones, and I was distressed to learn that transplant patients who have hip replacements often need "revisions," because without new bone growth to encompass the artificial joint, the metal-on-metal or ceramic-on-plastic femoral head often becomes loose. And with repetitive hip replacement surgeries for transplant patients there was "significant morbidity" due to infection. To fight graft versus host disease he took high-dose prednisone, but prednisone causes "necrosis." One step forward, two steps back.

Giovanni also was suffering from fibrosis of the fascia, a rare form of GVHD. Fascia is the connective tissue beneath the skin that surrounds and separates ligaments. "Scleroderma fasciitis" paralyzes the muscles, and Giovanni couldn't lift his arms very high or move his wrists. He could no longer play the guitar.

He could not put on his socks!

The disease can progress to the vital organs and has a high morbidity rate also. He had to begin a new routine of treatment to try to stop its progression. Three times a week he sits for four hours in a banana chair at the hospital while hooked up to an apheresis machine for a complex procedure called "ECP" or extracorporeal photopheresis. His whole blood is processed outside the body. His blood is siphoned into a bowl, and the white cells are exposed to UVA light in a separate plastic chamber, before they pump his blood back into him.

Even worse, when his graft versus host disease became so severe, Giovanni again started to say the word I dreaded to hear.

"I'll just *disappear*," he said, using the code word. "If I'm a cripple at twenty-six my life is over anyway."

Cancer therapy can kill you in many different ways. I remembered Picasso's deconstruction of his paintings, when he says his figures in paintings evaporate and in their place is just an "impression" of what they once had been. I feared my son would disappear this way. This is how I must curate our museum of despair.

I had a working title for this book. *Ghost Bike*. My publisher didn't like it. He said, "What does it mean?"

I said, "It's a metaphor—"

"Readers won't understand it."

I guess he was right. As a writer, I have always had a weakness for writing "extended" metaphors. It's a poet's hang-up. But having a child at risk, I make up metaphors, I guess, so I don't have to say what I fear directly.

SANDRINE WAS still beside him. After three years of cancer heartbreak, and with the news of a progressive decline, it was time he should pop the question. Sandrine had been all too patient. She had asked him, "Are we preengaged, or what?"

He said, "No one should get married on death's door."

I told him to look ahead. "Don't think the worst will happen."

He said, "She'll expect a ring. I don't have that kind of money."

"Let's go get one," I said.

A few weeks before Valentine's Day, Macy's has its yearly Diamond Jamboree. Diamonds were on sale. I had checked out the better jewelry stores in Boston, and some boutiques sold rings for only a few thousand dollars. But I discovered that these prices were just for the settings, and diamonds had to be purchased separately.

Macy's offered ready-to-wear diamond rings.

Giovanni and I spent an hour at the diamond counter. He asked me to slide each ring he examined on my own third finger, so he could see what it looked like.

My hands were battered. They showed hard work, my years, and new cuts across my knuckles after removing a rose bush earlier that week. The hand represents the journeys we have taken, both the high roads and the low. Each gorgeous ring I tried on exaggerated the miles I have gone. Examining sparkling gems on my own hand wasn't tragic, but all too cynical.

The clerk didn't like what she saw; upon my third finger the rings were diminished. She called over to another customer standing in line. She asked the pretty thing if she'd do us a small favor. The clerk said, "Would you try on a few rings for my customer here? He'd like to see them." The young girl came over, resting her elbows on the glass-topped cabinet. She was amused by the sudden obligation presented to her.

Giovanni said, "That one." He pointed to a ring under the glass. The clerk retrieved the half-karat stone, and the girl pushed the diamond over her smooth knuckle. Her hand was fresh and unlined, her skin so silky. The ring just "popped." It was beautiful.

With the young stranger as a stand-in, youth, itself, could be the final arbiter. It gave me a wallop of my mortality but I loved knowing my place, and my context in it. *Each of us alone on the breast of the earth / pierced by a ray of sun / And suddenly it's evening.*

I was happy to see the pretty stranger slip the ring off her finger and hand it to my son. A handsome young man who could not put on his socks. Unknown to us, graft versus host disease was secretly attacking his lungs. It can cause pulmonary fibrosis—another condition with a high rate of morbidity, or it could level out. Crispin tells us we have to wait to find out.

We left the department store with a tiny velvet box.

Giovanni explained his plans to me. He would take Sandrine to Harvard Square, to Harvard's Widener library where they had first met. I liked that their introduction was within a bastion of 3.5 million books. Barbara Tuchman called it her "Archimedes bathtub." But its namesake, Harry Elkins Widener, went down on the *Titanic*. The library has a forbidding entrance at the top of twenty-seven spiraling stone steps. He said he would let Sandrine walk ahead of him. When she was several steps higher, he'd call out her name. She'd turn around to see Giovanni below her, on his knees, holding out the little box.

THE BURNT SWAN

Freak accidents sometimes happen in the city. Just a few weeks ago a real estate agent had been killed on West Twelfth Street, struck by a piece of plywood that was blown off a security fence surrounding a 200-unit condominium complex under construction. Next a swath of brick facade broke free from a retirement complex on the Upper West Side ending the life of a two-year-old girl.

These events inspired me to stop seeing River-rat. I imagined a similar accident. The one sure way I could break it off with him was to create my own fiction.

River-rat is dead. It was a violent death, they say. Thank goodness my husband had nothing to do with it. Let's say it happened when a spirit-level plummeted from the rooftop of a high-rise. The silver stick bounced off an aluminum awning, and jettisoned into an intersection where River-rat was crossing Forty-Second Street. After River-rat's accident, police requested an authorized autopsy because of a building department and OSHA investigation, while work on the building was shut down indefinitely. Jewish law requires that burial take place as soon as possible, within twenty-four hours. The body should not be left alone during this time. With police matters, the ritual was delayed. The body wasn't yet released from the medical examiners. The Shemira was postponed. But I was permitted to see the body after explaining to someone at the desk, "I'm his author."

"Five minutes," they said, and they showed me into a cold anteroom paneled with subway tile. I wasn't family but I took my turn when no one was looking. The body had not yet been cleansed in a prescribed ceremony. They had not applied cosmetics or performed any embalming. He was lying supine on a steel table. I could not see signs of his head injury although his occipital lobe at the back of his skull had been crushed. His face was unmarked. I looked at its beautiful contours and delicate features that had once reminded me of my mother's Limoges. I kissed the blue sapphire on his lower lip. A friend had told me that I should participate in a rite that requires that mourners tear their own clothing. I ripped the lapel of my jacket, and its flap fell across my breast.

Sitting beside him, I thought of everything. I tried to sort my feelings. He had published four of my books and I was grateful to him. I recalled the little notes he had written in the margins. His tight handwriting had the appearance of a profusion of centipedes across my pages.

I took out my phone and thumbed through our last texts right before he was killed.

From Me: *did you read O'Brien's memoir yet? she looks like every Irish girl on the block in*

> *those early pix.* are you doing anything with
> my *new book? imagine how deeply i will kiss
> you next*

> From River-rat: *your message enlarged me,
> left me swollen. Edna would never use that
> word. Xo*

And I found an earlier message:

> From Me: *"Ash is the flesh of time" I love this
> line from Brodsky's book on Venice as if it
> were mine. Because it seems—you and I—
> have not a speck, other than. —m.*

> From River-rat: *dearest m, that is a great
> line. my son, the Greek scholar, loves to
> point to things etymological, the most recent.
> 'ephemeral' comes from the Greek word for
> day—which especially at this time of year
> when the light is so oblique at dusk and you
> can rest your eyes in the deepening azure of
> the sky, long for disappearance. i do miss
> you. —r-r.*

How disappointing that he brings his son into it.
Chicken!

But I was not above him. My MD, Marguerite, says,
*I used to watch what he did with me, how he used
me. He acted beyond my hope and in accordance
with my body's destiny.*

I didn't have much time left to sit beside him, but
I took out a little book. I read a poem out loud to

River-rat, a translation from Carmina Burana from the thirteenth century.

"Lament of the Roast Swan"

The lakes I swam upon,
My beauty—all is gone,
I was once a swan.

Alas, alack
Now I am black
And burnt both front and back

Whiter once than snow,
The fairest bird I know
Is blacker than a crow.

Alas, alack
Now I am black
And burnt both front and back

I wasn't permitted at the funeral. I wasn't family. I didn't attend the condolence meal back at the house, which usually consists of "round foods" like eggs, symbolic of the life cycle, served to mourners upon their return from the cemetery. Mourners are told not to wear leather shoes, and all of the mirrors in the house are to be draped by cloth. With River-rat I was familiar with the habit of keeping covered up, with no expression on my face, and with my feelings shrouded. I imagined his house, busy with blood relatives and his legitimate friends. I thought of the bureau drawers that Weensie would search to discard unwanted reminders—her black stockings, if she had any, and all their mementoes, knickknacks, and tchotchkes. His scuba diver undershorts would be a painful memory of him.

Of course, I was invited to a memorial service. All of his Random House authors received invitations. His most prominent writers will perform eulogies at the podium. I imagined the applesauce they would smear on us, with their personal stories about River-rat's essential contributions to their great works of literary genius.

I decided not to attend.

I see the ghost bike everywhere. My sister pumps the pedals. And with River-rat, Veronica, and the girl in the kitten hat, it has more than one set of handlebars.

THE GIFT

I discover the gun centered on the antique four-poster cannonball bed. He has arranged it to look like a romantic token, like expensive jewelry or a Fabergé egg. In foreplay he jokes and tries to put its nozzle in my mouth. He says, "This one's a Conceal Carry Government Model, .45-caliber ACP, or 'Automatic Colt Pistol,' with a five-inch barrel."

Shiny as chrome, it's made of stainless steel, with carved filigree on the grip. In its repose, the weapon is beautiful. He tells me, "Fully loaded, it holds seven rounds plus one in the chamber."

Beside the gun he has placed his most treasured fountain pen, and a pocket-sized booklet of blank paper. He encourages me to start a new novel. Instead the fancy pen and the empty diary invite someone to write a last note.

The pistol reflects splinters of light. So I click off the overhead.

In the darkened room, it glistens.

A group of figures lines up at the foot of the bed. Willis, with his arm still in a cast, his jet-black hair tousled and shoulder-length, is the ringleader. And there's Lux in a "freezing spell" of false paralysis until his mutism evaporates and he starts talking a blue streak. Cam jingles the keys to the Duster, daring us to pile in. Alden mocks authority, flashing her National Seashore ID. The Prince of Motown asks us to cosign his lease. Rennie Hopkins promises that she has enough morphine suppositories for everyone. April arrives late, but she had to wait for Blaze to feed the horses. He looks great. Even my sister shows up, wearing a garter belt that belonged to Veronica. Her trick, Horace, is holding a twenty. Fritz is trying to buy or sell something. They all like to needle me, trying to cheer me up. I know it's egocentric of me to bring my characters back to life. Of course they should fade away. But while I'm at it, I can invent what I want. Giovanni and Sandrine show up. Her diamond ring sparkles even more fiercely than the pistol left on the bed. All Smiles comes in. It's great to see his band all together again. Giovanni's graft versus host disease is in remission. He can move his wrists, use his hands, and play guitar again. The group has to connect their amps. "Let me do it," Willis says, finding some outlets. "Here we go," he announces. All Smiles tears into "I Hate the State."